STUDENT
WORLD
ATLAS

NATIONAL GEOGRAPHIC
WASHINGTON, D.C.

Table of Contents

Popocatépetl volcano,
page 55

Iguazú Falls, page 71

Lynx, page 88

Ha Long Bay, page 91

Cairo, Egypt, page 101

Koala, page 118

Southern elephant seals, page 125

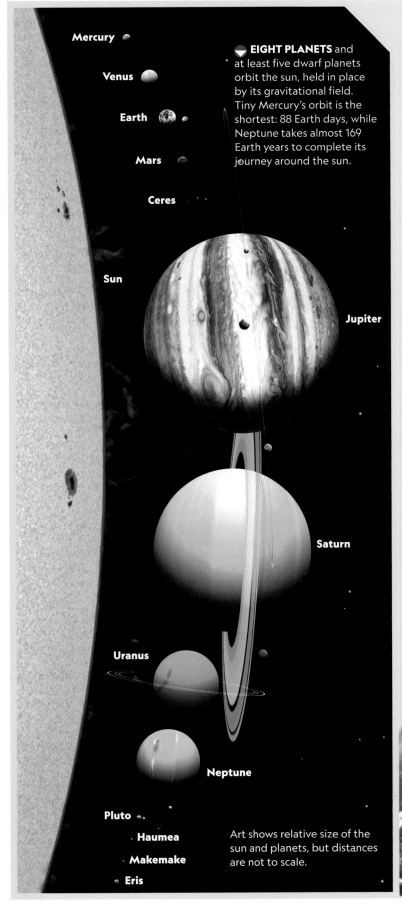

Mercury

Venus

Earth

Mars

Ceres

Sun

Jupiter

Saturn

Uranus

Neptune

Pluto

Haumea

Makemake

Eris

EIGHT PLANETS and at least five dwarf planets orbit the sun, held in place by its gravitational field. Tiny Mercury's orbit is the shortest: 88 Earth days, while Neptune takes almost 169 Earth years to complete its journey around the sun.

Art shows relative size of the sun and planets, but distances are not to scale.

Earth in Space

At the center of our solar system is the sun, a huge mass of hot gas that is the source of both light and warmth for Earth. Third in a group of eight planets that revolve around the sun, Earth is a terrestrial, or mostly rocky, planet. So are Mercury, Venus, and Mars. Earth is about 93 million miles (150 million km) from the sun, and its orbital journey, or revolution, around the sun takes 365 ¼ days. Farther away from the sun, four more planets—Jupiter, Saturn, Uranus, and Neptune (all made up primarily of gases)—plus at least five dwarf planets (Ceres, Pluto, Haumea, Makemake, and Eris) complete the main bodies of our solar system. The solar system, in turn, is part of the Milky Way galaxy.

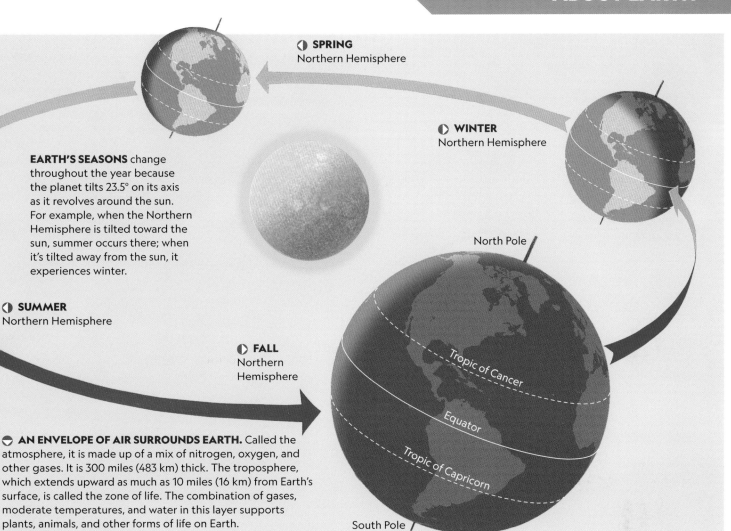

SPRING
Northern Hemisphere

WINTER
Northern Hemisphere

EARTH'S SEASONS change throughout the year because the planet tilts 23.5° on its axis as it revolves around the sun. For example, when the Northern Hemisphere is tilted toward the sun, summer occurs there; when it's tilted away from the sun, it experiences winter.

SUMMER
Northern Hemisphere

FALL
Northern Hemisphere

North Pole

Tropic of Cancer

Equator

Tropic of Capricorn

South Pole

AN ENVELOPE OF AIR SURROUNDS EARTH. Called the atmosphere, it is made up of a mix of nitrogen, oxygen, and other gases. It is 300 miles (483 km) thick. The troposphere, which extends upward as much as 10 miles (16 km) from Earth's surface, is called the zone of life. The combination of gases, moderate temperatures, and water in this layer supports plants, animals, and other forms of life on Earth.

EARTH ROTATES WEST TO EAST on its axis, an imaginary line that runs through Earth's center from pole to pole. Each rotation takes 24 hours, or one full cycle of day and night. One complete rotation equals one Earth day. One complete revolution around the sun equals one Earth year.

Map Projections

Maps tell a story about physical and human systems, places and regions, patterns and relationships. This atlas is a collection of maps that tell a story about Earth.

Understanding that story requires a knowledge of how maps are made and a familiarity with the special language used by cartographers, the people who create maps.

Globes present a model of Earth as it is—a sphere—but they are bulky and can be difficult to use and store. Flat maps are much more convenient, but certain problems result from transferring Earth's curved surface to a flat piece of paper, a process called projection. There are many different types of projections, all of which involve some form of distortion in area, distance, direction, or shape.

◔ **AZIMUTHAL MAP PROJECTION.** This kind of map is made by projecting a globe onto a flat surface that touches the globe at a single point, such as the North Pole. These maps accurately represent direction along any straight line extending from the point of contact. Away from the point of contact, shape is increasingly distorted.

◑ **MAKING A PROJECTION.** Imagine a globe that has been cut in half as this one has. If a light is shined into it, the lines of latitude and longitude and the shapes of the continents will cast shadows that can be "projected" onto a piece of paper, as shown here. Depending on how the paper is positioned, the shadows will be distorted in different ways.

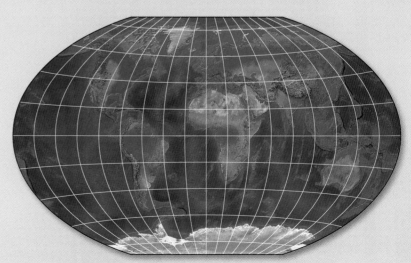

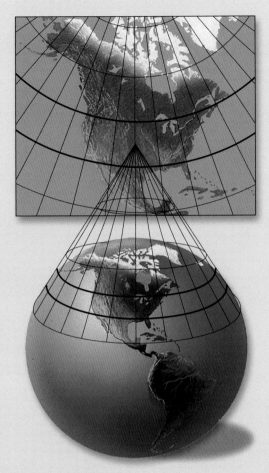

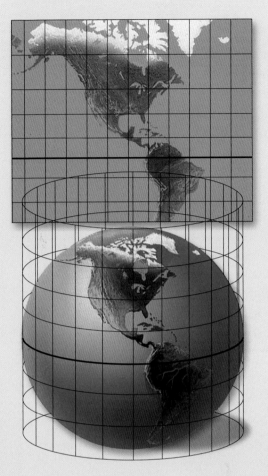

⬠ **CONIC MAP PROJECTION.** This kind of map is made by projecting a globe onto a cone. The part of Earth being mapped touches the sides of the cone. Lines of longitude appear as straight lines; lines of latitude appear as parallel arcs. Conic projections are often used to map mid-latitude areas with great east-west extent, such as North America.

⬠ **CYLINDRICAL MAP PROJECTION.** A cylindrical projection map is made by projecting a globe onto a cylinder that touches Earth's surface along the Equator. Latitude and longitude lines on this kind of map show true compass directions, which makes it useful for navigation. But there is great distortion in the size of high-latitude landmasses.

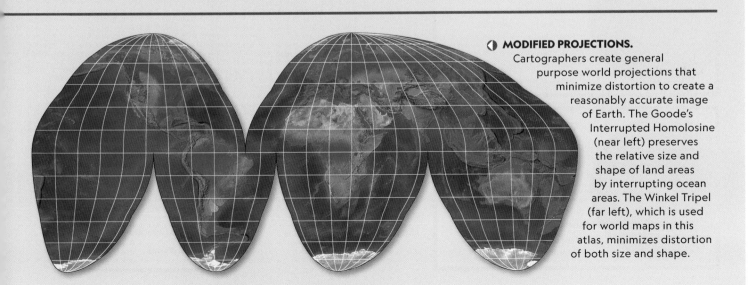

◗ **MODIFIED PROJECTIONS.** Cartographers create general purpose world projections that minimize distortion to create a reasonably accurate image of Earth. The Goode's Interrupted Homolosine (near left) preserves the relative size and shape of land areas by interrupting ocean areas. The Winkel Tripel (far left), which is used for world maps in this atlas, minimizes distortion of both size and shape.

Reading Maps

People can use maps to find locations, to determine direction or distance, and to understand information about places. Cartographers rely on a special graphic language to communicate through maps.

An imaginary system of lines, called the global grid, helps us locate particular points on Earth's surface. The global grid is made up of lines of latitude and longitude that are measured in degrees, minutes, and seconds. The point where these lines intersect identifies the absolute location of a place. No other place has the exact same address.

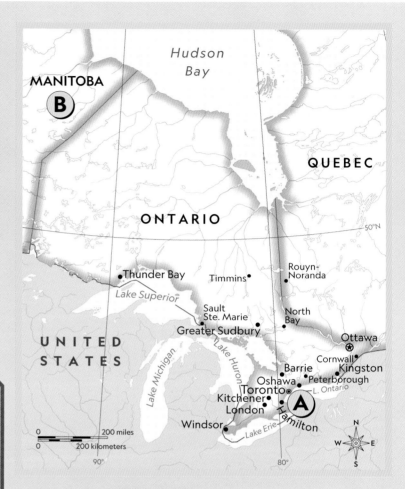

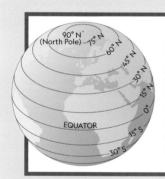

LATITUDE. Lines of latitude—also called parallels because they are parallel to the Equator— run east to west around the globe and measure location north or south of the Equator. The Equator is 0° latitude.

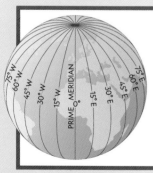

LONGITUDE. Lines of longitude—also called meridians—run from pole to pole and measure location east or west of the prime meridian. The prime meridian is 0° longitude, and it runs through Greenwich, near London, U.K.

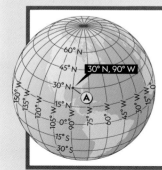

GLOBAL GRID. When used together, latitude and longitude form a grid that provides a system for determining the exact, or absolute, location of every place on Earth. For example, the absolute location of point A is 30° N, 90° W.

◗ **DIRECTION.** Cartographers put a north arrow or a compass rose, which shows the four cardinal directions— north, south, east, and west—on a map. On the map above, point Ⓑ is northwest (NW) of point Ⓐ. Northwest is an example of an intermediate direction, which means it is between two cardinal directions. Grid lines can also be used to indicate north.

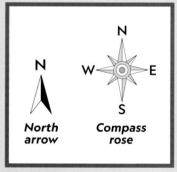

North arrow   **Compass rose**

◗ **SCALE.** A map represents a part of Earth's surface, but that part is greatly reduced. Cartographers include a map scale to show what distance on Earth is represented by a given length on the map. Scale can be graphic (a bar), verbal, or a ratio. To determine how many miles point Ⓐ is from point Ⓑ, place a piece of paper on the map above and mark the distance between Ⓐ and Ⓑ. Then compare the marks on the paper with the bar scale on the map.

Graphic, or bar scale

1 INCH represents 274 MILES
1 CENTIMETER represents 173 KILOMETERS

Verbal scale

SCALE 1:17,400,000

Ratio scale

SYMBOLS. Finally, cartographers use a variety of symbols, which are identified in a map key or legend, to tell us more about the places represented on the map. There are three general types of symbols:

• • **POINT SYMBOLS** show the exact location of places (such as cities) or their size (a large dot can mean a more populous city).

——— **LINE SYMBOLS** show boundaries or connections (such as roads, canals, and other trade links).

▢ **AREA SYMBOLS** show the form and extent of a feature (such as a lake, park, or swamp).

Additional information may be coded in color, size, and shape.

PUTTING IT ALL TOGETHER. We already know from the map on page 8 which provinces A and B are located in. But to find out more about city A, we need a larger-scale map—one that shows a smaller area in more detail (see above). The key below explains the symbols used on the map.

MAP KEY

▢	Metropolitan area	═══	Other road
▢	Lake or bay	**407**	Road number
▢	Tree-covered area	**Toronto**	City
───	Major road		

Types of Maps

This atlas includes many different types of maps so that a wide variety of information about Earth can be presented. Three of the most commonly used types of maps are physical, political, and thematic.

A **physical map** identifies natural features, such as mountains, deserts, oceans, and lakes. Area symbols of various colors and shadings may indicate height above sea level or, as in the example here, ecosystems. Similar symbols could also show water depth.

A **political map** shows how people have divided the world into countries. Political maps can also show states, counties, or cities within a country. Line symbols indicate boundaries, and point symbols show the locations and sometimes sizes of cities.

Thematic maps use a variety of symbols to show distributions and patterns on Earth. For example, a choropleth map uses shades of color to represent different values. The example here shows the main economic activity as a percentage of gross domestic product. Thematic maps can show many different things, such as patterns of vegetation, land use, and religions.

A **cartogram** is a special kind of thematic map in which the size of a country is based on some statistic other than land area. In the cartogram at far right, population size determines the size of each country. This is why Nigeria—the most populous country in Africa—appears much larger than Algeria, which has more than double the land area of Nigeria (see the political map). Cartograms allow for a quick visual comparison of countries in terms of a selected statistic.

▶ **THIS GLOBE** is useful for showing Africa's position and size relative to other landmasses, but very little detail is possible at this scale. By using different kinds of maps, mapmakers can show a variety of information in more detail.

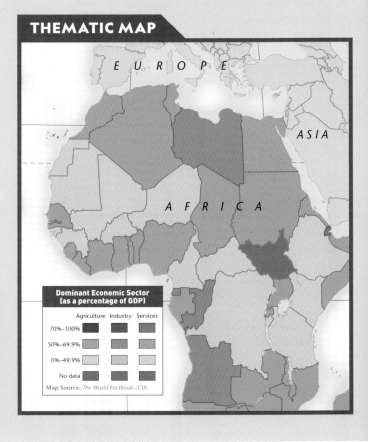

PHYSICAL MAP

THEMATIC MAP

Dominant Economic Sector (as a percentage of GDP)

	Agriculture	Industry	Services
70%–100%			
50%–69.9%			
0%–49.9%			
No data			

Map Source: *The World Factbook—CIA*

POLITICAL MAP

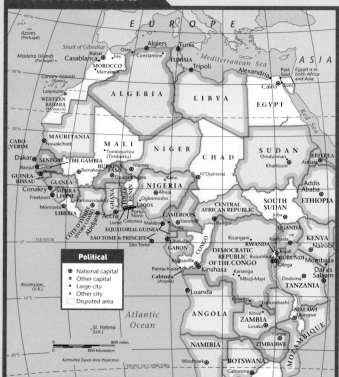

CARTOGRAM

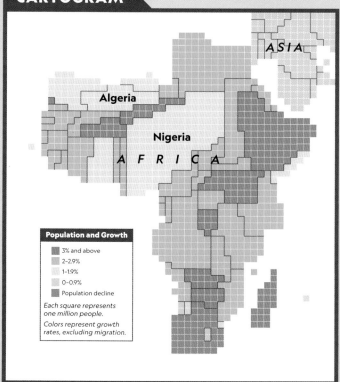

Population and Growth
- 3% and above
- 2–2.9%
- 1–1.9%
- 0–0.9%
- Population decline

Each square represents one million people.

Colors represent growth rates, excluding migration.

SATELLITE IMAGE MAPS

Satellites orbiting Earth transmit images of the surface to computers on the ground. These computers translate the information into special maps (below) that use colors to show various characteristics. Such maps are valuable tools for identifying patterns or comparing changes over time.

CLOUD COVERAGE

TOPOGRAPHY/BATHYMETRY

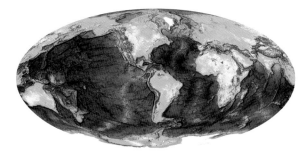

SEA LEVEL VARIABILITY

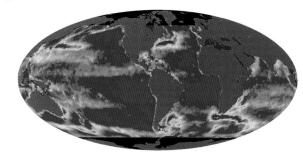

SEA SURFACE TEMPERATURE

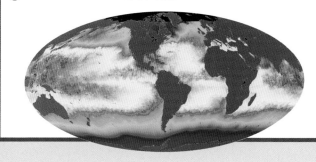

Time Zones

The people who live on the small island nations of Tonga, Samoa, and Kiribati are the first to ring in each new year. Why could fireworks light up their South Pacific skies before celebrations begin in other places around the globe? These islands lie just west of the date line, an invisible boundary designated to mark the beginning of each new day. The date line is part of the system we have adopted to keep track of the passage of days.

For most of human history, people determined time by observing the position of the sun in the sky. Slight differences in time did not matter until, in the mid-19th century, the spread of railroads and telegraph lines changed forever the importance of time. High-speed transportation and communications required schedules, and schedules required that everyone agree on the time.

In 1884, an international conference, convened in Washington, D.C., established an international system of 24 time zones based on the fact that Earth turns from west to east 15 degrees of longitude every hour. Each time zone has a central meridian and is 15 degrees wide, 7½ degrees to either side of the named central meridian.

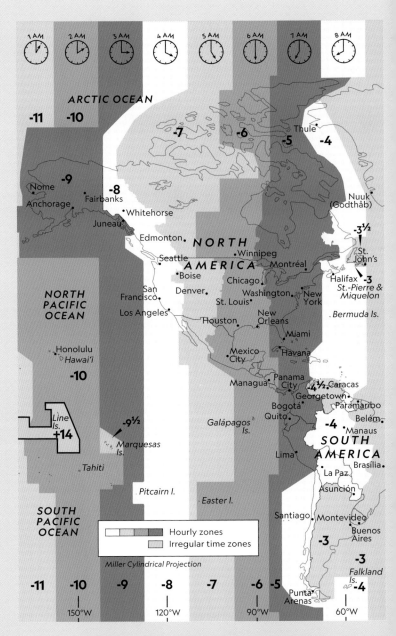

◐ WORLD TIME CLOCK, on Alexanderplatz in Berlin, Germany, features a large cylinder that is marked with the world's 24 time zones, as well as major cities found in each zone. The cylinder rises almost 33 feet (10 m) above the square and weighs 16 tons (14.5 t).

◒ A SYSTEM OF STANDARD TIME put trains on schedules, which helped reduce the chance of collisions and the loss of lives and property caused by them.

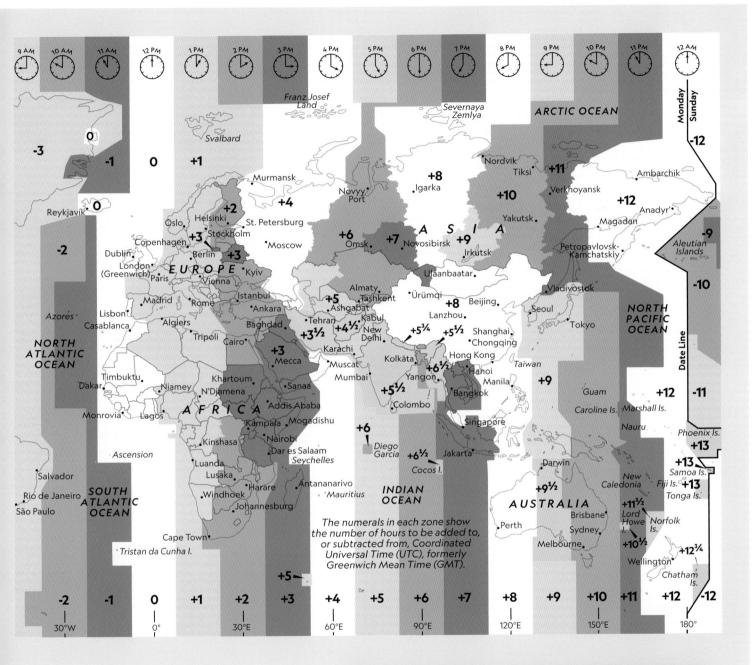

The numerals in each zone show the number of hours to be added to, or subtracted from, Coordinated Universal Time (UTC), formerly Greenwich Mean Time (GMT).

THE DATE LINE (180°) is directly opposite the prime meridian (0°). As Earth rotates, each new day officially begins as the 180° line passes midnight. If you travel west across the date line, you advance one day; if you travel east across the date line, you fall back one day. Notice on the map how the line zigs to the east as it passes through the South Pacific so that the islands of Fiji will not be split between two different days. Also notice that India is 5½ hours ahead of Coordinated Universal Time (UTC) (formerly Greenwich Mean Time, or GMT), and China has only one time zone, even though the country spans more than 60 degrees of longitude. These differences are the result of decisions made at the country level.

The Physical World

Realms of land and water make up the physical world. More than two-thirds of Earth's surface is covered by water: oceans, lakes, and rivers. The rest is land: continents and islands. Every continent is permanently inhabited except Antarctica, which lies frozen beneath a vast ice sheet at Earth's South Pole. Each continent is unique, but all show evidence of dynamic forces at work. Some forces build up mountains such as the Rockies, the Andes, and the Himalaya; other forces wear down Earth's surface, creating vast sedimentary plains and lowlands. Powerful rivers such as the Mississippi, the Congo, and the Yangtze cut through the land and empty billions of gallons of freshwater into the oceans and seas each day.

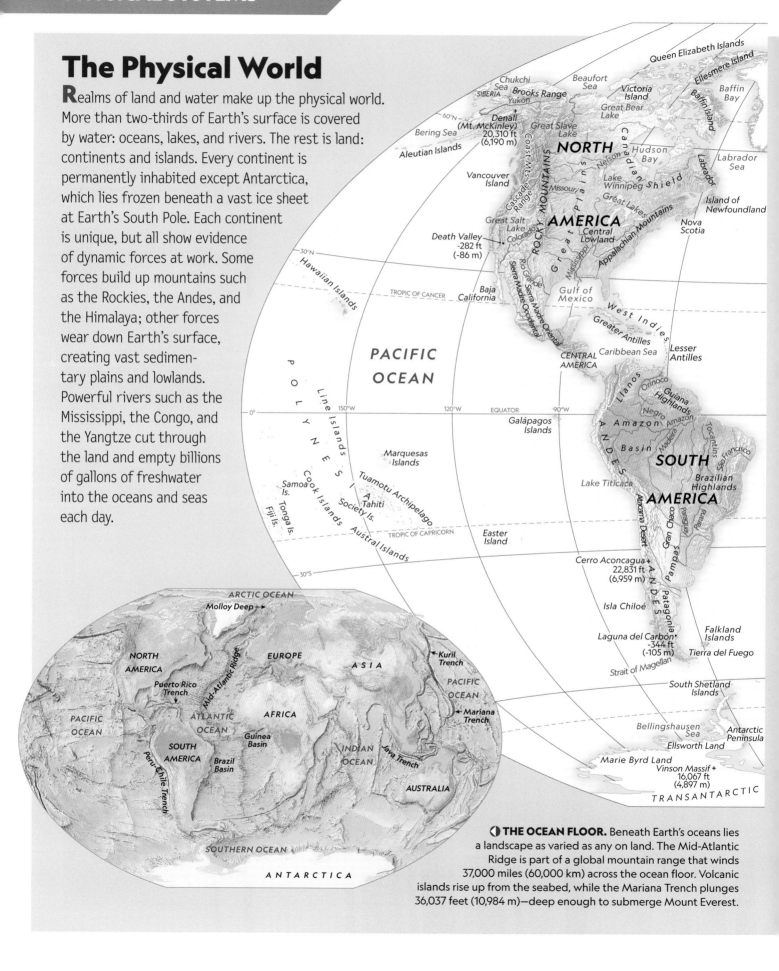

◖ **THE OCEAN FLOOR.** Beneath Earth's oceans lies a landscape as varied as any on land. The Mid-Atlantic Ridge is part of a global mountain range that winds 37,000 miles (60,000 km) across the ocean floor. Volcanic islands rise up from the seabed, while the Mariana Trench plunges 36,037 feet (10,984 m)—deep enough to submerge Mount Everest.

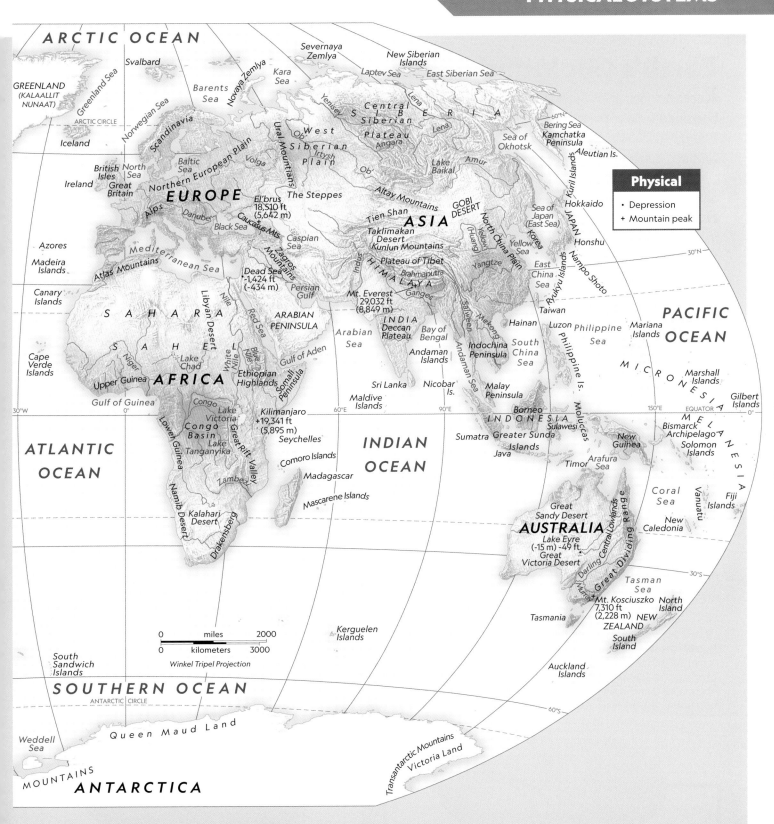

ARCTIC OCEAN

GREENLAND
(KALAALLIT
NUNAAT)

Svalbard

Severnaya
Zemlya

New Siberian
Islands

Greenland Sea

Barents
Sea

Novaya Zemlya

Kara
Sea

Laptev Sea

East Siberian Sea

ARCTIC CIRCLE

Iceland

Norwegian Sea

Scandinavia

Yenisey

C e n t r a l
S i b e r i a n
P l a t e a u

Lena

60°N

Bering Sea

Kamchatka
Peninsula

Aleutian Is.

Ob'

West

Angara

Lena

Sea of
Okhotsk

Kuril Islands

British
Isles

North
Sea

Baltic
Sea

Northern European Plain

Ural Mountains

Siberian
Plain

Irtysh

Ob'

Amur

Lake
Baikal

JAPAN

Hokkaido

Ireland

Great
Britain

EUROPE

Volga

Altay Mountains

GOBI
DESERT

North China Plain

Sea of
Japan
(East Sea)

Honshu

El'brus
18,510 ft
(5,642 m)

The Steppes

ASIA

Tien Shan

Korea

Yellow
(Huang)

Nampo Shoto

Alps

Danube

Black Sea

Caucasus Mts.

Taklimakan
Desert

Kunlun Mountains

Yellow
Sea

30°N

Azores

Mediterranean Sea

Caspian
Sea

Zagros Mountains

Plateau of Tibet

East
China
Sea

Madeira
Islands

Atlas Mountains

Dead Sea
-1,424 ft
(-434 m)

ARABIAN
PENINSULA

Persian
Gulf

H I M A L A Y A

Brahmaputra

Gangeș

Yangtze

Taiwan

PACIFIC
OCEAN

Canary
Islands

S A H A R A

Libyan Desert

Nile

Red Sea

Mt. Everest
29,032 ft
(8,849 m)

Arabian
Sea

INDIA
Deccan
Plateau

Salween

Mekong

Hainan

Luzon

Philippine
Sea

Mariana
Islands

Cape
Verde
Islands

S A H E L

Niger

White Nile

Lake
Chad

Blue Nile

Gulf of Aden

Bay of
Bengal

Indochina
Peninsula

South
China
Sea

Philippine Is.

M I C R O N E S I A

Marshall
Islands

Upper Guinea

AFRICA

Ethiopian
Highlands

Somali Peninsula

Andaman
Islands

Andaman Sea

Gilbert
Islands

Gulf of Guinea

0°

Congo

Lake
Victoria

Great Rift Valley

Kilimanjaro
+19,341 ft
(5,895 m)

Sri Lanka

Maldive
Islands

Nicobar
Is.

Malay
Peninsula

30°W

Congo
Basin

Lower Guinea

Lake
Tanganyika

60°E

90°E

Borneo

INDONESIA

Sulawesi

Moluccas

150°E

EQUATOR

Bismarck
Archipelago

0°

ATLANTIC
OCEAN

Seychelles

Comoro Islands

INDIAN
OCEAN

Sumatra

Greater Sunda
Islands

New
Guinea

Solomon
Islands

M E L A N E S I A

Zambezi

Madagascar

Java

Timor

Arafura
Sea

Coral
Sea

Vanuatu

Fiji
Islands

Namib Desert

Kalahari
Desert

Mascarene Islands

Great
Sandy Desert

AUSTRALIA

Darling

Central Lowlands

Great Dividing Range

New
Caledonia

Drakensberg

Lake Eyre
(-15 m) -49 ft
Great
Victoria Desert

Tasman
Sea

North
Island

miles   2000
0
0   kilometers   3000

Kerguelen
Islands

Murray

Mt. Kosciuszko
7,310 ft
(2,228 m)

Tasmania

NEW
ZEALAND

30°S

Winkel Tripel Projection

South
Island

South
Sandwich
Islands

Auckland
Islands

60°S

SOUTHERN OCEAN

ANTARCTIC CIRCLE

Weddell
Sea

Queen Maud Land

Transantarctic Mountains

Victoria Land

MOUNTAINS

ANTARCTICA

Physical
- Depression
+ Mountain peak

⬤ **THE PHYSICAL WORLD.** Great landmasses called continents break Earth's global ocean into four smaller ones. Each continent is unique in terms of the landforms and rivers that etch its surface and the ecosystems that lend colors to it, ranging from the deep greens of the tropical forests of northern South America and southeastern Asia to the browns and yellows of the arid lands of Africa and Australia. Most of Antarctica's features are hidden beneath its ice sheet.

Earth's Geologic History

Earth is a dynamic planet. Its outer shell, or crust, is broken into huge pieces called plates. These plates ride on the slowly moving molten rock, or magma, that lies beneath the crust. Their movement constantly changes Earth's surface. Along one convergent boundary—a place where two plates meet—the Indian Plate moves northward, colliding with the Eurasian Plate and heaving up the still growing Himalaya. Along another convergent boundary, the Nasca Plate dives beneath the South American Plate—a process called subduction that can trigger volcanoes, underwater earthquakes, and giant ocean waves called tsunamis. Along transform faults, such as California's San Andreas Fault, plates grind past each other, resulting in destructive earthquakes. Along divergent boundaries, plates are pushed apart, as in the Mid-Atlantic Ridge, where the ocean floor is spreading apart, allowing molten rock to rise, and Africa's Great Rift Valley, where the continental plate is separating.

🌐 **OUR CHANGING PLANET.** The Latin phrase *terra firma* implies planet Earth is solid and unchanging. However, Earth's surface has been anything but unchanging. Geologic evidence suggests that moving plates have collided and moved apart more than once over the course of the planet's long history. As the main map shows, the forces of change show no signs of stopping.

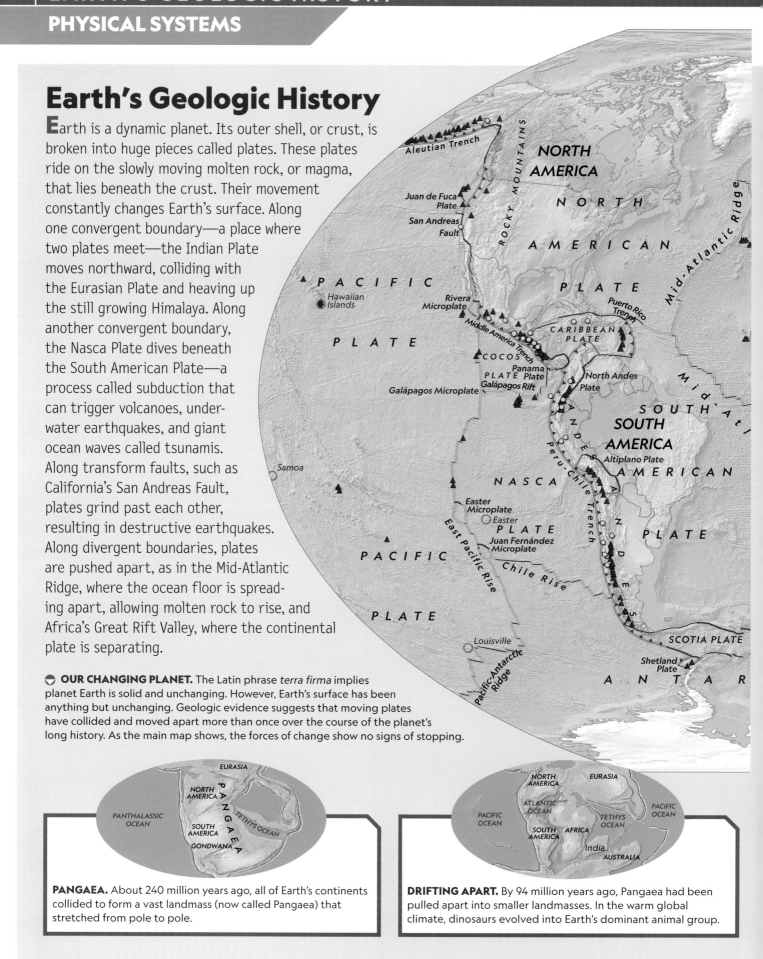

PANGAEA. About 240 million years ago, all of Earth's continents collided to form a vast landmass (now called Pangaea) that stretched from pole to pole.

DRIFTING APART. By 94 million years ago, Pangaea had been pulled apart into smaller landmasses. In the warm global climate, dinosaurs evolved into Earth's dominant animal group.

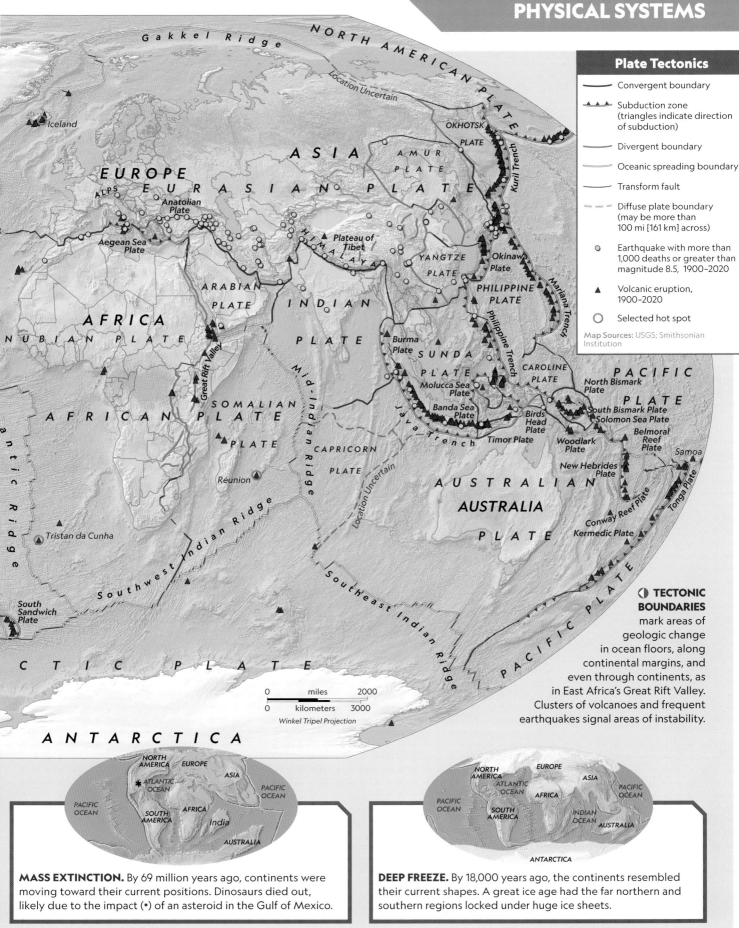

Plate Tectonics

— Convergent boundary

▲▲▲ Subduction zone (triangles indicate direction of subduction)

— Divergent boundary

— Oceanic spreading boundary

— Transform fault

- - - Diffuse plate boundary (may be more than 100 mi [161 km] across)

⊙ Earthquake with more than 1,000 deaths or greater than magnitude 8.5, 1900–2020

▲ Volcanic eruption, 1900–2020

○ Selected hot spot

Map Sources: USGS; Smithsonian Institution

◖ TECTONIC BOUNDARIES mark areas of geologic change in ocean floors, along continental margins, and even through continents, as in East Africa's Great Rift Valley. Clusters of volcanoes and frequent earthquakes signal areas of instability.

0 miles 2000
0 kilometers 3000
Winkel Tripel Projection

MASS EXTINCTION. By 69 million years ago, continents were moving toward their current positions. Dinosaurs died out, likely due to the impact (∗) of an asteroid in the Gulf of Mexico.

DEEP FREEZE. By 18,000 years ago, the continents resembled their current shapes. A great ice age had the far northern and southern regions locked under huge ice sheets.

Earth's Land & Water Features

The largest land and water features on Earth are the continents and the oceans, but many other features—large and small—make each place unique. Mountains, plateaus, and plains give texture to the land. The Rockies and the Andes rise high above the lowlands of North and South America. In Asia, the Himalaya and the Plateau of Tibet form the rugged core of Earth's largest continent. These features are the result of powerful forces within Earth pushing up the land. Other landforms, such as canyons and valleys, are created when weathering and erosion wear down parts of Earth's surface.

Dramatic features are not limited to Earth's continents. Deep beneath the surface of Earth's oceans, submarine mountains appear like pale blue threads in the dark blue water on the satellite map at right. These mountain chains rise from the sea-floor and trace zones of underwater geologic activity where plates converge. Deep trenches form in subduction zones where one plate dives beneath another.

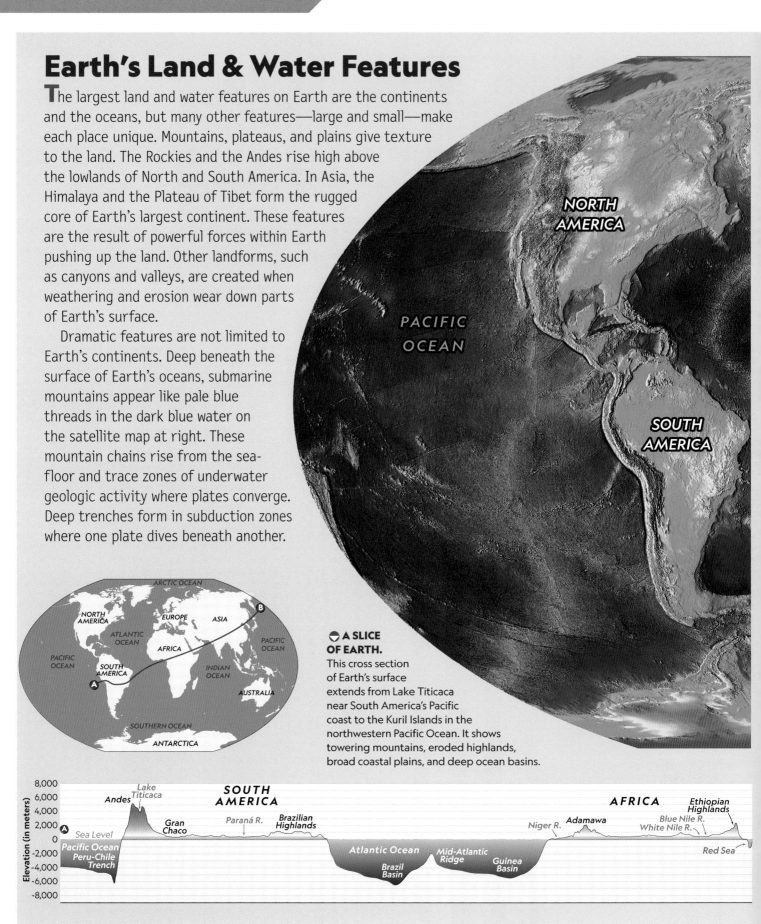

NORTH AMERICA

PACIFIC OCEAN

SOUTH AMERICA

ARCTIC OCEAN

NORTH AMERICA
EUROPE
ASIA
ATLANTIC OCEAN
AFRICA
PACIFIC OCEAN
PACIFIC OCEAN
SOUTH AMERICA
INDIAN OCEAN
AUSTRALIA
SOUTHERN OCEAN
ANTARCTICA

A SLICE OF EARTH.
This cross section of Earth's surface extends from Lake Titicaca near South America's Pacific coast to the Kuril Islands in the northwestern Pacific Ocean. It shows towering mountains, eroded highlands, broad coastal plains, and deep ocean basins.

Elevation (in meters)

8,000
6,000
4,000
2,000
0 — Sea Level
-2,000
-4,000
-6,000
-8,000

Andes
Lake Titicaca
SOUTH AMERICA
Gran Chaco
Paraná R.
Brazilian Highlands
Pacific Ocean Peru-Chile Trench
Atlantic Ocean
Brazil Basin
Mid-Atlantic Ridge
Guinea Basin
Niger R.
Adamawa
AFRICA
Ethiopian Highlands
Blue Nile R.
White Nile R.
Red Sea

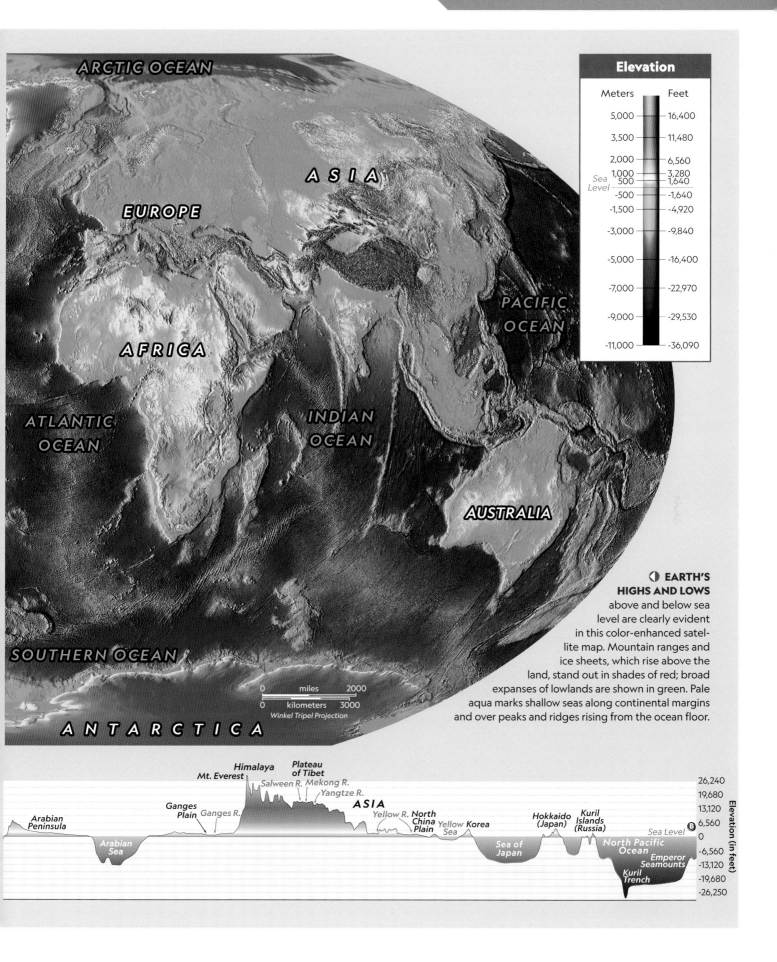

Elevation

Meters	Feet
5,000	16,400
3,500	11,480
2,000	6,560
1,000	3,280
Sea Level / 500	1,640
-500	-1,640
-1,500	-4,920
-3,000	-9,840
-5,000	-16,400
-7,000	-22,970
-9,000	-29,530
-11,000	-36,090

ARCTIC OCEAN — ASIA — EUROPE — AFRICA — ATLANTIC OCEAN — INDIAN OCEAN — PACIFIC OCEAN — AUSTRALIA — SOUTHERN OCEAN — ANTARCTICA

miles 2000 / kilometers 3000 / Winkel Tripel Projection

◖ EARTH'S HIGHS AND LOWS above and below sea level are clearly evident in this color-enhanced satellite map. Mountain ranges and ice sheets, which rise above the land, stand out in shades of red; broad expanses of lowlands are shown in green. Pale aqua marks shallow seas along continental margins and over peaks and ridges rising from the ocean floor.

Cross-section labels: Arabian Peninsula, Arabian Sea, Ganges Plain, Ganges R., Mt. Everest, Himalaya, Salween R., Mekong R., Plateau of Tibet, Yangtze R., ASIA, Yellow R., North China Plain, Yellow Sea, Korea, Sea of Japan, Hokkaido (Japan), Kuril Islands (Russia), North Pacific Ocean, Emperor Seamounts, Kuril Trench, Sea Level Ⓑ

Elevation (in feet): 26,240 / 19,680 / 13,120 / 6,560 / 0 / -6,560 / -13,120 / -19,680 / -26,250

Earth's Climates

Climate is not the same as weather. Climate is the long-term average of conditions in the atmosphere at a particular location on Earth's surface. Weather refers to the momentary conditions of the atmosphere. Climate is important because it influences vegetation and soil development. It also influences people's choices about how and where to live.

There are many different systems for classifying climates. One commonly used system was developed by Russian-born climatologist Wladimir Köppen and later modified by American climatologist Glenn Trewartha. Köppen's system identifies five major climate zones based on average precipitation and temperature, and a sixth zone for highland, or high elevation, areas. Except for continental climate, all climate zones occur in mirror image north and south of the Equator.

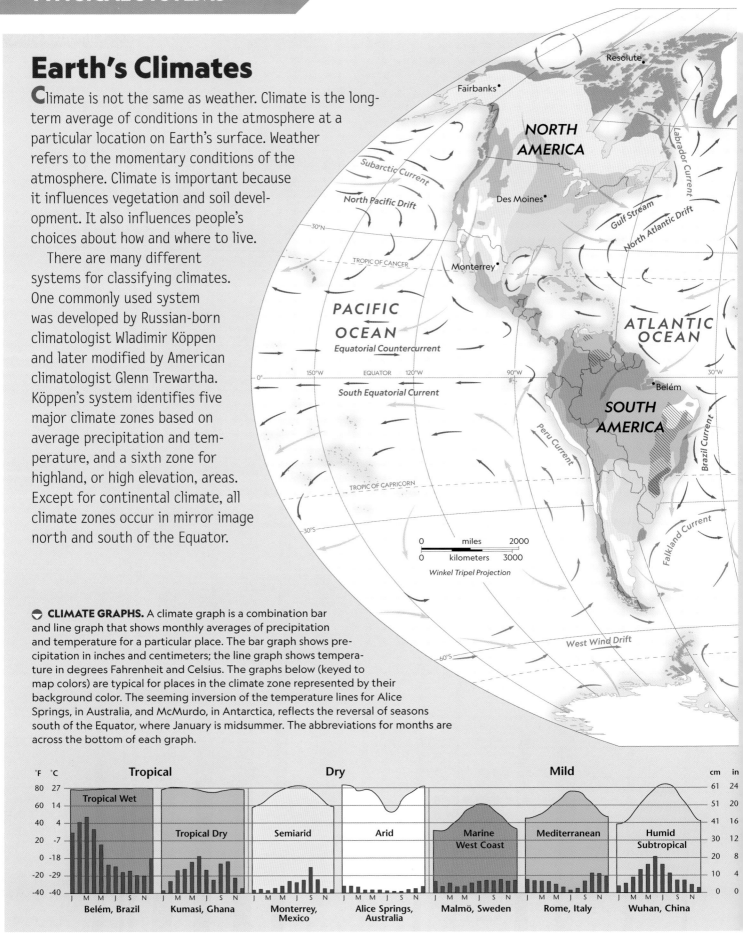

CLIMATE GRAPHS. A climate graph is a combination bar and line graph that shows monthly averages of precipitation and temperature for a particular place. The bar graph shows precipitation in inches and centimeters; the line graph shows temperature in degrees Fahrenheit and Celsius. The graphs below (keyed to map colors) are typical for places in the climate zone represented by their background color. The seeming inversion of the temperature lines for Alice Springs, in Australia, and McMurdo, in Antarctica, reflects the reversal of seasons south of the Equator, where January is midsummer. The abbreviations for months are across the bottom of each graph.

Tropical		Dry		Mild		
Tropical Wet	Tropical Dry	Semiarid	Arid	Marine West Coast	Mediterranean	Humid Subtropical
Belém, Brazil	Kumasi, Ghana	Monterrey, Mexico	Alice Springs, Australia	Malmö, Sweden	Rome, Italy	Wuhan, China

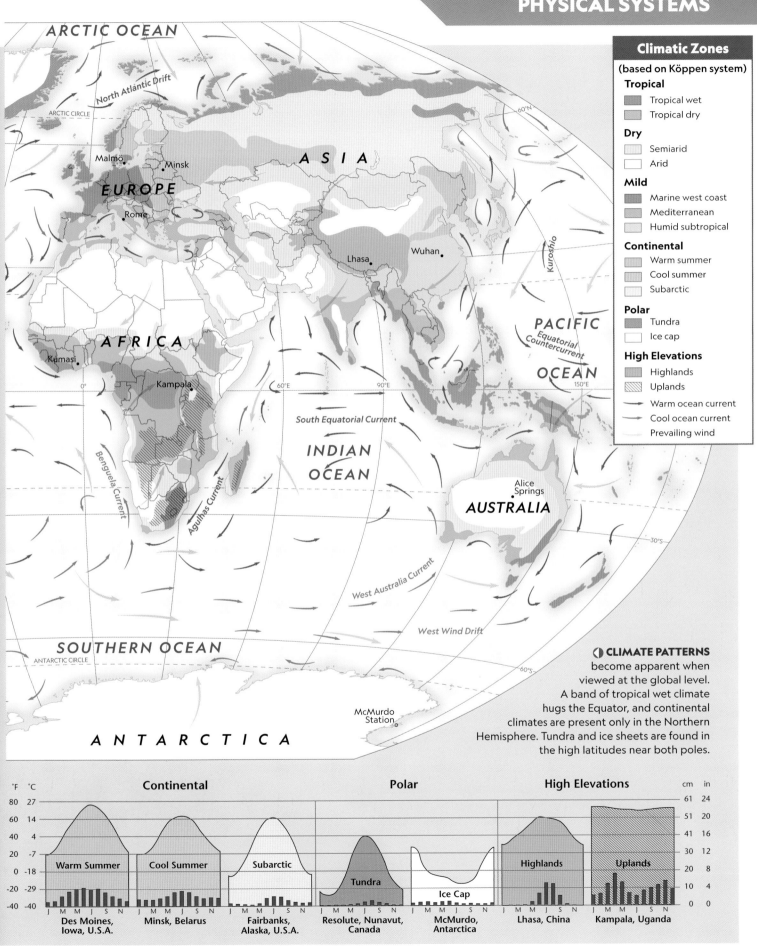

ARCTIC OCEAN

North Atlantic Drift

ARCTIC CIRCLE

60°N

ASIA

Malmö
Minsk

EUROPE

Rome

Lhasa
Wuhan

Kuroshio

PACIFIC

Equatorial
Countercurrent

OCEAN

150°E

AFRICA

Kumasi

Kampala

0°

60°E

90°E

South Equatorial Current

INDIAN

OCEAN

Benguela Current

Agulhas Current

Alice
Springs

AUSTRALIA

30°S

West Australia Current

West Wind Drift

SOUTHERN OCEAN

ANTARCTIC CIRCLE

60°S

McMurdo
Station

ANTARCTICA

Climatic Zones

(based on Köppen system)

Tropical
- Tropical wet
- Tropical dry

Dry
- Semiarid
- Arid

Mild
- Marine west coast
- Mediterranean
- Humid subtropical

Continental
- Warm summer
- Cool summer
- Subarctic

Polar
- Tundra
- Ice cap

High Elevations
- Highlands
- Uplands

- → Warm ocean current
- → Cool ocean current
- → Prevailing wind

◖ **CLIMATE PATTERNS** become apparent when viewed at the global level. A band of tropical wet climate hugs the Equator, and continental climates are present only in the Northern Hemisphere. Tundra and ice sheets are found in the high latitudes near both poles.

°F	°C	Continental			Polar		High Elevations		cm	in
80	27								61	24
60	14								51	20
40	4								41	16
20	-7	Warm Summer	Cool Summer	Subarctic			Highlands	Uplands	30	12
0	-18				Tundra				20	8
-20	-29					Ice Cap			10	4
-40	-40								0	0

J M M J S N — J M M J S N — J M M J S N — J M M J S N — J M M J S N — J M M J S N — J M M J S N

Des Moines, Iowa, U.S.A. | Minsk, Belarus | Fairbanks, Alaska, U.S.A. | Resolute, Nunavut, Canada | McMurdo, Antarctica | Lhasa, China | Kampala, Uganda

Climate Controls

The patterns of climate vary widely. Some climates, such as those near the Equator and the poles, are nearly constant year-round. Others experience great seasonal variations, such as the wet and dry patterns of the tropical dry zone and the monthly average temperature extremes of the subarctic.

Climate patterns are not random. They are the result of complex interactions of basic climate controls: latitude, elevation, prevailing winds, ocean currents, landforms, and location.

These controls combine in various ways to create the bands of climate that can be seen on the world climate map on pages 20–21 and on the climate maps in the individual continent sections of this atlas. At the local level, however, special conditions may create microclimates that differ from those that are more typical of a region.

ELEVATION

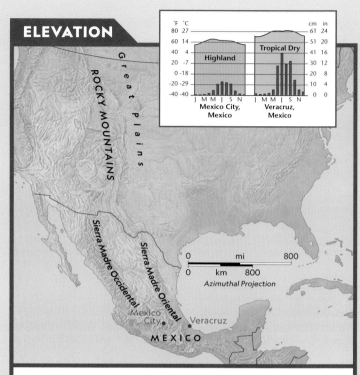

Not all locations at the same latitude experience similar climates. Air at higher elevations is cooler and holds less moisture than air at lower elevations. This explains why the climate at Veracruz, Mexico, which is near sea level, is warm and wet, and the climate at Mexico City, which is more than 7,000 feet (2,100 m) above sea level, is cooler and drier.

LATITUDE

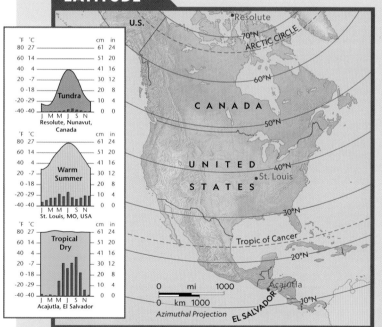

Latitude affects the amount of solar energy received. As latitude (distance north or south of the Equator) increases, the angle of the sun's energy becomes increasingly oblique, or slanted. Less energy is received from the sun, and annual average temperatures fall. Therefore, the annual average temperature decreases as latitude increases from Acajutla, El Salvador, to St. Louis, Missouri, U.S.A., to Resolute, Canada.

LANDFORMS

When air carried by prevailing winds blows across a large body of water, such as the ocean, it picks up moisture. If that air encounters a mountain when it reaches land, it is forced to rise and the air becomes cooler, causing precipitation on the windward side of the mountain (see Portland graph). When air descends on the side away from the wind—the leeward side—the air warms and absorbs available moisture. This creates a dry condition known as rain shadow (see Wallowa graph).

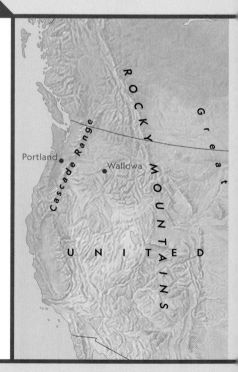

PREVAILING WINDS AND OCEAN CURRENTS

Earth's rotation, combined with heat energy from the sun, creates patterns of movement in Earth's atmosphere called prevailing winds. In the oceans, similar movements of water are called currents. Prevailing winds and ocean currents bring warm and cold temperatures to land areas. They also bring moisture or take it away. The Gulf Stream and the North Atlantic Drift, for example, are warm-water currents that influence average temperatures in eastern North America and northern Europe. Prevailing winds—trade winds, polar easterlies, and westerlies—also affect temperature and precipitation averages.

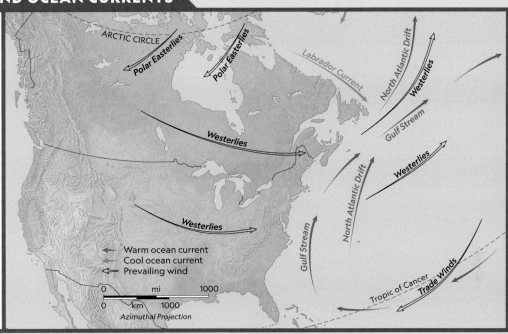

LOCATION

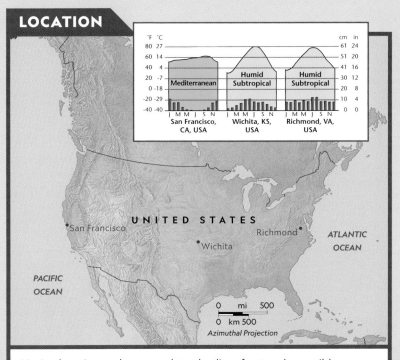

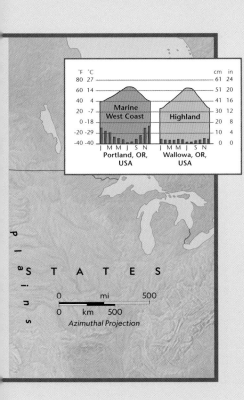

Marine locations—places near large bodies of water—have mild climates with little temperature variation because water gains and loses heat slowly (see San Francisco graph). Interior locations—places far from large water bodies—have much more extreme climates. There are great temperature variations because land gains and loses heat rapidly (see Wichita graph). Richmond, which is relatively near the Atlantic Ocean but which is also influenced by prevailing westerly winds blowing across the land, has the moderate characteristics of both conditions.

Earth's Natural Vegetation

Natural vegetation is plant life that would be found in an area if it were undisturbed by human activity. Natural vegetation varies widely depending on climate and soil conditions. In rainforests, trees tower as much as 200 feet (60 m) above the forest floor. In the humid mid-latitudes, deciduous trees shed their leaves during the cold season, while coniferous trees remain green throughout the year. Areas receiving too little rainfall to support trees have grasses. Dry areas have plants such as cacti that tolerate long periods without water. In the tundra, dwarf species of shrubs and flowers are adaptations to harsh conditions at high latitudes and high elevations.

Vegetation is important to human life. It provides oxygen, food, fuel, products with economic value, even lifesaving medicines. Human activities, however, have greatly affected natural vegetation (see pages 28–29). Huge forests have been cut to provide fuel and lumber. Grasslands have yielded to the plow as people extend agricultural lands.

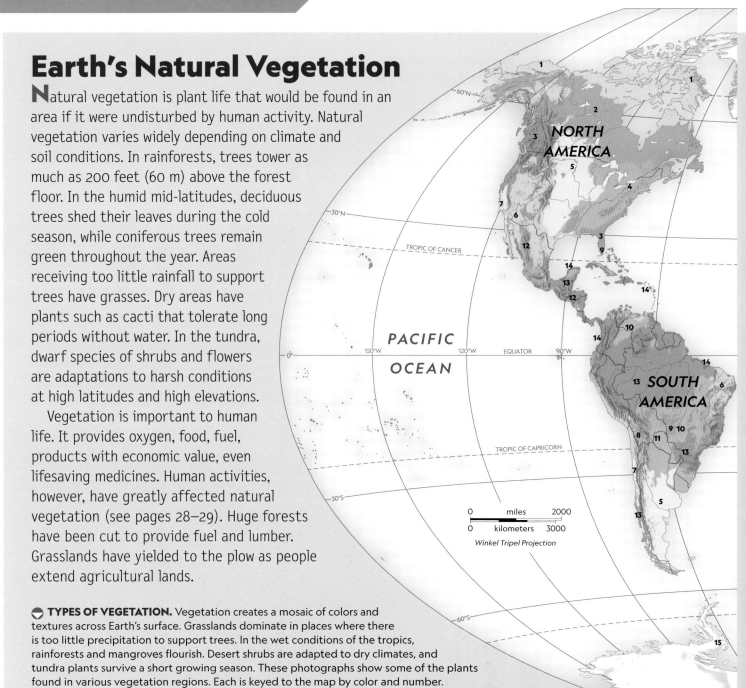

⬤ **TYPES OF VEGETATION.** Vegetation creates a mosaic of colors and textures across Earth's surface. Grasslands dominate in places where there is too little precipitation to support trees. In the wet conditions of the tropics, rainforests and mangroves flourish. Desert shrubs are adapted to dry climates, and tundra plants survive a short growing season. These photographs show some of the plants found in various vegetation regions. Each is keyed to the map by color and number.

1

TUNDRA

2

NORTHERN CONIFEROUS FOREST

4

TEMPERATE BROADLEAF FOREST

5

TEMPERATE GRASSLAND

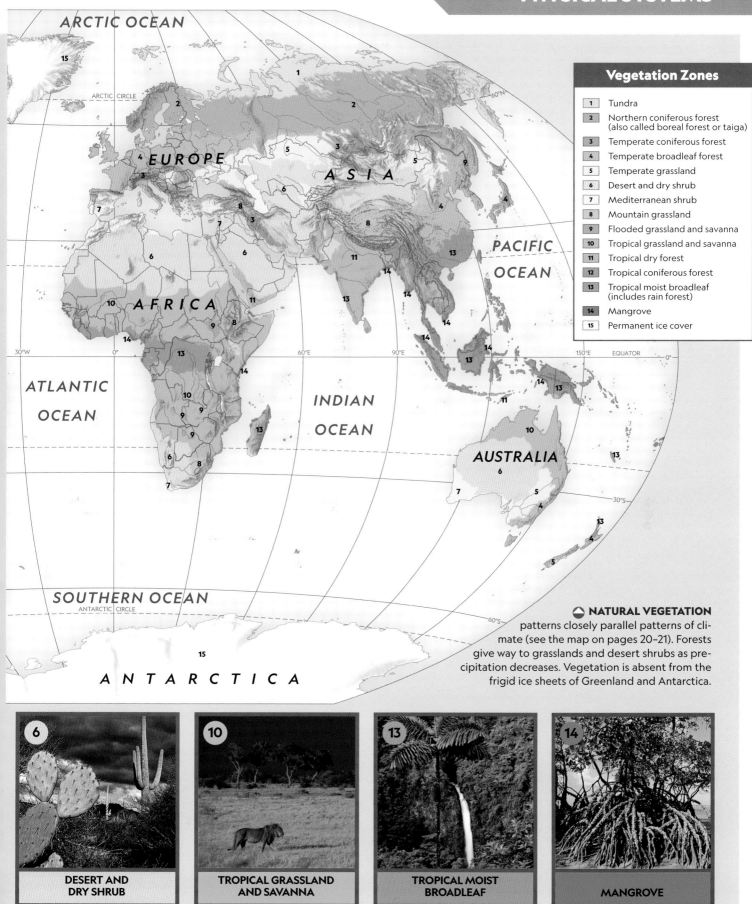

ARCTIC OCEAN

ARCTIC CIRCLE

EUROPE

ASIA

PACIFIC OCEAN

AFRICA

ATLANTIC OCEAN

INDIAN OCEAN

AUSTRALIA

SOUTHERN OCEAN

ANTARCTIC CIRCLE

ANTARCTICA

EQUATOR

Vegetation Zones

1	Tundra
2	Northern coniferous forest (also called boreal forest or taiga)
3	Temperate coniferous forest
4	Temperate broadleaf forest
5	Temperate grassland
6	Desert and dry shrub
7	Mediterranean shrub
8	Mountain grassland
9	Flooded grassland and savanna
10	Tropical grassland and savanna
11	Tropical dry forest
12	Tropical coniferous forest
13	Tropical moist broadleaf (includes rain forest)
14	Mangrove
15	Permanent ice cover

NATURAL VEGETATION patterns closely parallel patterns of climate (see the map on pages 20–21). Forests give way to grasslands and desert shrubs as precipitation decreases. Vegetation is absent from the frigid ice sheets of Greenland and Antarctica.

6 DESERT AND DRY SHRUB

10 TROPICAL GRASSLAND AND SAVANNA

13 TROPICAL MOIST BROADLEAF

14 MANGROVE

Earth's Water

Water is essential for life and is one of Earth's most valuable natural resources. It is even more important than food. More than 70 percent of Earth's surface is covered with water in the form of oceans, lakes, rivers, and streams, but most of this water—about 97 percent—is salty and without treatment is unusable for drinking or growing crops. The remaining 3 percent is fresh, but most of this is either trapped in glaciers or ice sheets or lies too deep underground to be tapped economically.

Water is a renewable resource that can be used over and over because the hydrologic, or water, cycle purifies water as it moves through the processes of evaporation, condensation, precipitation, runoff, and infiltration. However, careless use can diminish the supply of usable freshwater when pollution results from industrial dumping, runoff of fertilizers or pesticides from cultivated fields, or discharge of urban sewage. Like other natural resources, water is unevenly distributed on Earth. Some regions, such as the eastern United States, have sufficient water to meet the needs of the people living there. But in other regions, the demand for water places great stress on available supply (see the map).

NORTH AMERICA

PACIFIC OCEAN

ATLANTIC OCEAN

SOUTH AMERICA

TROPIC OF CANCER

30°N

150°W   EQUATOR   120°W   90°W   30°W

30°S

60°S

Overall Water Risk

Measure of all water-related risks

- Extremely high
- High
- Medium to high
- Low to medium
- Extremely low
- No data

Map Source: WRI

WATER USES

DOMESTIC. Youth activists gather at the World Economic Forum in Davos, Switzerland, to talk about efforts to protect water that people need for daily use.

AGRICULTURAL. Irrigation has made agriculture possible in dry areas such as the San Pedro Valley in Arizona, U.S.A., shown here.

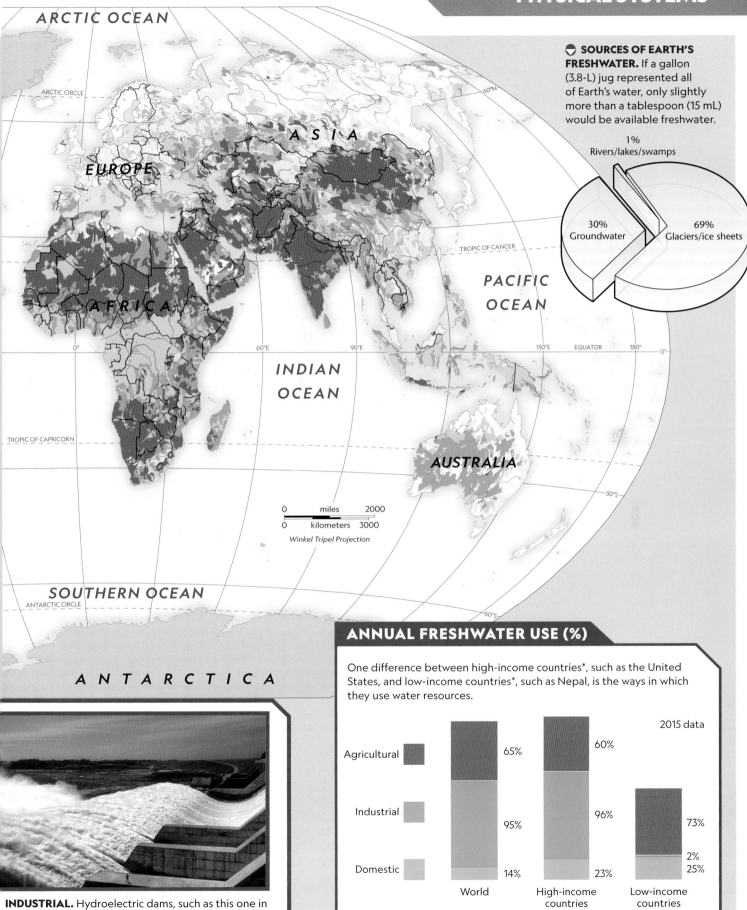

ARCTIC OCEAN

ARCTIC CIRCLE

ASIA

EUROPE

AFRICA

0°   60°E   90°E   150°E   EQUATOR   180°

TROPIC OF CANCER

PACIFIC OCEAN

INDIAN OCEAN

TROPIC OF CAPRICORN

AUSTRALIA

60°N

30°S

0°

0   miles   2000
0   kilometers   3000
Winkel Tripel Projection

SOUTHERN OCEAN
ANTARCTIC CIRCLE

60°S

ANTARCTICA

SOURCES OF EARTH'S FRESHWATER. If a gallon (3.8-L) jug represented all of Earth's water, only slightly more than a tablespoon (15 mL) would be available freshwater.

1%
Rivers/lakes/swamps

30%
Groundwater

69%
Glaciers/ice sheets

INDUSTRIAL. Hydroelectric dams, such as this one in Tucuruí, Brazil, generate electricity to power industry.

ANNUAL FRESHWATER USE (%)

One difference between high-income countries*, such as the United States, and low-income countries*, such as Nepal, is the ways in which they use water resources.

2015 data

Agricultural

Industrial

Domestic

	World	High-income countries	Low-income countries
Agricultural	65%	60%	73%
Industrial	95%	96%	2%
Domestic	14%	23%	25%

*According to the World Bank, high-income countries have gross national incomes per capita of more than $12,235 (US$), and low-income countries have GNI/capita incomes of $1,005 (US$) or less.

Environmental Hot Spots

As Earth's human population increases, pressures on the natural environment also increase. In industrialized countries, landfills overflow with the volume of trash produced. Industries generate waste and pollution that foul the air and water. Farmers use chemical fertilizers and pesticides that run off into streams and groundwater. Cars release exhaust fumes that pollute the air, contributing to global climate change.

In countries, forests are cut and not replanted, making the land vulnerable to erosion. Fragile grasslands turn into deserts when farmers and herders move onto marginal land as they try to make a living. And cities struggle with issues such as water safety, sanitation, and basic services that accompany the explosive urban growth that characterizes many countries.

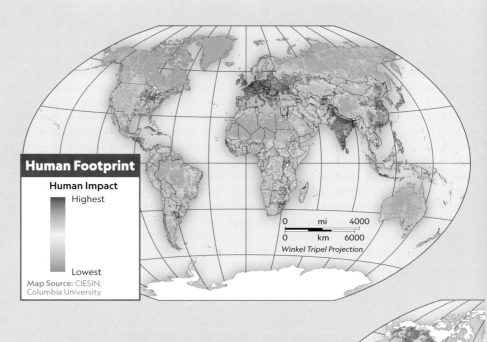

Human Footprint

Human Impact

Highest

Lowest

Map Source: CIESIN, Columbia University

0 mi 4000
0 km 6000
Winkel Tripel Projection

○ **HUMAN ACTIVITY** has altered nearly 75 percent of Earth's habitable surface. Referred to as the "human footprint," this disturbance is greatest in areas of high population.

◑ **FORESTS** play a critical role in Earth's natural systems. They regulate water flow, release oxygen and retain carbon, cycle nutrients, and build soils. But humans have cut, burned, altered, and removed half of all forests that stood 8,000 years ago.

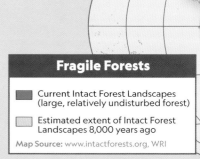

Fragile Forests

◼ Current Intact Forest Landscapes (large, relatively undisturbed forest)

☐ Estimated extent of Intact Forest Landscapes 8,000 years ago

Map Source: www.intactforests.org, WRI

DESERT SANDS, moved by high winds, cover large areas of Mauritania. The shifting sands threaten to cover an important transportation route (upper right), which must be cleared daily. A grid of branches has been laid over the sand to try to slow the advancing desert, which has been expanding since the mid-1960s.

DEFORESTATION in Haiti (left side of photograph above) clearly defines its border with the Dominican Republic. Haiti was once 30 percent forested, but loss of trees for timber and subsistence agriculture has reduced forest cover to less than 2 percent.

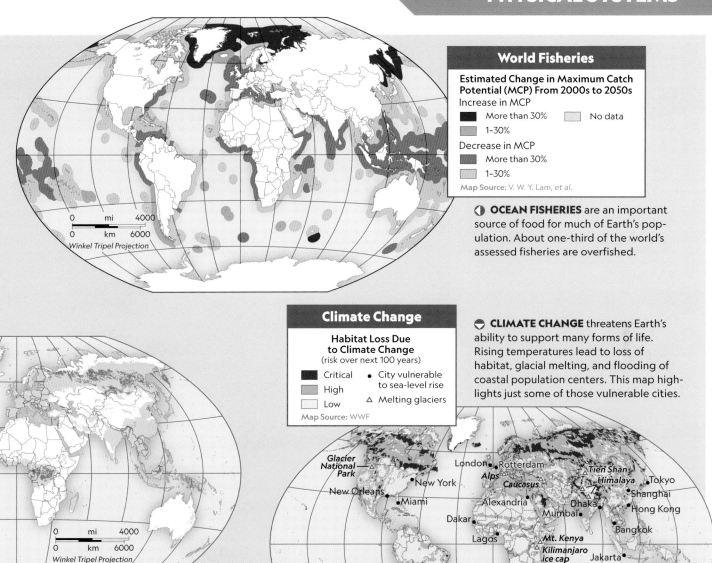

World Fisheries

Estimated Change in Maximum Catch Potential (MCP) From 2000s to 2050s

Increase in MCP
- More than 30%
- 1–30%
- No data

Decrease in MCP
- More than 30%
- 1–30%

Map Source: V. W. Y. Lam, et al.

OCEAN FISHERIES are an important source of food for much of Earth's population. About one-third of the world's assessed fisheries are overfished.

Climate Change

Habitat Loss Due to Climate Change
(risk over next 100 years)
- Critical
- High
- Low
- • City vulnerable to sea-level rise
- △ Melting glaciers

Map Source: WWF

CLIMATE CHANGE threatens Earth's ability to support many forms of life. Rising temperatures lead to loss of habitat, glacial melting, and flooding of coastal population centers. This map highlights just some of those vulnerable cities.

Glacier National Park
London
Rotterdam
Tien Shan
Himalaya
Tokyo
Alps
Caucasus
New York
Shanghai
New Orleans
Alexandria
Dhaka
Hong Kong
Miami
Mumbai
Dakar
Bangkok
Lagos
Mt. Kenya
Kilimanjaro ice cap
Jakarta
Quelccaya Ice Cap
Rio de Janeiro
Buenos Aires

AN OIL SPILL along the coast of Wales, in the United Kingdom, left this beach and the wildlife living there covered with potentially toxic crude oil.

SMOG hangs over Los Angeles, California, U.S.A. This type of air pollution is formed by a combination of vehicle emissions, terrain that traps pollution, and a warm, sunny climate.

The Political World

A map with the names and boundaries of countries shows the political world. Boundaries—some arrived at peacefully, others after years of conflict and war—carve up the land into 195 independent units, or countries. Boundaries are dynamic, meaning they change over time as political power shifts. For example, in 1990, West and East Germany became one country, removing a boundary that had separated them since 1949. In 2011, a boundary was established to separate the new country of South Sudan from Sudan.

Countries vary greatly in size. Russia, the largest, stretches across northern Asia into Europe. Other countries are small enough to fit inside another country. For instance, the country of Lesotho lies entirely within the country of South Africa, and tiny Vatican City lies within the city of Rome, Italy.

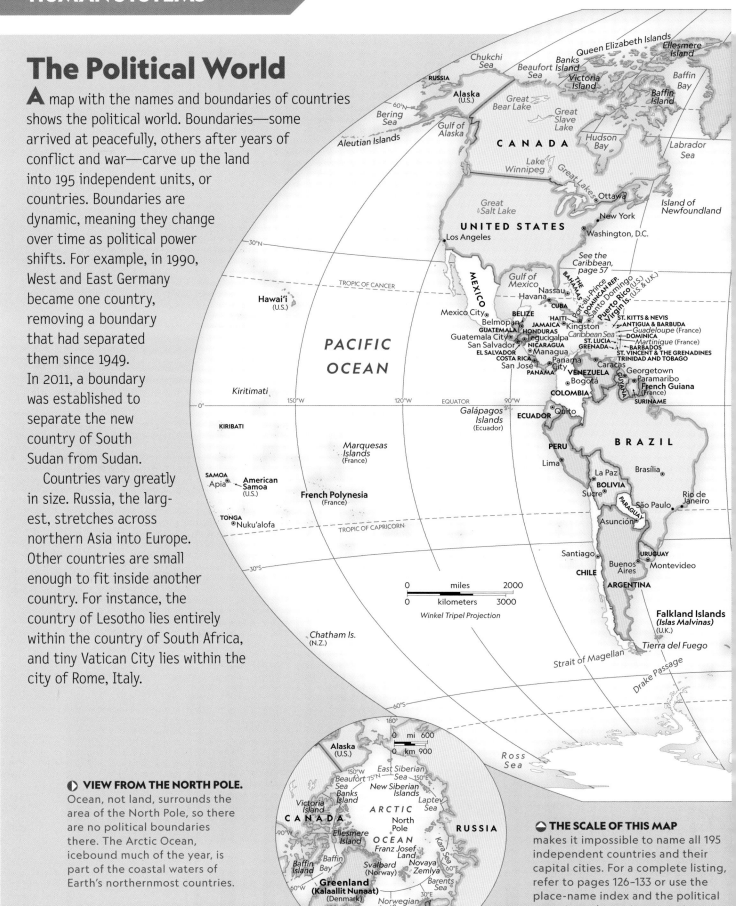

Winkel Tripel Projection

● **VIEW FROM THE NORTH POLE.** Ocean, not land, surrounds the area of the North Pole, so there are no political boundaries there. The Arctic Ocean, icebound much of the year, is part of the coastal waters of Earth's northernmost countries.

◗ **THE SCALE OF THIS MAP** makes it impossible to name all 195 independent countries and their capital cities. For a complete listing, refer to pages 126–133 or use the place-name index and the political maps in each continent section.

Cities
- ⊛ National capital
- • Other major city

TAIWAN
The People's Republic of China claims Taiwan as its 23rd province. Taiwan's government (Republic of China) maintains that there are two political entities.

● **VIEW FROM THE SOUTH POLE.** Covered by ice, the continent of Antarctica has been set aside by treaty for scientific research. It has no permanent population and no political boundaries, although seven countries claim territory there and 20 operate year-round research stations (see map, page 124).

See Europe, pp. 82-83

0 mi 600
0 km 900

World Population

In 2020, the United Nations estimated Earth's population at more than 7.7 billion. Although more than 83 million people are added each year, the rate, or annual percentage, at which the population is growing (1.1 percent) is gradually decreasing. Earth's population is unevenly distributed, with huge clusters in Asia and in Europe. Population density, the average number of people living in each square mile (or square kilometer), is high in these regions. For example, on average, there are more than 2,700 people per square mile (1,265 per sq km) in Bangladesh. Other areas, such as deserts and Arctic tundra, have fewer than two people per square mile (one person per sq km).

◗ **CROWDED STREETS,** like this one in Shanghai, China, may become commonplace as Earth's population continues to increase and as more people move to urban areas.

NORTH AMERICA

New York

Los Angeles

30°N

TROPIC OF CANCER

Mexico City

PACIFIC OCEAN

ATLANTIC OCEAN

Bogotá

150°W EQUATOR 120°W 90°W 30°W 0°

SOUTH AMERICA

Lima

Rio de Janeiro

São Paulo

Buenos Aires

THREE POPULATION PYRAMIDS

A population pyramid is a special type of bar graph that shows the distribution of a country's population by sex and age. Italy has a very narrow pyramid, which shows that most people are in middle age. Its population is said to be aging, meaning the median age is increasing. The United States also has a narrow pyramid, but one that shows some growth due to a median age of almost 38 years and a young immigrant population. By contrast, Nigeria's pyramid has a broad base, showing it has a young population. Almost half of its people are younger than 15 years.

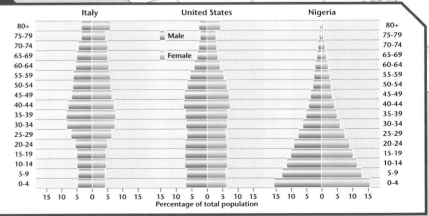

Italy — United States — Nigeria

Male

Female

80+
75-79
70-74
65-69
60-64
55-59
50-54
45-49
40-44
35-39
30-34
25-29
20-24
15-19
10-14
5-9
0-4

15 10 5 0 5 10 15   15 10 5 0 5 10 15   15 10 5 0 5 10 15
Percentage of total population

C.E. 1 50 100 150 200 250 300 350 400 450 500 550 600 650 700 750 800
Year

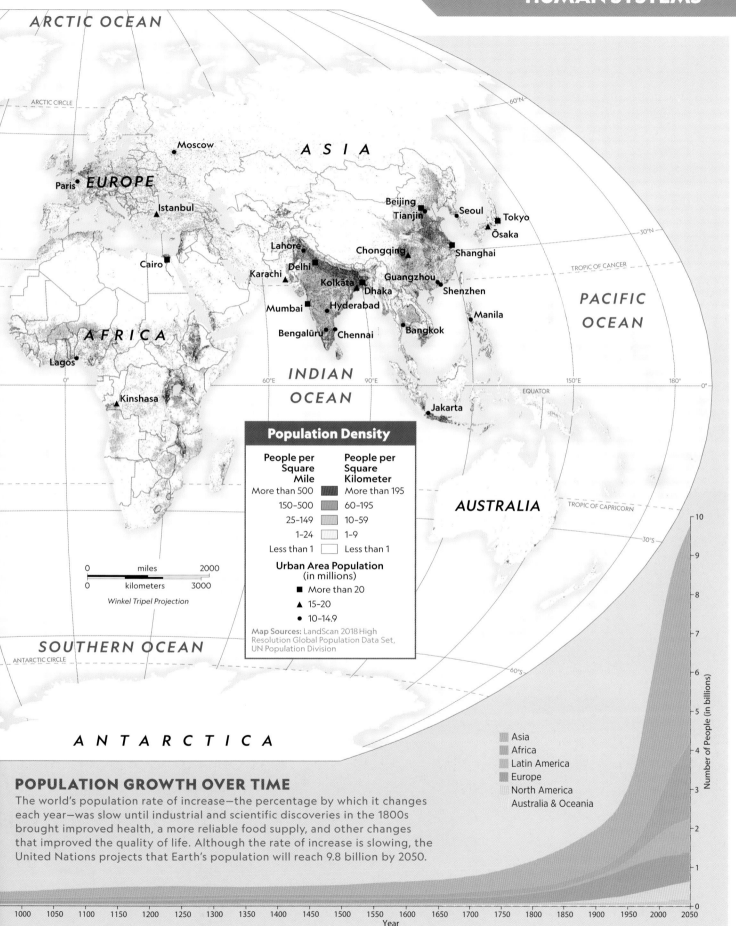

ARCTIC OCEAN

ARCTIC CIRCLE

Moscow

ASIA

Paris EUROPE

Istanbul

Beijing
Tianjin
Seoul
Tokyo
Ōsaka

Lahore
Chongqing
Shanghai

Cairo

Delhi
Karachi
Kolkāta
Guangzhou
Dhaka
Shenzhen

Mumbai
Hyderabad

AFRICA

Bengalūru
Chennai
Bangkok

Manila

PACIFIC
OCEAN

Lagos

INDIAN
OCEAN

Kinshasa

Jakarta

TROPIC OF CANCER

EQUATOR

AUSTRALIA

TROPIC OF CAPRICORN

SOUTHERN OCEAN

ANTARCTIC CIRCLE

ANTARCTICA

Population Density

People per Square Mile	People per Square Kilometer
More than 500	More than 195
150–500	60–195
25–149	10–59
1–24	1–9
Less than 1	Less than 1

Urban Area Population (in millions)
■ More than 20
▲ 15–20
● 10–14.9

Map Sources: LandScan 2018 High Resolution Global Population Data Set, UN Population Division

0 — miles — 2000
0 — kilometers — 3000

Winkel Tripel Projection

POPULATION GROWTH OVER TIME

The world's population rate of increase—the percentage by which it changes each year—was slow until industrial and scientific discoveries in the 1800s brought improved health, a more reliable food supply, and other changes that improved the quality of life. Although the rate of increase is slowing, the United Nations projects that Earth's population will reach 9.8 billion by 2050.

Asia
Africa
Latin America
Europe
North America
Australia & Oceania

Number of People (in billions)

Year
1000 1050 1100 1150 1200 1250 1300 1350 1400 1450 1500 1550 1600 1650 1700 1750 1800 1850 1900 1950 2000 2050

World Refugees

Every day, people relocate. Most people move by choice, but some people, called refugees, move to escape war, persecution, or natural disasters that make it impossible to remain where they are. Such forced movement creates severe hardship for families who must leave behind their possessions. They may find themselves in a place where they do not speak the local language, where customs are unfamiliar, and where basic necessities, such as food, shelter, and medical services, are in short supply.

The High Commissioner for Refugees (UNHCR), an agency of the United Nations, is responsible for the safety and well-being of refugees worldwide and for protecting their rights.

Since 2010, the number of refugees has doubled. In 2020, the UNHCR estimated that there were more than 26.4 million refugees worldwide, and another 48 million internally displaced persons—people still living within their country, but forced to leave their homes.

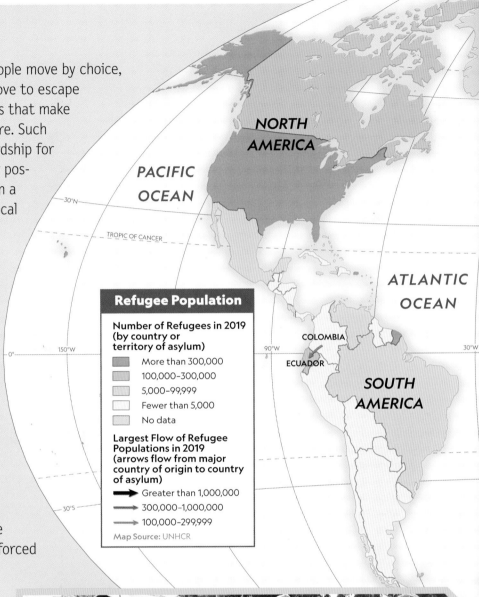

Refugee Population

Number of Refugees in 2019 (by country or territory of asylum)

- More than 300,000
- 100,000–300,000
- 5,000–99,999
- Fewer than 5,000
- No data

Largest Flow of Refugee Populations in 2019 (arrows flow from major country of origin to country of asylum)

- Greater than 1,000,000
- 300,000–1,000,000
- 100,000–299,999

Map Source: UNHCR

REFUGEE HOST COUNTRIES

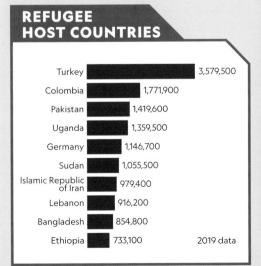

Turkey	3,579,500
Colombia	1,771,900
Pakistan	1,419,600
Uganda	1,359,500
Germany	1,146,700
Sudan	1,055,500
Islamic Republic of Iran	979,400
Lebanon	916,200
Bangladesh	854,800
Ethiopia	733,100

2019 data

REFUGEES fleeing hostilities in the Democratic Republic of the Congo (DRC) receive food in a transit camp in Uganda. Almost four million people have been displaced—many within the DRC, others crossing into neighboring countries.

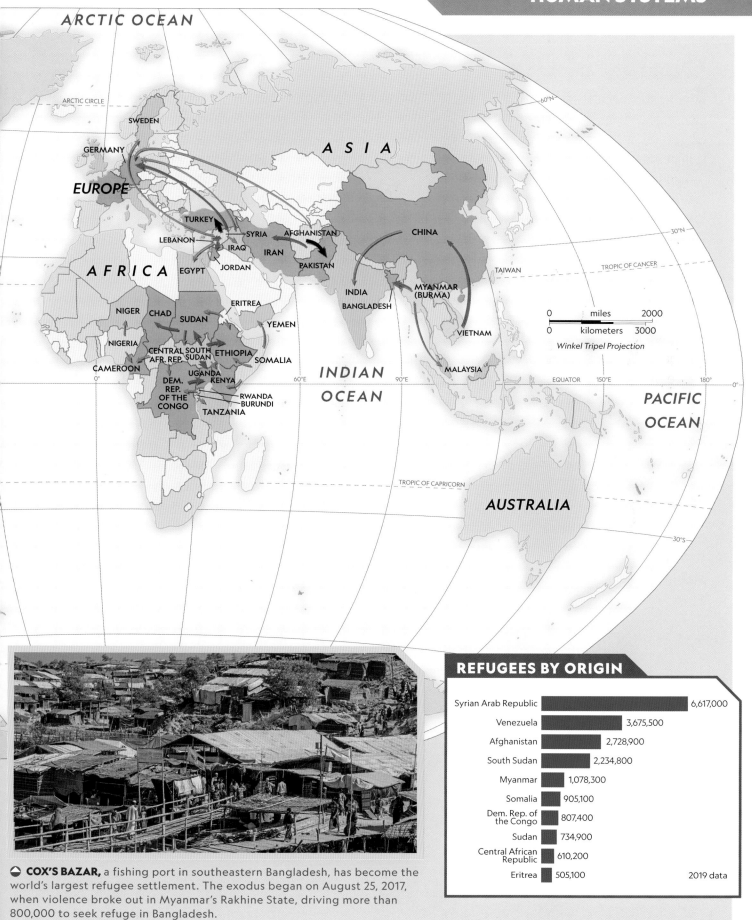

ARCTIC OCEAN

ARCTIC CIRCLE 60°N

SWEDEN

GERMANY

EUROPE

ASIA

TURKEY

LEBANON
IRAQ
SYRIA   AFGHANISTAN   CHINA   30°N

EGYPT   JORDAN   IRAN   PAKISTAN

AFRICA

TAIWAN   TROPIC OF CANCER

NIGER   CHAD   SUDAN   ERITREA

NIGERIA   YEMEN   INDIA   MYANMAR (BURMA)

CENTRAL   SOUTH
AFR. REP.   SUDAN   ETHIOPIA   SOMALIA

CAMEROON   0°   60°E   90°E   INDIAN   EQUATOR   150°E   180°   0°
UGANDA   KENYA   OCEAN   VIETNAM

DEM.
REP.
OF THE
CONGO   RWANDA
BURUNDI   MALAYSIA   PACIFIC
TANZANIA   OCEAN

| 0 | miles | 2000 |
| 0 | kilometers | 3000 |

Winkel Tripel Projection

TROPIC OF CAPRICORN

AUSTRALIA

30°S

COX'S BAZAR, a fishing port in southeastern Bangladesh, has become the world's largest refugee settlement. The exodus began on August 25, 2017, when violence broke out in Myanmar's Rakhine State, driving more than 800,000 to seek refuge in Bangladesh.

REFUGEES BY ORIGIN

Origin	Refugees
Syrian Arab Republic	6,617,000
Venezuela	3,675,500
Afghanistan	2,728,900
South Sudan	2,234,800
Myanmar	1,078,300
Somalia	905,100
Dem. Rep. of the Congo	807,400
Sudan	734,900
Central African Republic	610,200
Eritrea	505,100

2019 data

Quality of Life

The world's population is unevenly distributed (see map on pages 32–33), and not everyone experiences the same quality of life. The level of development in countries is often measured in economic terms, but beginning in 1990, the United Nations Development Program introduced a different and more complete way to evaluate the condition of life in the world's countries: the Human Development Index (HDI). The HDI combines both social and economic factors to rank the world's countries based on three indicators: health, education, and living standard (see map at right). Health is measured by life expectancy at birth (see map below). Education is measured by average years of schooling. And living standard is measured using gross national income (GNI) per capita—the total income earned in a country each year divided by the country's population (see graph on facing page).

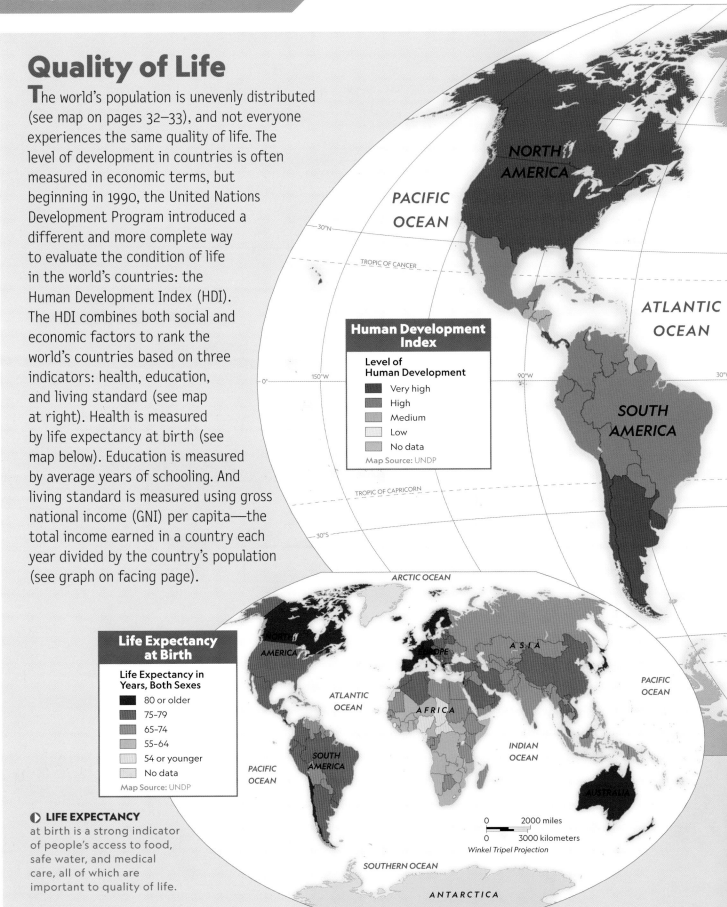

Human Development Index

Level of Human Development
- Very high
- High
- Medium
- Low
- No data

Map Source: UNDP

Life Expectancy at Birth

Life Expectancy in Years, Both Sexes
- 80 or older
- 75–79
- 65–74
- 55–64
- 54 or younger
- No data

Map Source: UNDP

0 — 2000 miles
0 — 3000 kilometers
Winkel Tripel Projection

◗ **LIFE EXPECTANCY** at birth is a strong indicator of people's access to food, safe water, and medical care, all of which are important to quality of life.

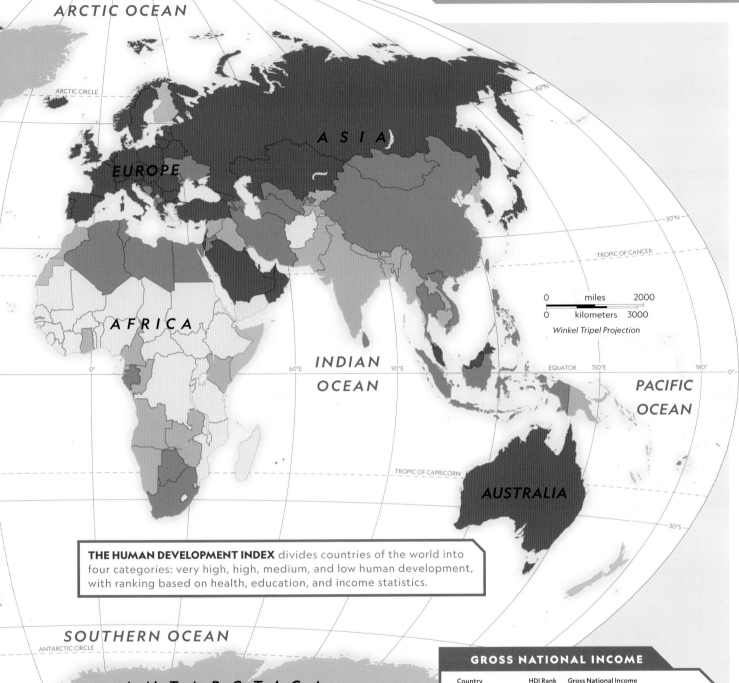

ARCTIC OCEAN

ARCTIC CIRCLE

ASIA

EUROPE

AFRICA

INDIAN
OCEAN

PACIFIC
OCEAN

AUSTRALIA

60°N

30°N

TROPIC OF CANCER

EQUATOR

TROPIC OF CAPRICORN

30°S

0   miles   2000
0   kilometers   3000

Winkel Tripel Projection

THE HUMAN DEVELOPMENT INDEX divides countries of the world into four categories: very high, high, medium, and low human development, with ranking based on health, education, and income statistics.

SOUTHERN OCEAN

ANTARCTIC CIRCLE

ANTARCTICA

◖ **EDUCATION** opens doors to employment and a better standard of living.

GROSS NATIONAL INCOME

Country (10 most populous)	HDI Rank (2020)	Gross National Income per capita
China	85	$10,410
India	131	$2,120
United States	17	$65,850
Indonesia	107	$4,050
Pakistan	154	$1,410
Nigeria	161	$2,030
Brazil	84	$9,130
Bangladesh	133	$1,940
Russia	52	$11,260
Mexico	74	$9,480

◓ **QUALITY OF LIFE,** as measured in terms of income per person, varies greatly among the world's 10 most populous countries.

World Cities

Throughout most of history, people have lived spread across the land, first as hunters and gatherers, later as farmers. But urban geographers—people who study cities—have determined that today more than half of Earth's population lives in urban areas. Urban areas include one or more cities and their surrounding suburbs. Large urban areas are sometimes called metropolitan areas. People living there are employed primarily in industry or service/technology-related jobs. In some countries, such as Belgium, almost everyone lives in cities. But throughout much of Africa and Asia, many people still live in rural areas. Even so, some of the world's fastest growing urban areas are towns and small cities in Africa and Asia.

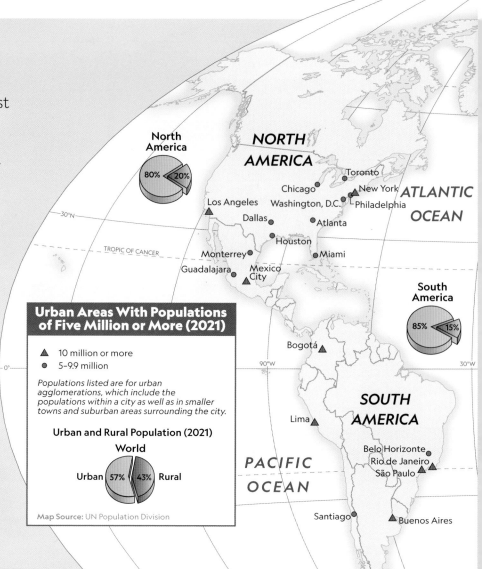

North America 80% 20%

NORTH AMERICA

Toronto
Chicago • New York ATLANTIC
Los Angeles ▲ Washington, D.C. ▲ Philadelphia OCEAN
Dallas • Atlanta
Houston
Monterrey • Miami
Guadalajara • Mexico City ▲

South America 85% 15%

Bogotá ▲

SOUTH AMERICA

Lima ▲

Belo Horizonte •
Rio de Janeiro ▲
São Paulo ▲

PACIFIC OCEAN

Santiago • Buenos Aires ▲

Urban Areas With Populations of Five Million or More (2021)

▲ 10 million or more
● 5–9.9 million

Populations listed are for urban agglomerations, which include the populations within a city as well as in smaller towns and suburban areas surrounding the city.

Urban and Rural Population (2021)
World

Urban 57% 43% Rural

Map Source: UN Population Division

MOST POPULOUS URBAN AREAS

In 1970, only New York, Tokyo, and Osaka, each with populations greater than 10 million, qualified as megacities. By 2018, there were 33 megacities. By 2030, the list is projected to include 43 cities, still led by Tokyo despite a projected decline in its population to 37 million people.

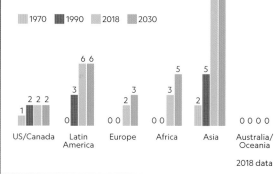

Urban areas with populations greater than 10 million for the years:

■ 1970 ■ 1990 ■ 2018 ■ 2030

US/Canada 1 2 2 2
Latin America 0 3 6 6
Europe 0 0 2 3 3
Africa 0 0 3 5
Asia 2 5 20 27
Australia/Oceania 0 0 0 0

2018 data

⬢ **CENTRAL TOKYO,** viewed from high above crowded city streets, contains a mix of modern high-rise and older low-rise buildings. With almost 38 million people, Tokyo is Japan's largest and most densely populated urban area and the world's largest urban agglomeration.

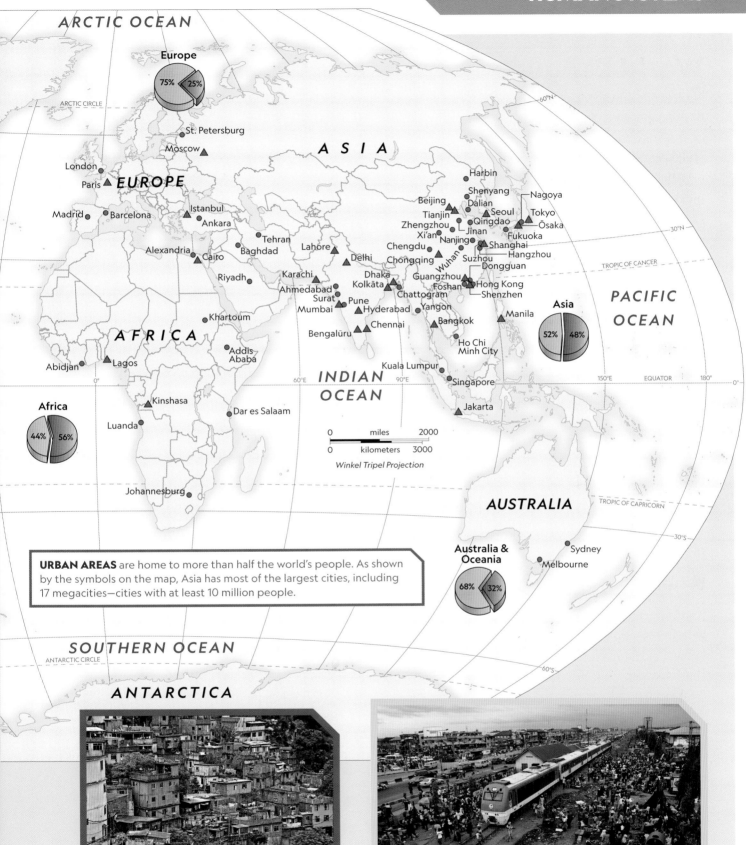

ARCTIC OCEAN

Europe
75% 25%

ARCTIC CIRCLE

St. Petersburg
Moscow ▲

London
Paris ▲ **EUROPE**

A S I A

Harbin
Shenyang
Beijing ● Dalian ● Nagoya
Tianjin ● Seoul ▲ Tokyo
Madrid ● Barcelona ● Istanbul Zhengzhou ● Jinan Qingdao Ōsaka ▲
Ankara Xi'an ● Nanjing ● Fukuoka
Tehran Lahore Chengdu ● ● Shanghai ▲
Alexandria ▲ Baghdad Delhi ▲ Chongqing ▲ Wuhan ● Hangzhou
Cairo ▲ Suzhou
Riyadh ● Karachi ▲ Dongguan
Ahmedabad ● Dhaka ▲ Guangzhou ● TROPIC OF CANCER
Surat ● Kolkāta ▲ Foshan ● Hong Kong
Mumbai ▲ Pune ▲ Chattogram Shenzhen
Khartoum ● Hyderabad ▲ Yangon ▲ **Asia**
Bengalūru ▲▲ Chennai ▲ Bangkok ▲ Manila ▲ 52% 48%

AFRICA Manila ▲ PACIFIC OCEAN

Addis Ho Chi
Abidjan ● Lagos ▲ Ababa ● Minh City ●
Kuala Lumpur ●
Africa *INDIAN* Singapore ●
44% 56% Kinshasa ▲ *OCEAN* EQUATOR
Luanda ● Jakarta ●
Dar es Salaam ●

0 miles 2000
0 kilometers 3000
Winkel Tripel Projection

AUSTRALIA TROPIC OF CAPRICORN

Johannesburg ●

Australia & Sydney ●
Oceania Melbourne ●
68% 32%

> **URBAN AREAS** are home to more than half the world's people. As shown by the symbols on the map, Asia has most of the largest cities, including 17 megacities—cities with at least 10 million people.

SOUTHERN OCEAN
ANTARCTIC CIRCLE

ANTARCTICA

◐ **RAPID URBAN GROWTH** in Rio de Janeiro, Brazil, has resulted in the spread of slums, called favelas, up the steep hillsides around the city.

◐ **AFRICA'S GROWING** cities are expected to add almost 350 million residents by 2030. Cities like Nairobi, Kenya, are working to improve transportation infrastructure to keep up with the growth.

World Languages

Culture is all the shared traits that make different groups of people around the world unique. For example, customs, food and clothing preferences, housing styles, and music and art forms are all a part of each group's culture. Language is one of the most defining characteristics of culture.

Language reflects what people value and the way they understand the world. It also reveals how certain groups of people may have had common roots at some point in history. English and German, for example, are two very different languages, but both are part of the same Indo-European language family. This means that these two languages share certain characteristics that suggest they have evolved from a common ancestor language.

Patterns on the world language families map (right) offer clues to the diffusion, or movement, of groups of people. For example, the widespread use of English, extending from the United States to India and Australia, reflects the far-reaching effects of the British colonial empire. Today, English is the main language of the internet.

About 5,000 languages are spoken in the world today, but experts think many may become extinct as more people become involved in global trade, communications, and travel.

MOST COMMONLY SPOKEN LANGUAGES

Among the 10 most widely spoken languages by number of first-language speakers, seven—including English—belong to the Indo-European language family.

Population of first-language speakers (in millions)

English	1,348
Mandarin Chinese	1,120
Hindi	600
Spanish	543
Standard Arabic	274
Bengali	268
French	267
Russian	258
Portuguese	258
Urdu	230

2021 data

▷ **THE GOLDEN ARCHES** icon helps you identify this restaurant in Moscow even if you don't know how to read the Cyrillic alphabet of the Russian language.

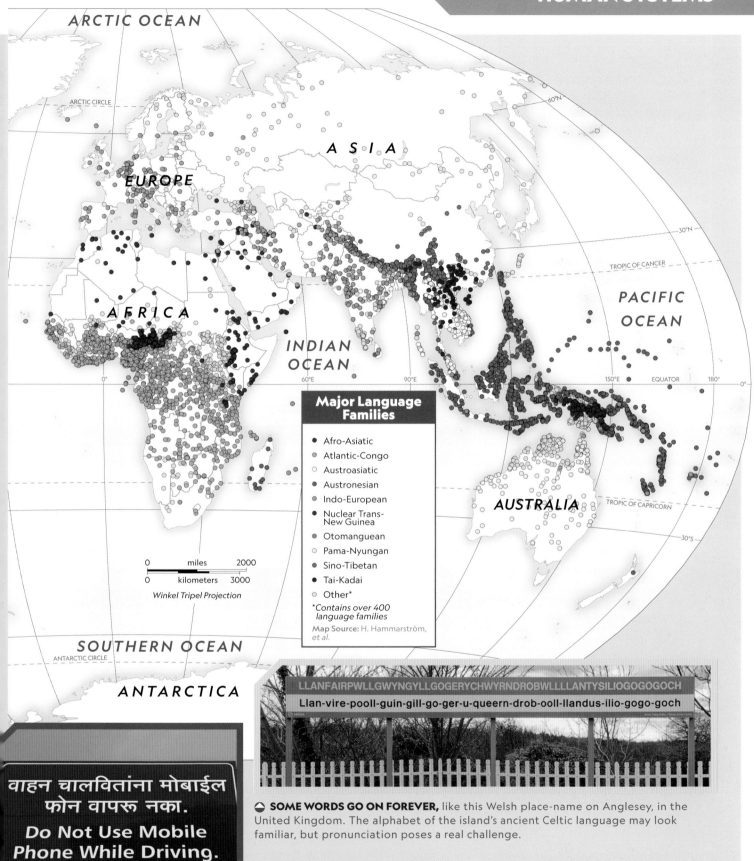

ARCTIC OCEAN

ARCTIC CIRCLE

ASIA

EUROPE

AFRICA

PACIFIC OCEAN

INDIAN OCEAN

TROPIC OF CANCER

AUSTRALIA

TROPIC OF CAPRICORN

Major Language Families

- Afro-Asiatic
- Atlantic-Congo
- Austroasiatic
- Austronesian
- Indo-European
- Nuclear Trans-New Guinea
- Otomanguean
- Pama-Nyungan
- Sino-Tibetan
- Tai-Kadai
- Other*

*Contains over 400 language families

Map Source: H. Hammarström, et al.

0 miles 2000
0 kilometers 3000

Winkel Tripel Projection

SOUTHERN OCEAN

ANTARCTIC CIRCLE

ANTARCTICA

LLANFAIRPWLLGWYNGYLLGOGERYCHWYRNDROBWLLLLANTYSILIOGOGOGOCH

Llan-vire-pooll-guin-gill-go-ger-u-queern-drob-ooll-llandus-ilio-gogo-goch

◯ **SOME WORDS GO ON FOREVER,** like this Welsh place-name on Anglesey, in the United Kingdom. The alphabet of the island's ancient Celtic language may look familiar, but pronunciation poses a real challenge.

वाहन चालवितांना मोबाईल फोन वापरु नका.
Do Not Use Mobile Phone While Driving.

◖ **MARATHI,** an Indo-European language derived from ancient Sanskrit, appears on a highway sign in Pune, Maharashtra, India, warning drivers about a safety issue that is a worldwide problem.

World Religions

Religion is a central element of culture. Religious beliefs and practices help people deal with the unknown. But people in different places have developed a variety of belief systems.

Universalizing religions, such as Christianity, Islam, and Buddhism, seek converts. Carried by migration, colonization, and global trade, these religions have spread throughout the world from their places of origin in different parts of Asia. Ethnic religions, including Judaism, Hinduism, and Shinto, tend to be associated with particular groups of people and are generally concentrated in certain places. Some groups, especially Indigenous, or Native, people living in remote areas, believe that spirits inhabit all things in the natural world. These kinds of belief systems are known as animistic religions.

Places of worship are often a distinctive part of the cultural landscape. A cathedral, mosque, or temple can reveal much about the people who live in a particular place.

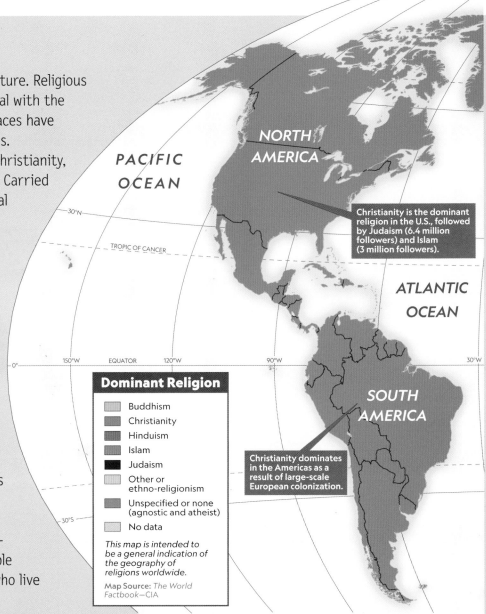

NORTH AMERICA

PACIFIC OCEAN

ATLANTIC OCEAN

SOUTH AMERICA

Christianity is the dominant religion in the U.S., followed by Judaism (6.4 million followers) and Islam (3 million followers).

Christianity dominates in the Americas as a result of large-scale European colonization.

Dominant Religion

- Buddhism
- Christianity
- Hinduism
- Islam
- Judaism
- Other or ethno-religionism
- Unspecified or none (agnostic and atheist)
- No data

This map is intended to be a general indication of the geography of religions worldwide.

Map Source: *The World Factbook*—CIA

⬥ **MOST OF HINDUISM'S** one billion followers live in India and other South Asian countries. The goddess Durga (above) is regarded as Mother of the Universe and protector of the righteous.

⬥ **JERUSALEM IS HOLY** to Jews, Christians, and Muslims, a fact that has led to tension and conflict. Below, a Russian Orthodox church (foreground) overlooks the Western Wall, sacred to Jews, while sunlight reflects off the Dome of the Rock, a Muslim shrine.

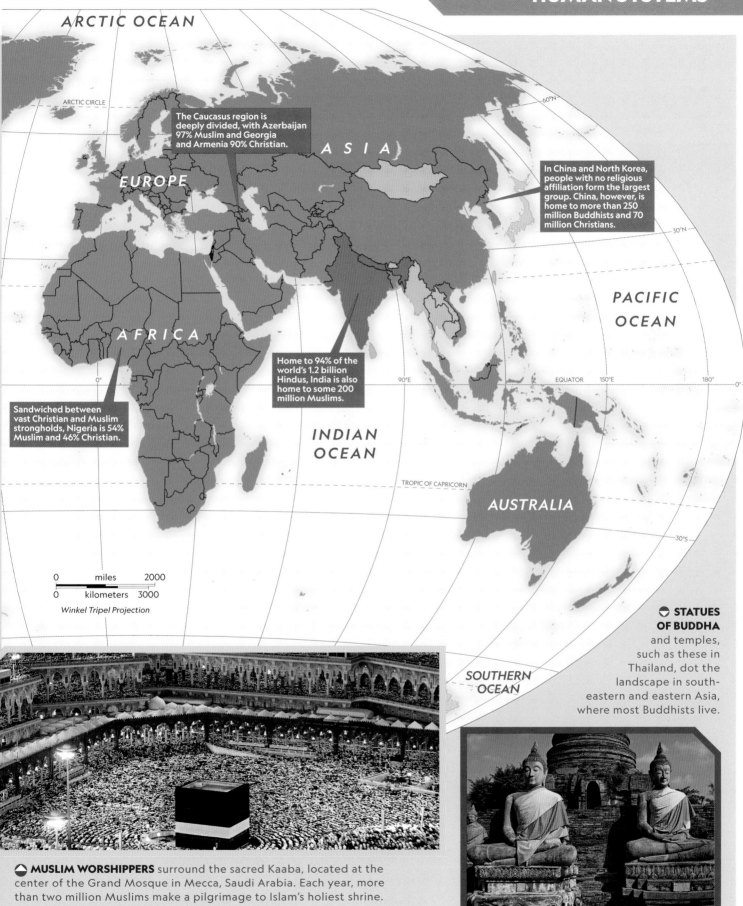

ARCTIC OCEAN

ARCTIC CIRCLE

ASIA

EUROPE

The Caucasus region is deeply divided, with Azerbaijan 97% Muslim and Georgia and Armenia 90% Christian.

In China and North Korea, people with no religious affiliation form the largest group. China, however, is home to more than 250 million Buddhists and 70 million Christians.

PACIFIC OCEAN

AFRICA

Home to 94% of the world's 1.2 billion Hindus, India is also home to some 200 million Muslims.

Sandwiched between vast Christian and Muslim strongholds, Nigeria is 54% Muslim and 46% Christian.

INDIAN OCEAN

AUSTRALIA

0 miles 2000
0 kilometers 3000

Winkel Tripel Projection

SOUTHERN OCEAN

◆ STATUES OF BUDDHA and temples, such as these in Thailand, dot the landscape in southeastern and eastern Asia, where most Buddhists live.

◆ MUSLIM WORSHIPPERS surround the sacred Kaaba, located at the center of the Grand Mosque in Mecca, Saudi Arabia. Each year, more than two million Muslims make a pilgrimage to Islam's holiest shrine.

Predominant World Economies

People generate income to meet their needs and wants through a variety of activities that can be grouped into four categories, or sectors: primary (agriculture, fishing, and forestry); secondary (manufacturing and processing activities); tertiary (services ranging from retail sales to teaching, banking, and medicine); and quaternary (information creation and exchange and e-commerce—buying and selling over the internet). Services and industry generate higher incomes, and therefore account for a greater share of a country's gross domestic product (GDP), although not necessarily a greater percentage of the workforce. In many countries, a large part of the workforce is still engaged in agriculture, which generates low income and perpetuates poverty.

PACIFIC OCEAN

NORTH AMERICA

ATLANTIC OCEAN

SOUTH AMERICA

30°N
TROPIC OF CANCER
0°
30°S
90°W
30°W

Dominant Economic Sector (as a percentage of GDP)

	Agriculture	Industry	Services
70%–100%			
50%–69.9%			
0%–49.9%			
No data			

Map Source: *The World Factbook—CIA*

⬥ **SUBSISTENCE AGRICULTURE.** Many people, such as these farmers in Bhutan, use traditional methods to grow crops for their daily food requirements rather than for commercial sale.

⬥ **MANUFACTURING.** This mill in Slovakia processes raw materials such as coal and iron ore to make steel. Industries use steel to produce cars and other manufactured goods.

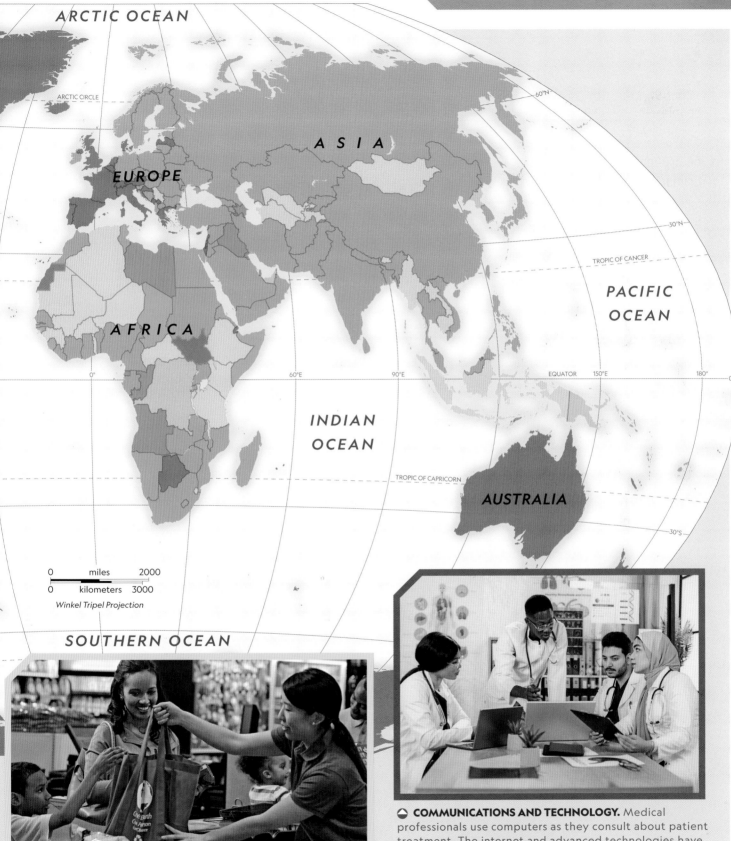

ARCTIC OCEAN

ARCTIC CIRCLE

ASIA

EUROPE

AFRICA

TROPIC OF CANCER

PACIFIC OCEAN

EQUATOR

INDIAN OCEAN

TROPIC OF CAPRICORN

AUSTRALIA

0 miles 2000
0 kilometers 3000

Winkel Tripel Projection

SOUTHERN OCEAN

⬭ **SERVICES.** Ranging from banking to education to retail sales, service, or tertiary, jobs involve interacting with people, such as this grocery clerk handing over a family's purchases.

⬭ **COMMUNICATIONS AND TECHNOLOGY.** Medical professionals use computers as they consult about patient treatment. The internet and advanced technologies have introduced new ways of exchanging information in order to solve problems. Email and social media connect people near and far, while e-commerce makes possible buying and selling from home or office.

World Food

In 2019, the world's population topped 7.7 billion people—all needing to be fed. However, the productive potential of Earth's surface varies greatly from place to place. Some areas are good for growing crops; some are better for grazing animals; and others have little or no agricultural potential. Grains, such as rice, corn, and wheat, are main sources of food calories, while meat, poultry, and fish are sources of protein.

RICE is an important staple food crop, especially in eastern and southern Asia. Although China produces more than 40 percent of the world's rice, it is also a major importer of rice to feed its population of more than a billion people.

PACIFIC OCEAN

NORTH AMERICA

ATLANTIC OCEAN

30°N

TROPIC OF CANCER

SOUTH AMERICA

Agricultural Land Use

Pasture — Cropland
☐ No data

Map Source: University of Minnesota

0° 150°W 90°W 30°W

TROPIC OF CAPRICORN

30°S

CORN, which originated in the Americas, is an important food grain for people and livestock. Corn is also used to make ethanol, which is added to gasoline to make a cleaner fuel.

WHEAT, the world's leading export grain, is a main ingredient in bread and pasta and is grown on every inhabited continent. Each year, trade in this grain exceeds 175 million tons (159 million t).

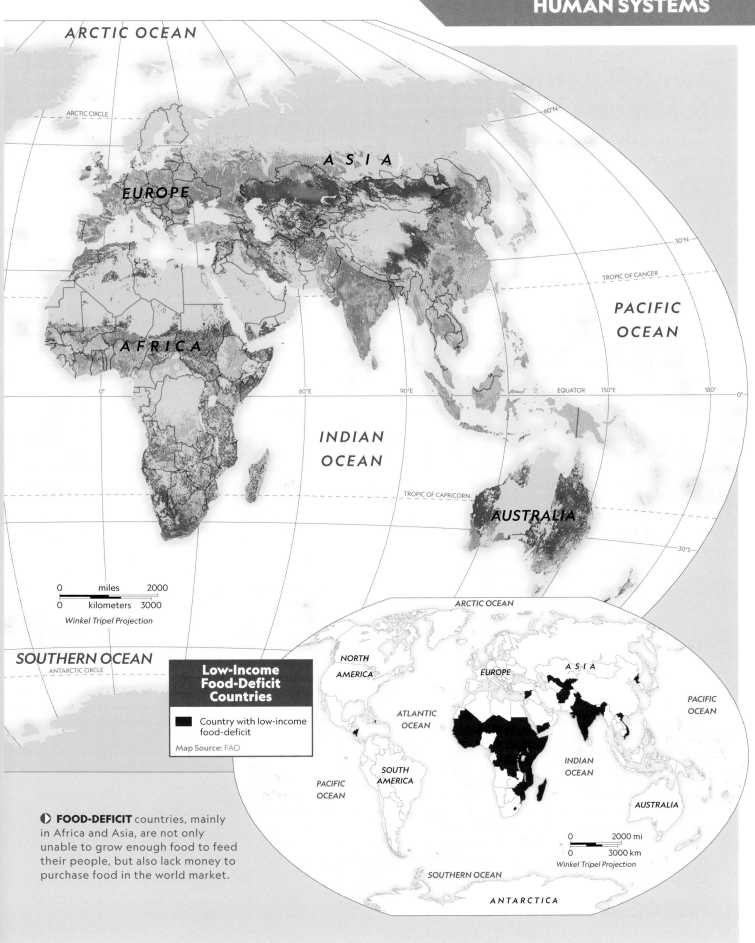

ARCTIC OCEAN

ARCTIC CIRCLE

ASIA

EUROPE

60°N

30°N

TROPIC OF CANCER

PACIFIC
OCEAN

AFRICA

0°

60°E

90°E

EQUATOR

150°E

180°

0°

INDIAN
OCEAN

TROPIC OF CAPRICORN

AUSTRALIA

30°S

0   miles   2000
0   kilometers   3000
Winkel Tripel Projection

SOUTHERN OCEAN

ANTARCTIC CIRCLE

Low-Income Food-Deficit Countries

■ Country with low-income food-deficit

Map Source: FAO

ARCTIC OCEAN

NORTH
AMERICA

EUROPE

ASIA

ATLANTIC
OCEAN

PACIFIC
OCEAN

SOUTH
AMERICA

INDIAN
OCEAN

PACIFIC
OCEAN

AUSTRALIA

0   2000 mi
0   3000 km
Winkel Tripel Projection

SOUTHERN OCEAN

ANTARCTICA

◗ **FOOD-DEFICIT** countries, mainly
in Africa and Asia, are not only
unable to grow enough food to feed
their people, but also lack money to
purchase food in the world market.

World Energy & Mineral Resources

Beginning in the 19th century, as the industrial revolution spread across Europe and around the world, the demand for energy and non-fuel mineral resources skyrocketed. Fossil fuels—first coal, then oil and natural gas—have provided the energy that keeps the wheels of industry turning. Non-fuel minerals such as iron ore (essential for steel production) and copper (for electrical wiring) have become increasingly important.

Energy and non-fuel minerals, like all nonrenewable resources, are in limited supply and are unevenly distributed. Exporting countries with major deposits can influence both supply and prices of these resources, thus playing an important role in the global economy.

RENEWABLE ENERGY, including energy from the sun, wind, running water, and heat from within Earth, is an important alternative to fossil fuels. Some examples are shown below.

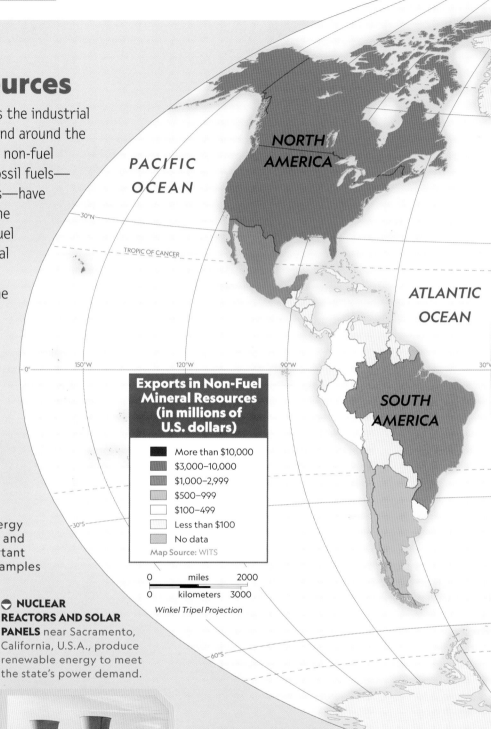

Exports in Non-Fuel Mineral Resources (in millions of U.S. dollars)

- ■ More than $10,000
- ■ $3,000–10,000
- ■ $1,000–2,999
- ■ $500–999
- □ $100–499
- □ Less than $100
- ■ No data

Map Source: WITS

0 miles 2000
0 kilometers 3000

Winkel Tripel Projection

● **WINDMILLS** rising above ancient temples near Jaisalmer, India, generate electricity by capturing the energy of winds blowing off the Indian Ocean.

● **NUCLEAR REACTORS AND SOLAR PANELS** near Sacramento, California, U.S.A., produce renewable energy to meet the state's power demand.

◖ **A GEOTHERMAL POWER PLANT,** fueled by heat from within Earth, produces energy to heat homes in Iceland. Runoff creates a warm pool for bathers.

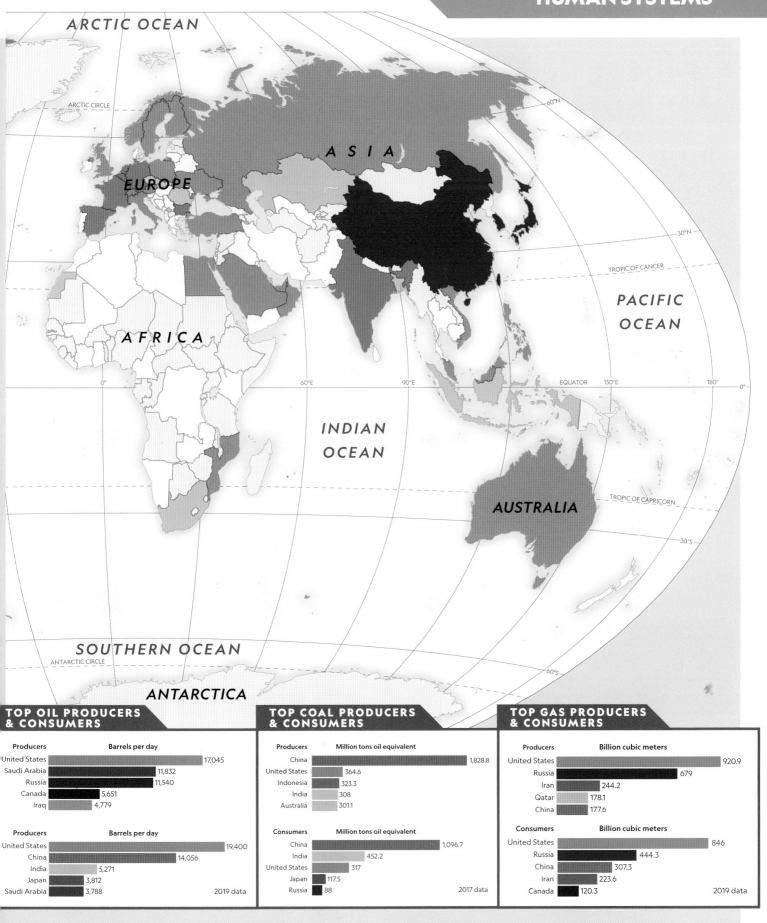

ARCTIC OCEAN

ARCTIC CIRCLE

60°N

ASIA

EUROPE

30°N

TROPIC OF CANCER

AFRICA

PACIFIC
OCEAN

0°

60°E

90°E

EQUATOR

150°E

180°

0°

INDIAN
OCEAN

AUSTRALIA

TROPIC OF CAPRICORN

30°S

SOUTHERN OCEAN

ANTARCTIC CIRCLE

60°S

ANTARCTICA

TOP OIL PRODUCERS & CONSUMERS

Producers	Barrels per day	
United States		17,045
Saudi Arabia		11,832
Russia		11,540
Canada	5,651	
Iraq	4,779	

Producers	Barrels per day	
United States		19,400
China		14,056
India	5,271	
Japan	3,812	
Saudi Arabia	3,788	2019 data

TOP COAL PRODUCERS & CONSUMERS

Producers	Million tons oil equivalent	
China		1,828.8
United States	364.6	
Indonesia	323.3	
India	308	
Australia	301.1	

Consumers	Million tons oil equivalent	
China		1,096.7
India	452.2	
United States	317	
Japan	117.5	
Russia	88	2017 data

TOP GAS PRODUCERS & CONSUMERS

Producers	Billion cubic meters	
United States		920.9
Russia		679
Iran	244.2	
Qatar	178.1	
China	177.6	

Consumers	Billion cubic meters	
United States		846
Russia	444.3	
China	307.3	
Iran	223.6	
Canada	120.3	2019 data

Globalization

The early years of the 21st century have seen a technology revolution that has changed the way people and countries relate to each other. This revolution in technology is part of a process known as globalization.

Globalization refers to the complex network of interconnections linking people, companies, and places without regard for national boundaries. Although it began when some countries became increasingly active in international trade, the process of globalization has gained momentum in recent years, expanding to include political and social interactions. But not all countries are major players in the global arena.

Improvements in communications and transportation have made it possible for companies to employ workers in distant countries. Some workers make clothing; some perform accounting tasks; and others work in call centers answering inquiries about products or services. Technology also allows banking transactions to take place faster and over greater distances than ever before. Companies that conduct business in multiple countries around the world are called transnational companies.

An important part of today's global communications system is the internet, a vast system of computer networks that allows people to access information around the world in seconds. Ideas and images now travel over the internet, introducing change and making places more and more alike.

◐ **MAQUILADORAS,** foreign-owned assembly plants located in Mexico, import parts and materials duty-free to produce finished goods for consumers in the U.S. and around the world. Maquiladoras, such as this one in Ciudad Juárez, employ a large workforce.

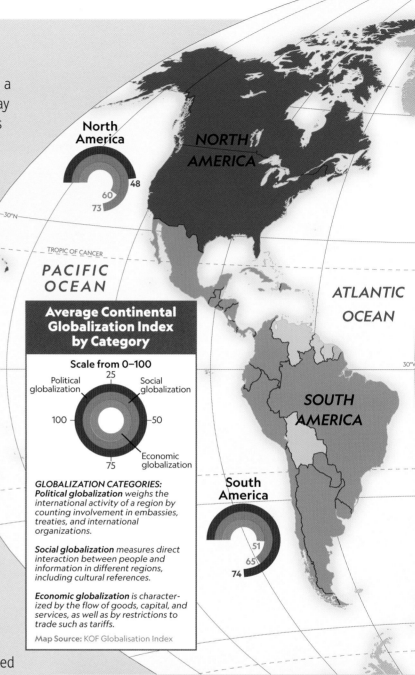

North America

48
60
73

Average Continental Globalization Index by Category

Scale from 0–100

Political globalization — 25 — Social globalization

100 — — 50

75

Economic globalization

GLOBALIZATION CATEGORIES:
Political globalization *weighs the international activity of a region by counting involvement in embassies, treaties, and international organizations.*

Social globalization *measures direct interaction between people and information in different regions, including cultural references.*

Economic globalization *is characterized by the flow of goods, capital, and services, as well as by restrictions to trade such as tariffs.*

Map Source: KOF Globalisation Index

South America

51
65
74

(Map labels: NORTH AMERICA, SOUTH AMERICA, PACIFIC OCEAN, ATLANTIC OCEAN, TROPIC OF CANCER, 30°N, 0°, 30°W)

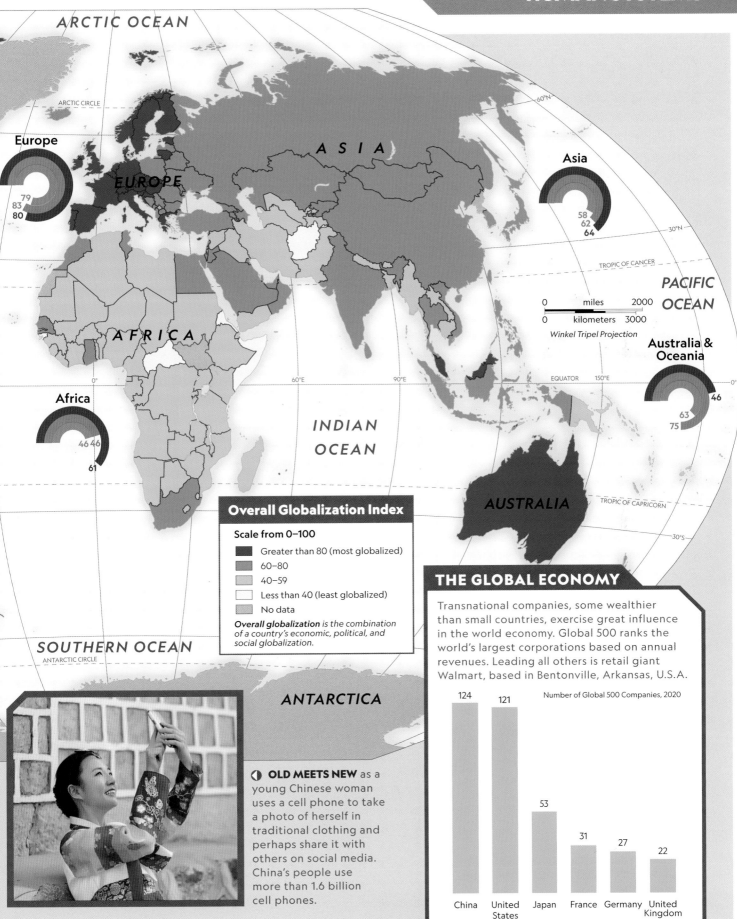

ARCTIC OCEAN

ARCTIC CIRCLE

Europe
79
83
80

EUROPE

A S I A

Asia
58
62
64

AFRICA

Africa
46 46
61

INDIAN
OCEAN

PACIFIC
OCEAN

Winkel Tripel Projection

Australia &
Oceania
46
63
75

AUSTRALIA

TROPIC OF CANCER

TROPIC OF CAPRICORN

EQUATOR

SOUTHERN OCEAN

ANTARCTIC CIRCLE

ANTARCTICA

Overall Globalization Index
Scale from 0–100

- Greater than 80 (most globalized)
- 60–80
- 40–59
- Less than 40 (least globalized)
- No data

Overall globalization is the combination of a country's economic, political, and social globalization.

THE GLOBAL ECONOMY

Transnational companies, some wealthier than small countries, exercise great influence in the world economy. Global 500 ranks the world's largest corporations based on annual revenues. Leading all others is retail giant Walmart, based in Bentonville, Arkansas, U.S.A.

Number of Global 500 Companies, 2020

China	124
United States	121
Japan	53
France	31
Germany	27
United Kingdom	22

◖ **OLD MEETS NEW** as a young Chinese woman uses a cell phone to take a photo of herself in traditional clothing and perhaps share it with others on social media. China's people use more than 1.6 billion cell phones.

Cultural Diffusion

In the past, when groups of people lived in relative isolation, cultures varied widely from place to place. Customs, styles, and preferences were handed down from one generation to the next.

Today, as a result of globalization, cultures all around the world are encountering and adopting new ideas. New customs, clothing and music trends, food habits, and life-styles are being introduced into cultures everywhere at almost the same time. Some people are concerned that this trend may result in a loss of cultural distinctiveness that makes places unique. For example, fast-food chains once found only in the United States can now be seen in major cities around the world. And denim jeans, once a distinctively American clothing style, are worn by young people everywhere in place of more traditional clothing.

An important key to the spread, or diffusion, of popular culture is the increasing contact between people and places around the world. Cellular phones, digital television, social media, and cybercafes have introduced styles and trends popular in local markets to people and places all around the world. And tourists, traveling to places once considered remote and isolated, carry with them ideas and fashions that are catalysts for two-way cultural exchange.

International Tourism

International Tourist Arrivals (2019)

- More than 25,000,000
- 5,000,000–25,000,000
- 500,000–4,999,999
- 100,000–499,999
- Less than 100,000
- No data

Map Source: World Bank

◗ THE INFLUENCE OF IMMIGRANT CULTURES on the American cultural landscape is evident in ethnic communities such as Chinatown in the heart of New York City, U.S.A.

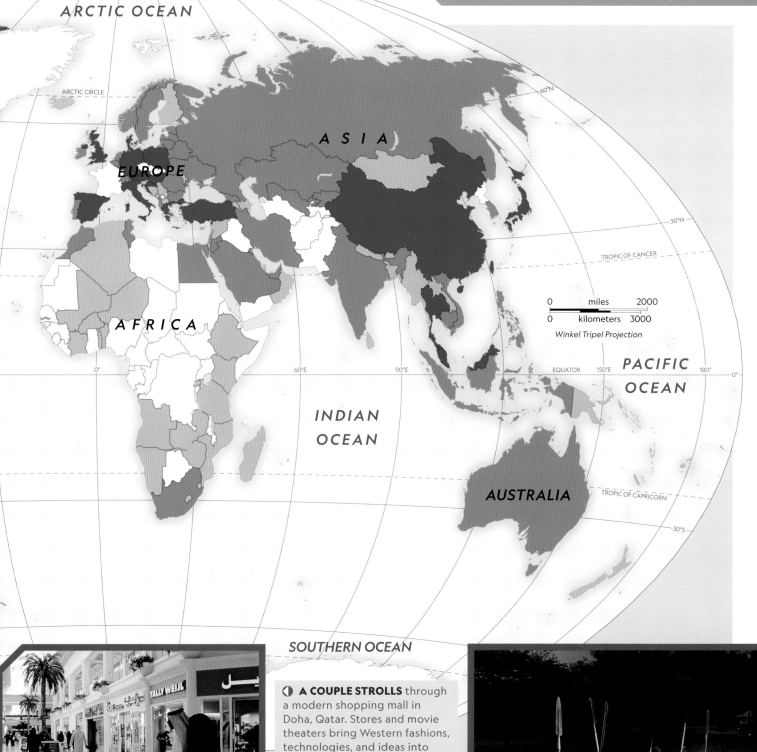

ARCTIC OCEAN

ARCTIC CIRCLE

60°N

EUROPE

A S I A

30°N

TROPIC OF CANCER

A F R I C A

0°

60°E

90°E

0   miles   2000
0   kilometers   3000

Winkel Tripel Projection

INDIAN
OCEAN

EQUATOR   150°E   PACIFIC
180°
0°
OCEAN

AUSTRALIA

TROPIC OF CAPRICORN

30°S

SOUTHERN OCEAN

◑ A COUPLE STROLLS through a modern shopping mall in Doha, Qatar. Stores and movie theaters bring Western fashions, technologies, and ideas into contact with long-established Arab culture and values.

◑ A GROUP OF MAASAI PEOPLE IN TANZANIA gather to tell stories. Stories told by Indigenous peoples are being studied for their "biocultural" capacity to help preserve Earth's landscapes.

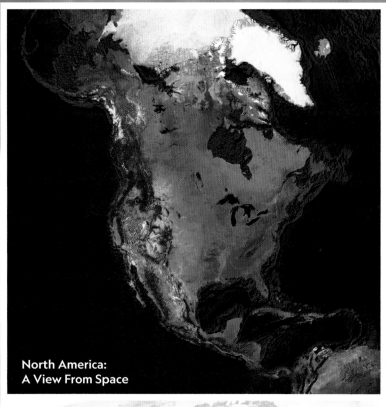

North America:
A View From Space

Viewed from space, North America stretches from the frozen expanses of the Arctic Ocean and Greenland to the lush green of Panama's tropical forests. Hudson Bay and the Great Lakes, finger-prints of long-departed glaciers, dominate the continent's east, while the brown land-scapes of the west and southwest tell of dry lands where water is scarce.

Popocatépetl, a volcano outside of Mexico City, Mexico, sends up a plume of gas, steam, and ash.

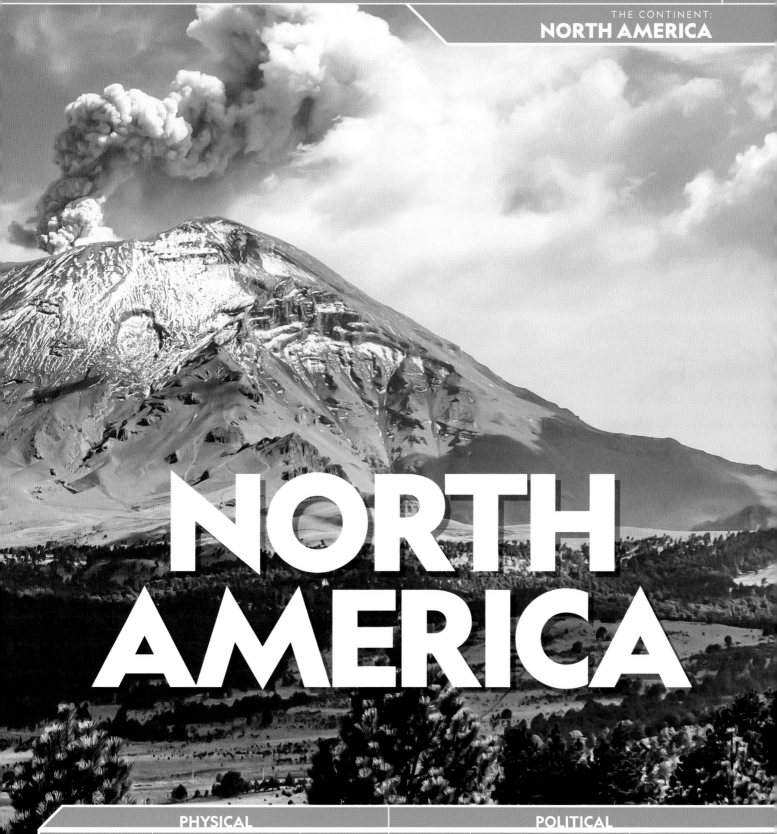

NORTH AMERICA

PHYSICAL			POLITICAL		
Land area 9,449,000 sq mi (24,474,000 sq km)	**Lowest point** Death Valley, California, U.S.A. -282 ft (-86 m)	**Largest lake** Lake Superior, U.S.A.-Canada 31,700 sq mi (82,100 sq km)	**Population** 594,228,000 **Number of** **independent** **countries** 23	**Largest country** Canada 3,855,103 sq mi (9,984,670 sq km)	**Most populous country** United States Pop. 334,998,000
Highest point Denali (Mt. McKinley), Alaska, U.S.A. 20,310 ft (6,190 m)	**Longest river** Mississippi-Missouri, United States 3,710 mi (5,971 km)			**Smallest country** St. Kitts and Nevis 101 sq mi (261 sq km)	**Least populous country** St. Kitts and Nevis Pop. 54,000

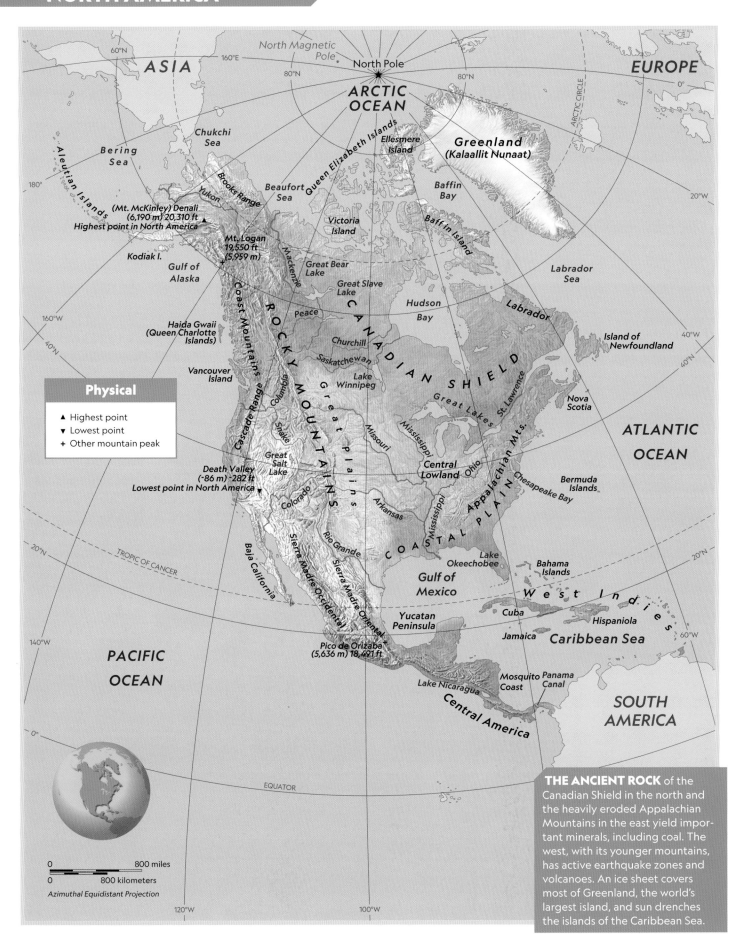

ASIA

North Magnetic Pole

North Pole

EUROPE

ARCTIC OCEAN

ARCTIC CIRCLE

Chukchi Sea

Bering Sea

Aleutian Islands

Brooks Range

Queen Elizabeth Islands

Ellesmere Island

Greenland (Kalaallit Nunaat)

Beaufort Sea

Baffin Bay

Yukon

(Mt. McKinley) Denali (6,190 m) 20,310 ft
Highest point in North America ▲

Mt. Logan 19,550 ft (5,959 m) +

Victoria Island

Baffin Island

Kodiak I.

Gulf of Alaska

Mackenzie

Great Bear Lake

Great Slave Lake

Labrador Sea

Peace

Hudson Bay

Labrador

Haida Gwaii (Queen Charlotte Islands)

Churchill

Saskatchewan

CANADIAN SHIELD

Island of Newfoundland

Vancouver Island

Coast Mountains

Lake Winnipeg

Great Lakes

St. Lawrence

Nova Scotia

Physical

▲ Highest point
▼ Lowest point
+ Other mountain peak

ROCKY MOUNTAINS

Columbia

Great Plains

Missouri

Mississippi

Ohio

Appalachian Mts.

ATLANTIC OCEAN

Cascade Range

Snake

Great Salt Lake

Central Lowland

Chesapeake Bay

Bermuda Islands

Death Valley (-86 m) -282 ft
Lowest point in North America ▼

Colorado

Arkansas

Mississippi

COASTAL PLAIN

TROPIC OF CANCER

Baja California

Rio Grande

Lake Okeechobee

Bahama Islands

20°N

Sierra Madre Occidental

Sierra Madre Oriental

Gulf of Mexico

West Indies

Cuba

PACIFIC OCEAN

Yucatan Peninsula

Hispaniola

Jamaica

Caribbean Sea

Pico de Orizaba (5,636 m) 18,491 ft

Lake Nicaragua

Mosquito Coast

Panama Canal

SOUTH AMERICA

Central America

EQUATOR

0 — 800 miles
0 — 800 kilometers

Azimuthal Equidistant Projection

THE ANCIENT ROCK of the Canadian Shield in the north and the heavily eroded Appalachian Mountains in the east yield important minerals, including coal. The west, with its younger mountains, has active earthquake zones and volcanoes. An ice sheet covers most of Greenland, the world's largest island, and sun drenches the islands of the Caribbean Sea.

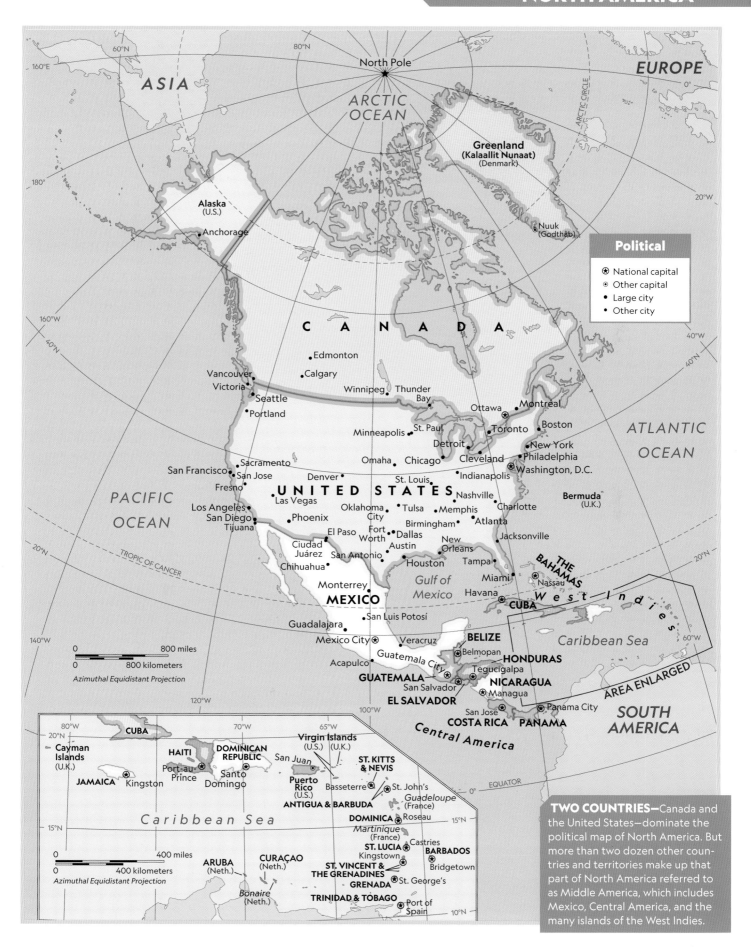

Political
- ⊛ National capital
- ◉ Other capital
- • Large city
- • Other city

North Pole

ASIA

EUROPE

ARCTIC OCEAN

Greenland
(Kalaallit Nunaat)
(Denmark)

Nuuk
(Godthåb)

Alaska
(U.S.)

Anchorage

C A N A D A

Edmonton

Calgary

Vancouver
Victoria
Seattle
Portland

Winnipeg · Thunder Bay

Ottawa ⊛ · Montreal
Toronto · Boston
Minneapolis · St. Paul
Detroit · New York
Omaha · Chicago · Cleveland · Philadelphia
Washington, D.C. ⊛

ATLANTIC OCEAN

PACIFIC OCEAN

San Francisco
San Jose
Fresno
Sacramento

Denver
St. Louis
Indianapolis

U N I T E D   S T A T E S
Las Vegas
Nashville
Bermuda
(U.K.)

Los Angeles
San Diego
Tijuana

Oklahoma City
Tulsa
Memphis
Charlotte

Phoenix
Birmingham
Atlanta

El Paso
Fort Worth
Dallas
Austin
New Orleans
Jacksonville

Ciudad Juárez
San Antonio

Chihuahua

Houston
Tampa

Monterrey

Gulf of Mexico

Miami
Havana ⊛

THE BAHAMAS
Nassau ◉

West Indies

CUBA

Guadalajara

San Luis Potosí

MEXICO

Mexico City ⊛
Veracruz

BELIZE
Belmopan ◉

Caribbean Sea

Acapulco
Guatemala City ⊛
HONDURAS
Tegucigalpa ⊛

AREA ENLARGED

GUATEMALA
San Salvador ⊛
NICARAGUA
Managua ⊛

SOUTH AMERICA

EL SALVADOR
San José ⊛
COSTA RICA   PANAMA
Panama City ⊛

Central America

0   800 miles
0   800 kilometers
Azimuthal Equidistant Projection

Inset map (Caribbean / West Indies)

CUBA

Cayman Islands
(U.K.)

HAITI
Port-au-Prince ⊛

DOMINICAN REPUBLIC
Santo Domingo ⊛

San Juan

Virgin Islands
(U.S.) (U.K.)

ST. KITTS & NEVIS

JAMAICA
Kingston ⊛

Puerto Rico
(U.S.)

Basseterre ⊛

St. John's ⊛

ANTIGUA & BARBUDA

Guadeloupe
(France)

DOMINICA
Roseau ⊛

Martinique
(France)

Caribbean Sea

ST. LUCIA
Castries ⊛
BARBADOS
Kingstown ⊛
Bridgetown ⊛

ARUBA
(Neth.)
CURAÇAO
(Neth.)
ST. VINCENT & THE GRENADINES

GRENADA
St. George's ⊛

Bonaire
(Neth.)

TRINIDAD & TOBAGO
Port of Spain ⊛

0   400 miles
0   400 kilometers
Azimuthal Equidistant Projection

TWO COUNTRIES—Canada and the United States—dominate the political map of North America. But more than two dozen other countries and territories make up that part of North America referred to as Middle America, which includes Mexico, Central America, and the many islands of the West Indies.

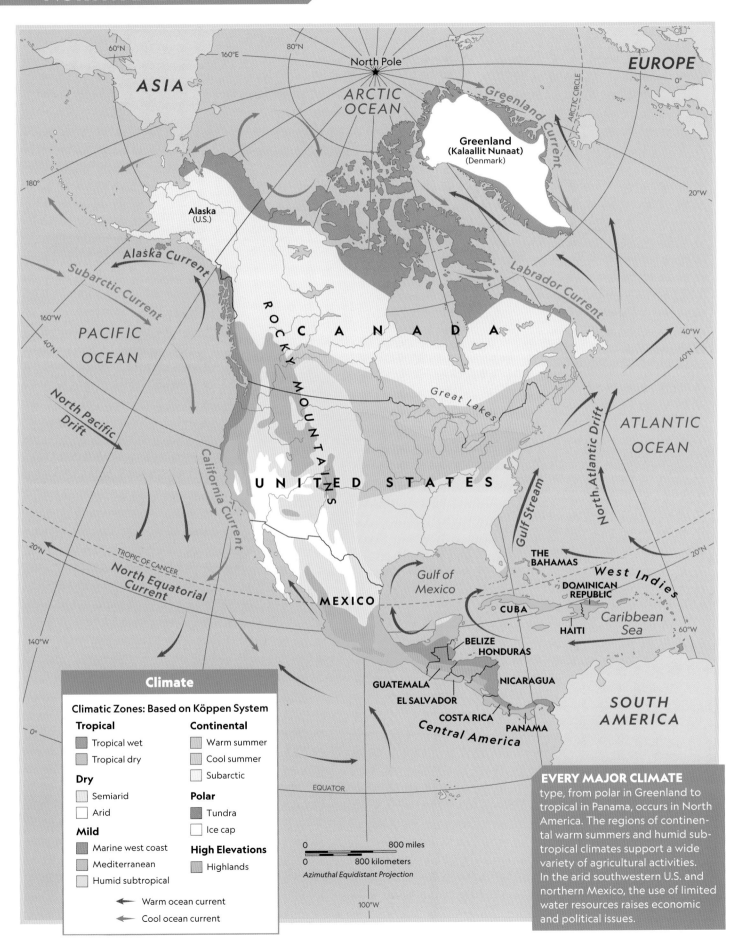

ASIA

North Pole

ARCTIC OCEAN

EUROPE

Greenland Current

Greenland
(Kalaallit Nunaat)
(Denmark)

Alaska
(U.S.)

Alaska Current

Subarctic Current

PACIFIC OCEAN

Labrador Current

CANADA

ROCKY MOUNTAINS

North Pacific Drift

California Current

Great Lakes

ATLANTIC OCEAN

North Atlantic Drift

UNITED STATES

TROPIC OF CANCER

North Equatorial Current

Gulf Stream

Gulf of Mexico

MEXICO

THE BAHAMAS

West Indies

DOMINICAN REPUBLIC

CUBA

Caribbean Sea

HAITI

BELIZE
HONDURAS

GUATEMALA

NICARAGUA

SOUTH AMERICA

EL SALVADOR

COSTA RICA

PANAMA

Central America

EQUATOR

Climate

Climatic Zones: Based on Köppen System

Tropical
- Tropical wet
- Tropical dry

Dry
- Semiarid
- Arid

Mild
- Marine west coast
- Mediterranean
- Humid subtropical

Continental
- Warm summer
- Cool summer
- Subarctic

Polar
- Tundra
- Ice cap

High Elevations
- Highlands

← Warm ocean current
← Cool ocean current

0   800 miles
0   800 kilometers
Azimuthal Equidistant Projection

EVERY MAJOR CLIMATE type, from polar in Greenland to tropical in Panama, occurs in North America. The regions of continental warm summers and humid subtropical climates support a wide variety of agricultural activities. In the arid southwestern U.S. and northern Mexico, the use of limited water resources raises economic and political issues.

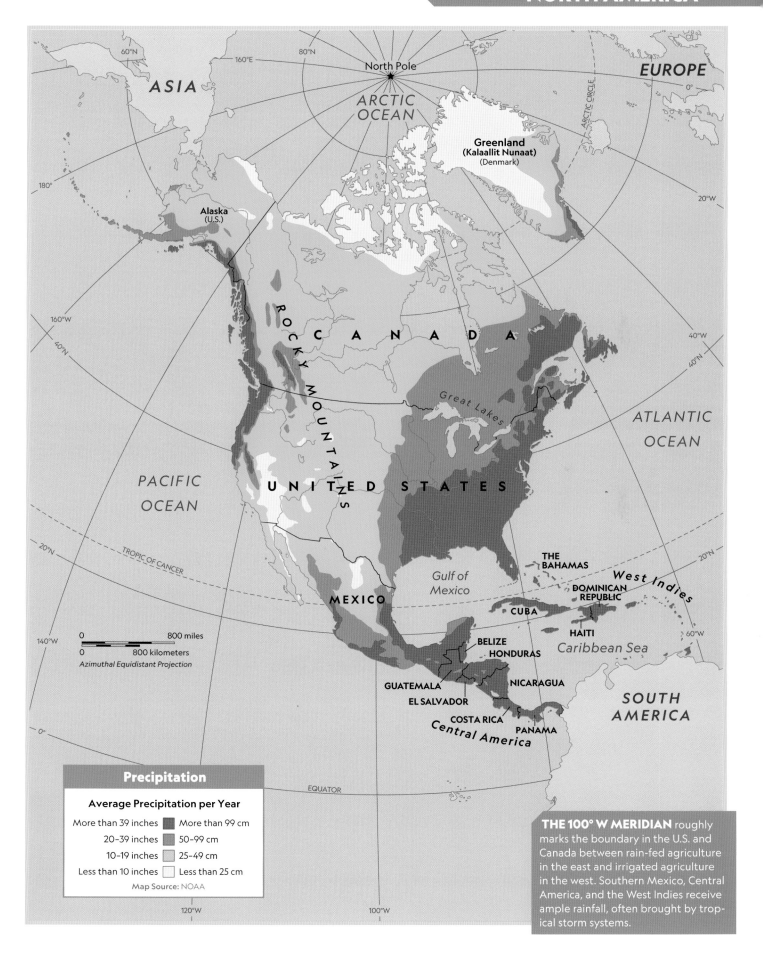

ASIA

ARCTIC
OCEAN

North Pole

EUROPE

Greenland
(Kalaallit Nunaat)
(Denmark)

Alaska
(U.S.)

ROCKY MOUNTAINS

C A N A D A

Great Lakes

ATLANTIC
OCEAN

PACIFIC
OCEAN

U N I T E D   S T A T E S

TROPIC OF CANCER

MEXICO

Gulf of
Mexico

THE
BAHAMAS

West Indies

DOMINICAN
REPUBLIC

CUBA

HAITI

Caribbean Sea

BELIZE
HONDURAS

GUATEMALA

EL SALVADOR

NICARAGUA

COSTA RICA

PANAMA

SOUTH
AMERICA

Central America

EQUATOR

0   800 miles
0   800 kilometers
Azimuthal Equidistant Projection

Precipitation

Average Precipitation per Year

More than 39 inches	More than 99 cm
20–39 inches	50–99 cm
10–19 inches	25–49 cm
Less than 10 inches	Less than 25 cm

Map Source: NOAA

THE 100° W MERIDIAN roughly marks the boundary in the U.S. and Canada between rain-fed agriculture in the east and irrigated agriculture in the west. Southern Mexico, Central America, and the West Indies receive ample rainfall, often brought by tropical storm systems.

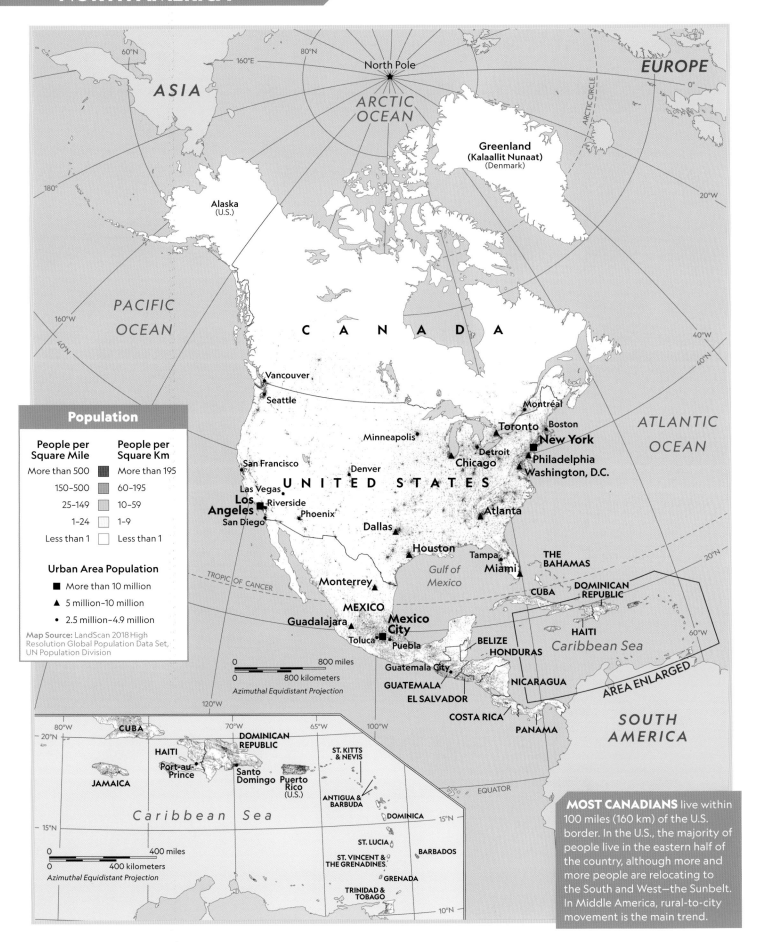

Population

People per Square Mile		People per Square Km	
More than 500		More than 195	
150–500		60–195	
25–149		10–59	
1–24		1–9	
Less than 1		Less than 1	

Urban Area Population

- ■ More than 10 million
- ▲ 5 million–10 million
- • 2.5 million–4.9 million

Map Source: LandScan 2018 High Resolution Global Population Data Set, UN Population Division

0   800 miles
0   800 kilometers
Azimuthal Equidistant Projection

0   400 miles
0   400 kilometers
Azimuthal Equidistant Projection

MOST CANADIANS live within 100 miles (160 km) of the U.S. border. In the U.S., the majority of people live in the eastern half of the country, although more and more people are relocating to the South and West—the Sunbelt. In Middle America, rural-to-city movement is the main trend.

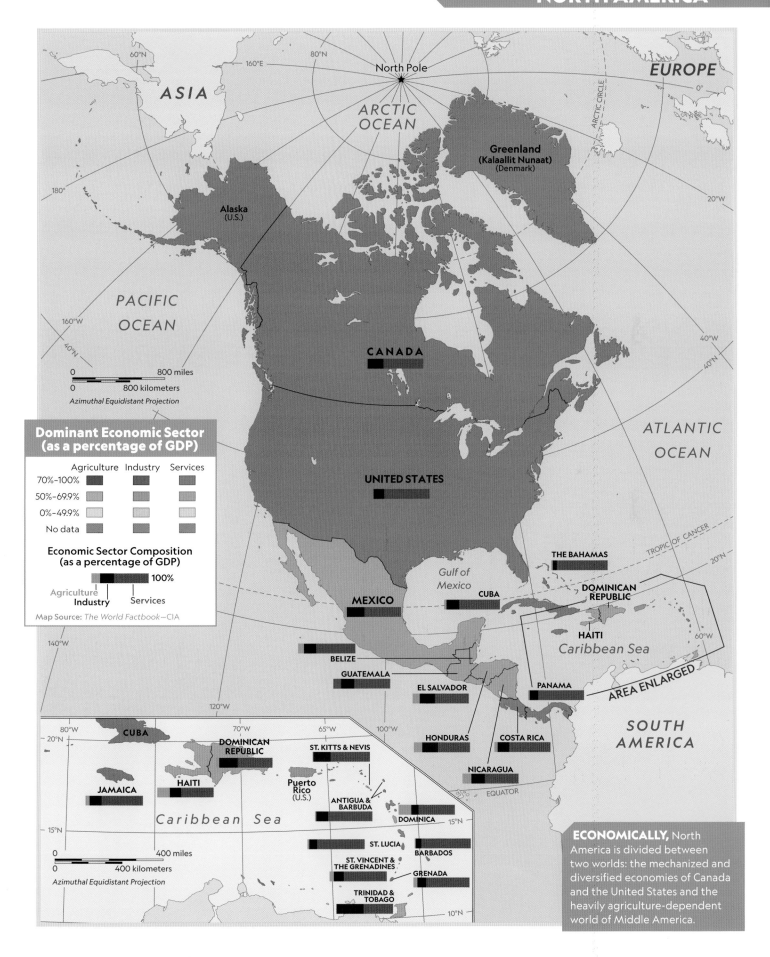

**Dominant Economic Sector
(as a percentage of GDP)**

	Agriculture	Industry	Services
70%–100%			
50%–69.9%			
0%–49.9%			
No data			

**Economic Sector Composition
(as a percentage of GDP)**

100%

Agriculture
Industry   Services

Map Source: *The World Factbook—CIA*

ECONOMICALLY, North America is divided between two worlds: the mechanized and diversified economies of Canada and the United States and the heavily agriculture-dependent world of Middle America.

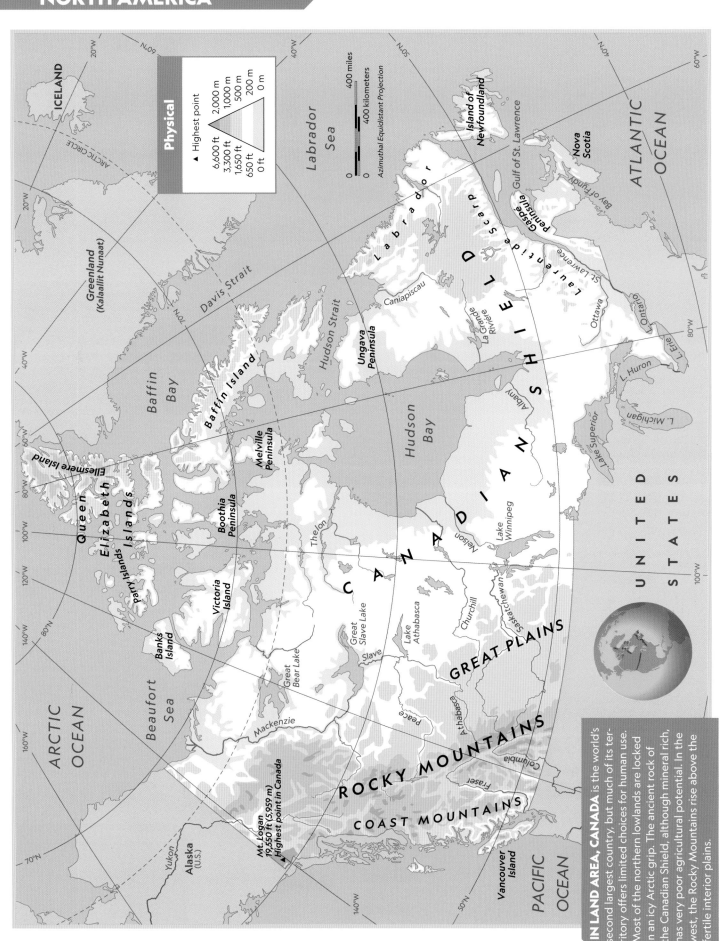

Physical

▲ Highest point

6,600 ft — 2,000 m
3,300 ft — 1,000 m
1,650 ft — 500 m
650 ft — 200 m
0 ft — 0 m

400 miles
400 kilometers
Azimuthal Equidistant Projection

ICELAND

ARCTIC CIRCLE

Greenland
(Kalaallit Nunaat)

Davis Strait

Labrador
Sea

Labrador

Island of
Newfoundland

Gulf of St. Lawrence

Nova
Scotia

Bay of Fundy

ATLANTIC
OCEAN

Baffin
Bay

Baffin Island

Hudson Strait

Ungava
Peninsula

Caniapiscau

La Grande
Rivière

Gaspé
Peninsula

St. Lawrence

Laurentide Scarp

Ottawa

L. Ontario

L. Erie

Ellesmere Island

Queen
Elizabeth
Islands

Parry Islands

Melville
Peninsula

Boothia
Peninsula

Hudson
Bay

Albany

C A N A D I A N   S H I E L D

Lake Superior

L. Huron

L. Michigan

Banks
Island

Victoria
Island

Thelon

Nelson

Lake
Winnipeg

Great
Bear Lake

Great
Slave Lake

Slave

Lake
Athabasca

Churchill

Saskatchewan

GREAT PLAINS

U N I T E D
S T A T E S

Beaufort
Sea

Mackenzie

Athabasca

Peace

ROCKY MOUNTAINS

Columbia

Fraser

COAST MOUNTAINS

Vancouver
Island

ARCTIC
OCEAN

Mt. Logan
19,550 ft (5,959 m)
Highest point in Canada ▲

Yukon

Alaska
(U.S.)

PACIFIC
OCEAN

IN LAND AREA, CANADA is the world's second largest country, but much of its territory offers limited choices for human use. Most of the northern lowlands are locked in an icy Arctic grip. The ancient rock of the Canadian Shield, although mineral rich, has very poor agricultural potential. In the west, the Rocky Mountains rise above the fertile interior plains.

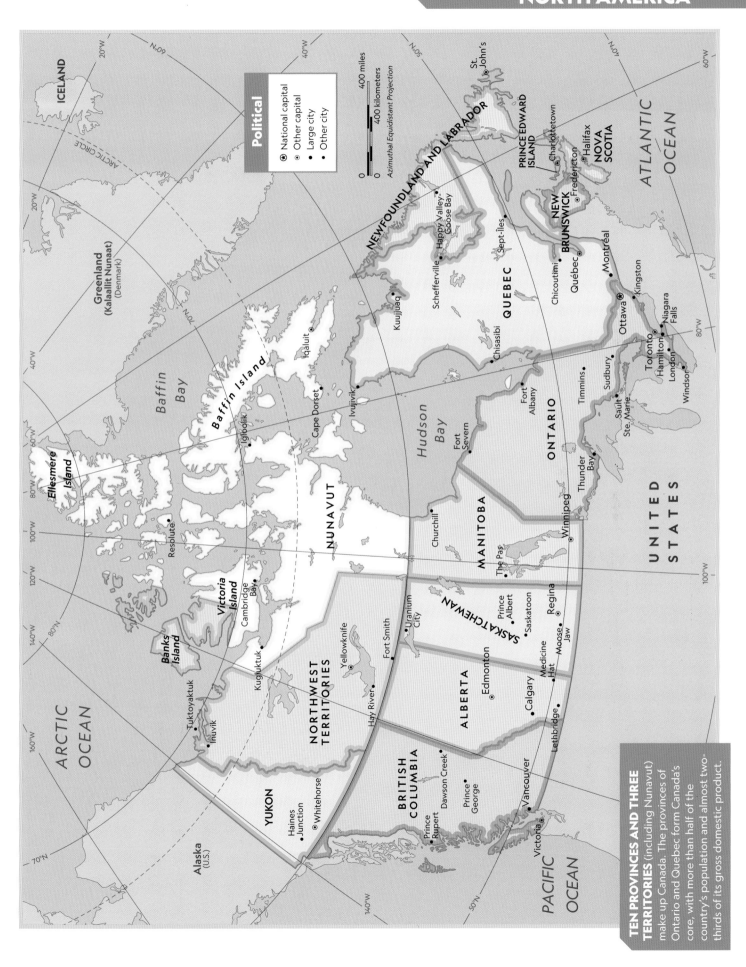

Political

⊛ National capital
◉ Other capital
● Large city
• Other city

400 miles
400 kilometers
Azimuthal Equidistant Projection

ICELAND

ARCTIC CIRCLE

Greenland
(Kalaallit Nunaat)
(Denmark)

Ellesmere
Island

Baffin
Bay

Baffin Island

Iqaluit ⊛

Cape Dorset

Igloolik

Ivujivik

Resolute

Victoria
Island

Cambridge
Bay

Banks
Island

Kugluktuk

NUNAVUT

Hudson
Bay

NEWFOUNDLAND AND LABRADOR

St.
John's

PRINCE EDWARD
ISLAND

Charlottetown

Halifax
NOVA
SCOTIA

NEW
BRUNSWICK

Fredericton

ATLANTIC
OCEAN

Happy Valley-
Goose Bay

Sept-Îles

Montréal

Schefferville

Kuujjuaq

QUEBEC

Chicoutimi

Québec

Kingston

Chisasibi

Ottawa ⊛

Niagara
Falls

Toronto

Hamilton

London

Windsor

Fort
Albany

Timmins

Sudbury

Sault
Ste.
Marie

ONTARIO

Thunder
Bay

UNITED
STATES

Fort
Severn

Churchill

MANITOBA

The Pas

Winnipeg

Tuktoyaktuk

Inuvik

Kugluktuk

NORTHWEST
TERRITORIES

Yellowknife

Fort Smith

Hay River

Uranium
City

SASKATCHEWAN

Prince
Albert

Saskatoon

Regina

Moose
Jaw

Medicine
Hat

ALBERTA

Edmonton

Calgary

Lethbridge

ARCTIC
OCEAN

YUKON

Haines
Junction

Whitehorse

BRITISH
COLUMBIA

Dawson Creek

Prince
Rupert

Prince
George

Vancouver

Victoria ◉

PACIFIC
OCEAN

Alaska
(U.S.)

**TEN PROVINCES AND THREE
TERRITORIES** (including Nunavut)
make up Canada. The provinces of
Ontario and Quebec form Canada's
core, with more than half of the
country's population and almost two-
thirds of its gross domestic product.

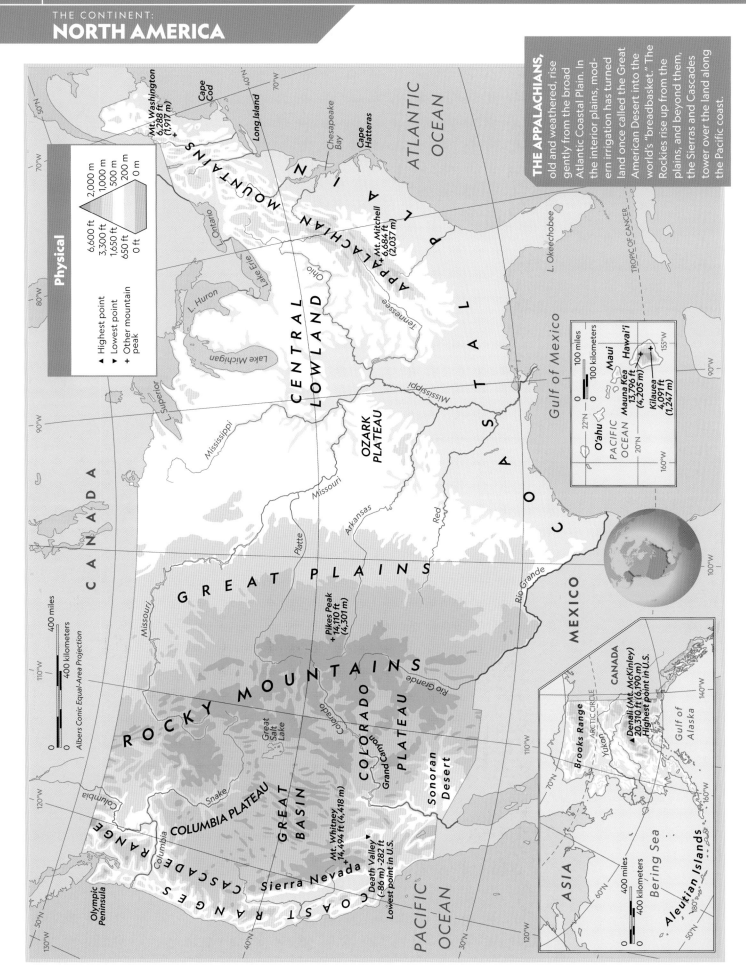

THE APPALACHIANS, old and weathered, rise gently from the broad Atlantic Coastal Plain. In the interior plains, modern irrigation has turned land once called the Great American Desert into the world's "breadbasket." The Rockies rise up from the plains, and beyond them, the Sierras and Cascades tower over the land along the Pacific coast.

Physical

2,000 m
1,000 m
500 m
200 m
0 m

6,600 ft
3,300 ft
1,650 ft
650 ft
0 ft

▲ Highest point
▼ Lowest point
+ Other mountain peak

400 miles
400 kilometers
Albers Conic Equal-Area Projection

CANADA

ATLANTIC OCEAN

Mt. Washington 6,288 ft (1,917 m) +
Cape Cod
Long Island
Chesapeake Bay
Cape Hatteras

L. Ontario
Lake Erie
L. Huron
Lake Michigan
L. Superior

Ohio
Tennessee

APPALACHIAN MOUNTAINS

COASTAL PLAIN

+ Mt. Mitchell 6,684 ft (2,037 m)

CENTRAL LOWLAND

OZARK PLATEAU

Mississippi
Missouri
Arkansas
Red

Gulf of Mexico

L. Okeechobee

TROPIC OF CANCER

MEXICO

Rio Grande

GREAT PLAINS

Pikes Peak + 14,110 ft (4,301 m)

ROCKY MOUNTAINS

Great Salt Lake
Colorado

COLORADO PLATEAU

Grand Canyon

Sonoran Desert

Platte

Snake
Columbia
COLUMBIA PLATEAU

GREAT BASIN

Mt. Whitney ▲ 14,494 ft (4,418 m)

Death Valley ▼ -282 ft (-86 m) Lowest point in U.S.

Sierra Nevada

COAST RANGES
CASCADE RANGE

Olympic Peninsula

PACIFIC OCEAN

Hawaii inset
100 miles
100 kilometers

PACIFIC OCEAN
O'ahu
Maui
Mauna Kea 13,796 ft (4,205 m) +
Hawai'i
Kīlauea 4,091 ft (1,247 m) +
22°N
20°N
160°W
155°W

Alaska inset
CANADA
Brooks Range
Yukon
Denali (Mt. McKinley) ▲ 20,310 ft (6,190 m) Highest point in U.S.
ARCTIC CIRCLE
Gulf of Alaska
ASIA
Bering Sea
Aleutian Islands
400 miles
400 kilometers
70°N
60°N
50°N
180°
170°W
160°W
150°W
140°W
130°W

THE CONTINENT:
NORTH AMERICA

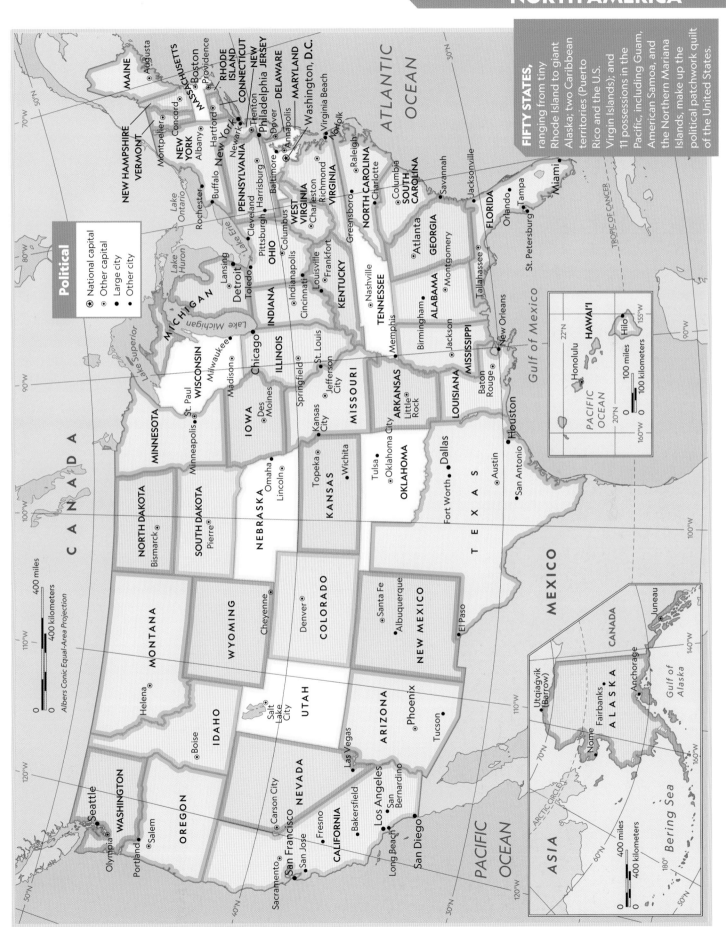

FIFTY STATES, ranging from tiny Rhode Island to giant Alaska; two Caribbean territories (Puerto Rico and the U.S. Virgin Islands); and 11 possessions in the Pacific, including Guam, American Samoa, and the Northern Mariana Islands, make up the political patchwork quilt of the United States.

Political
⊛ National capital
⊙ Other capital
● Large city
• Other city

ATLANTIC OCEAN

CANADA

PACIFIC OCEAN

MEXICO

Gulf of Mexico

Albers Conic Equal-Area Projection

MAINE
Augusta
NEW HAMPSHIRE
VERMONT
Montpelier
Concord
MASSACHUSETTS
Boston
RHODE ISLAND
Providence
CONNECTICUT
NEW JERSEY
Hartford
NEW YORK
Albany
Buffalo
Rochester
PENNSYLVANIA
Harrisburg
Pittsburgh
Philadelphia
Trenton
Newark
DELAWARE
Dover
MARYLAND
Baltimore
Annapolis
Washington, D.C.
Virginia Beach
Norfolk
WEST VIRGINIA
Charleston
VIRGINIA
Richmond
NORTH CAROLINA
Raleigh
Greensboro
Charlotte
SOUTH CAROLINA
Columbia
Savannah
Jacksonville
GEORGIA
Atlanta
Montgomery
ALABAMA
Birmingham
Jackson
MISSISSIPPI
FLORIDA
Tallahassee
Orlando
Tampa
St. Petersburg
Miami
New Orleans
Baton Rouge
LOUISIANA
Houston
San Antonio
Austin
TEXAS
Fort Worth
Dallas
El Paso
Tulsa
Oklahoma City
OKLAHOMA
NEW MEXICO
Albuquerque
Santa Fe
ARKANSAS
Little Rock
Memphis
TENNESSEE
Nashville
KENTUCKY
Frankfort
Louisville
Cincinnati
Indianapolis
INDIANA
OHIO
Columbus
Cleveland
Toledo
Detroit
Lansing
MICHIGAN
Lake Michigan
ILLINOIS
Chicago
Springfield
St. Louis
MISSOURI
Jefferson City
Kansas City
KANSAS
Topeka
Wichita
Omaha
Lincoln
NEBRASKA
IOWA
Des Moines
WISCONSIN
Madison
Milwaukee
MINNESOTA
St. Paul
Minneapolis
SOUTH DAKOTA
Pierre
NORTH DAKOTA
Bismarck
MONTANA
Helena
WYOMING
Cheyenne
COLORADO
Denver
UTAH
Salt Lake City
IDAHO
Boise
NEVADA
Carson City
Las Vegas
ARIZONA
Phoenix
Tucson
CALIFORNIA
Sacramento
San Francisco
San Jose
Fresno
Bakersfield
Las Vegas
Los Angeles
San Bernardino
Long Beach
San Diego
OREGON
Salem
Portland
WASHINGTON
Olympia
Seattle

Lake Ontario
Lake Erie
Lake Huron
Lake Superior

TROPIC OF CANCER

Inset: Hawai'i
HAWAI'I
Honolulu
Hilo
PACIFIC OCEAN
22°N
20°N
160°W
155°W
0   100 miles
0   100 kilometers

Inset: Alaska
ALASKA
CANADA
Juneau
Anchorage
Fairbanks
Nome
Utqiaġvik (Barrow)
Gulf of Alaska
ASIA
Bering Sea
ARCTIC CIRCLE
70°N
60°N
50°N
180°
160°W
140°W
0   400 miles
0   400 kilometers

0   400 miles
0   400 kilometers

70°N
60°N
50°N
40°N
30°N
120°W
110°W
100°W
90°W
80°W
70°W

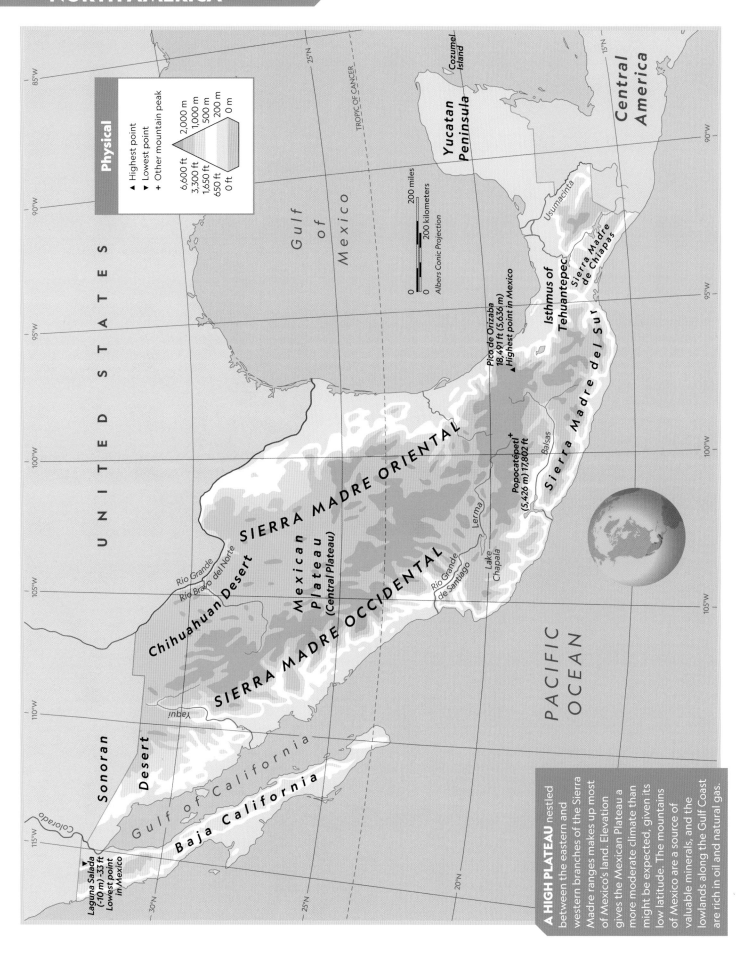

Physical

▲ Highest point
▼ Lowest point
+ Other mountain peak

6,600 ft	2,000 m
3,300 ft	1,000 m
1,650 ft	500 m
650 ft	200 m
0 ft	0 m

UNITED STATES

TROPIC OF CANCER

Gulf of Mexico

200 miles
200 kilometers
Albers Conic Projection

Yucatan Peninsula

Cozumel Island

Central America

Pico de Orizaba
18,491 ft (5,636 m)
▲ Highest point in Mexico

Isthmus of Tehuantepec

Sierra Madre de Chiapas

Usumacinta

SIERRA MADRE ORIENTAL

Mexican Plateau
(Central Plateau)

Chihuahuan Desert

Rio Grande
Rio Bravo del Norte

SIERRA MADRE OCCIDENTAL

Popocatépetl +
(5,426 m) 17,802 ft

Balsas

Sierra Madre del Sur

Lerma

Rio Grande
de Santiago

Lake Chapala

PACIFIC OCEAN

Yaqui

Sonoran Desert

Gulf of California

Baja California

Colorado

▲ Laguna Salada
(-10 m) -33 ft
Lowest point in Mexico

A HIGH PLATEAU nestled between the eastern and western branches of the Sierra Madre ranges makes up most of Mexico's land. Elevation gives the Mexican Plateau a more moderate climate than might be expected, given its low latitude. The mountains of Mexico are a source of valuable minerals, and the lowlands along the Gulf Coast are rich in oil and natural gas.

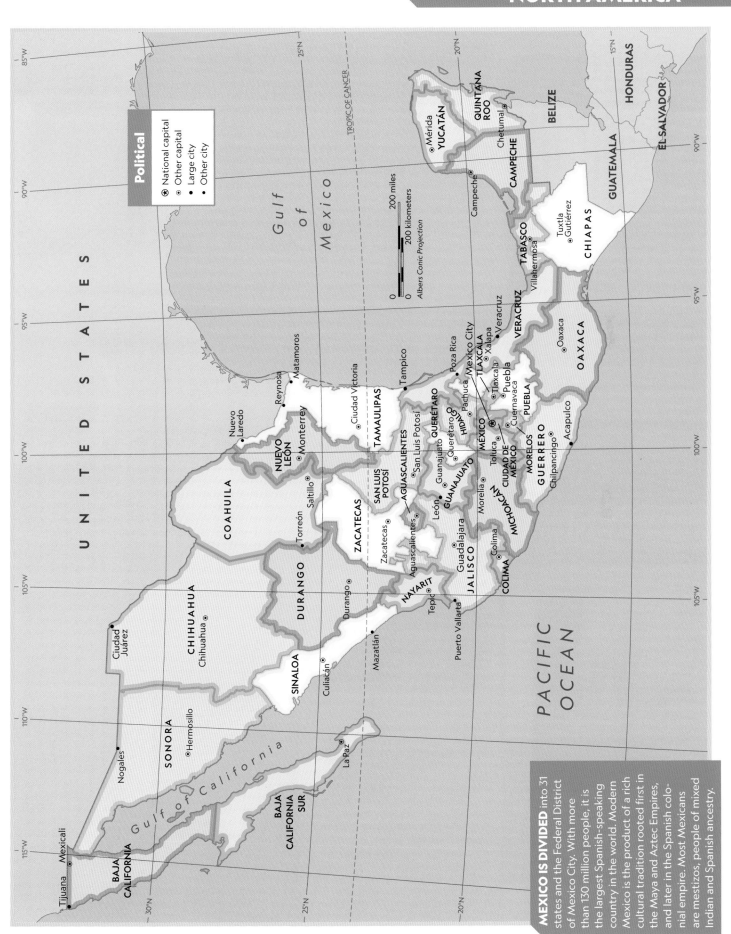

Political
⊛ National capital
⊙ Other capital
● Large city
● Other city

UNITED STATES

Gulf of Mexico

PACIFIC OCEAN

Gulf of California

200 miles
200 kilometers
Albers Conic Projection
0

TROPIC OF CANCER

Tijuana
Mexicali
BAJA CALIFORNIA
Nogales
SONORA
Hermosillo
Ciudad Juárez
CHIHUAHUA
Chihuahua
La Paz
BAJA CALIFORNIA SUR
Culiacán
SINALOA
Mazatlán
DURANGO
Durango
Torreón
COAHUILA
Saltillo
ZACATECAS
Zacatecas
Puerto Vallarta
Tepic
NAYARIT
JALISCO
Guadalajara
Aguascalientes
AGUASCALIENTES
San Luis Potosí
SAN LUIS POTOSÍ
León
Guanajuato
GUANAJUATO
Colima
COLIMA
Morelia
MICHOACÁN
Querétaro
QUERÉTARO
Nuevo Laredo
Reynosa
Matamoros
Monterrey
NUEVO LEÓN
Ciudad Victoria
TAMAULIPAS
Tampico
Poza Rica
Pachuca
HIDALGO
Toluca
MÉXICO
CIUDAD DE MÉXICO
Mexico City
TLAXCALA
Tlaxcala
Puebla
PUEBLA
Cuernavaca
MORELOS
Chilpancingo
GUERRERO
Acapulco
Xalapa
Veracruz
VERACRUZ
Oaxaca
OAXACA
Villahermosa
TABASCO
Tuxtla Gutiérrez
CHIAPAS
Campeche
CAMPECHE
Mérida
YUCATÁN
Chetumal
QUINTANA ROO
BELIZE
GUATEMALA
HONDURAS
EL SALVADOR

MEXICO IS DIVIDED into 31 states and the Federal District of Mexico City. With more than 130 million people, it is the largest Spanish-speaking country in the world. Modern Mexico is the product of a rich cultural tradition rooted first in the Maya and Aztec Empires, and later in the Spanish colonial empire. Most Mexicans are mestizos, people of mixed Indian and Spanish ancestry.

BILLION-DOLLAR DISASTERS, 1980-2020

The National Oceanic and Atmospheric and Administration (NOAA) tracked storms in the United States that each cost a billion dollars or more in damage, recovery, and overall economic impact.

O There were 290 billion-dollar disasters in the U.S. from 1980 to 2020.

O These 290 disasters cost more than $1.9 trillion in total.

O In just one decade, from 2010 to 2019, there were 123 billion-dollar disasters in the U.S.

O In 2020, the U.S. had 22 billion-dollar disasters, the most on record.

O All 50 states have had at least one billion-dollar disaster since 1980.

O From 2015 to 2020, there were an average of 15.1 billion-dollar disasters per year.

O Since 1980, severe storms, tropical cyclones, and flooding have caused the highest number of billion-dollar disaster events. But tropical cyclones caused the most damage and had the highest average event cost.

PROJECTED COST OF CLIMATE CHANGE IN THE CARIBBEAN

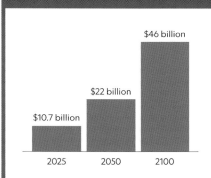

$46 billion

$22 billion

$10.7 billion

2025   2050   2100

The Caribbean islands are especially vulnerable to the effects of climate change. Coastal erosion, storm surges, and saltwater coming into freshwater aquifers impact farming and cause a loss in tourism. Promoting sustainable development and limiting sea-level rise is essential to these islands' survival.

Climate and Weather

The World Risk Index is a statistical model that assesses the global risk of disasters that arise from natural hazards such as earthquakes, tornadoes, floods, droughts, and storms, as well as sea-level rise caused by climate change. The index does not just measure the risk level of these events in and of themselves. It assesses the social, political, and economic structures that could help people recover from the effects of a natural hazard. The World Risk Index looks at 27 indicators, including the likelihood of the risk itself (how vulnerable a place is to a natural hazard); how frequently the risk might occur; susceptibility (the degree of suffering that a society might experience); coping ability (how well a society can respond to the effects of a natural hazard); and the ability of a society to create structural changes to lessen future damage, such as building stronger buildings that can withstand high winds. As the map illustrates, in North America, some island states in the Caribbean face very high risk due to poverty and inequality combined with geographic location and susceptibility to sea-level rise.

◖ TO CREATE CLIMATE-RESILIENT infrastructure, Mexico City plans to plant 20 million trees, reduce emissions by 30 percent, build a new clean energy transportation system, and expand the use of solar energy in public buildings, among other improvements.

◖ JOURNALISTS IN ST. LUCIA report on the social, cultural, and economic impacts of climate change on their island— such as that warmer weather can cause more mosquito-borne diseases—which helps convey the tangible and local impacts of climate change.

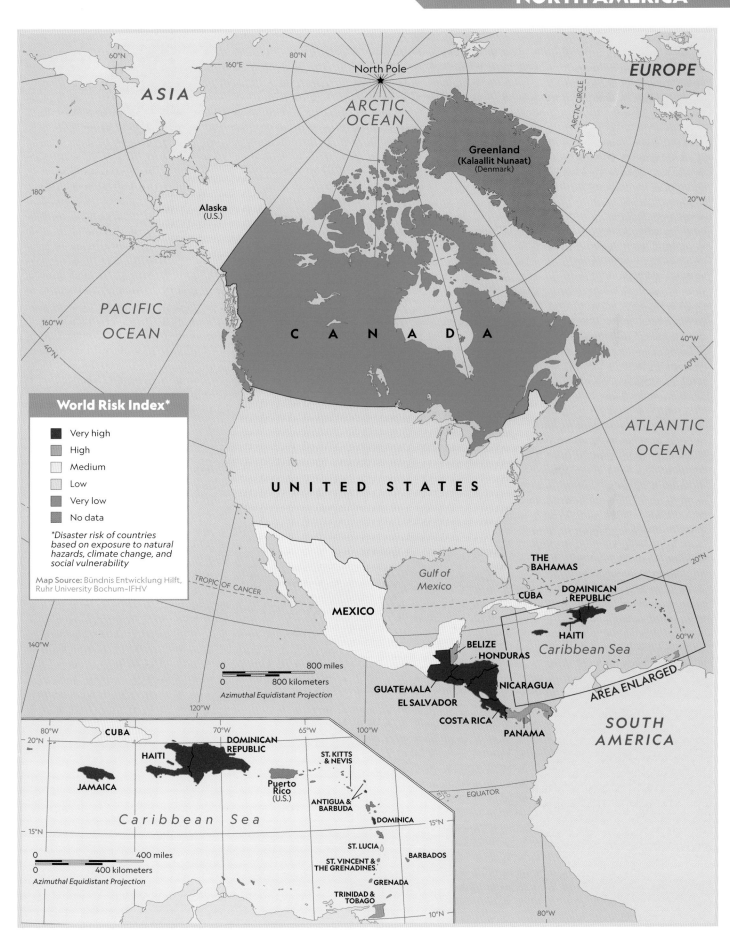

ASIA

ARCTIC OCEAN

North Pole

EUROPE

Greenland
(Kalaallit Nunaat)
(Denmark)

Alaska
(U.S.)

PACIFIC OCEAN

C A N A D A

ATLANTIC OCEAN

World Risk Index*

- Very high
- High
- Medium
- Low
- Very low
- No data

*Disaster risk of countries based on exposure to natural hazards, climate change, and social vulnerability

Map Source: Bündnis Entwicklung Hilft, Ruhr University Bochum–IFHV

U N I T E D   S T A T E S

TROPIC OF CANCER

Gulf of Mexico

THE BAHAMAS

CUBA

DOMINICAN REPUBLIC

HAITI

Caribbean Sea

MEXICO

BELIZE
HONDURAS

AREA ENLARGED

0   800 miles
0   800 kilometers
Azimuthal Equidistant Projection

GUATEMALA
EL SALVADOR

NICARAGUA

COSTA RICA

PANAMA

SOUTH AMERICA

CUBA

DOMINICAN REPUBLIC

HAITI

ST. KITTS & NEVIS

Puerto Rico
(U.S.)

JAMAICA

ANTIGUA & BARBUDA

Caribbean Sea

DOMINICA

EQUATOR

ST. LUCIA

BARBADOS

ST. VINCENT & THE GRENADINES

GRENADA

0   400 miles
0   400 kilometers
Azimuthal Equidistant Projection

TRINIDAD & TOBAGO

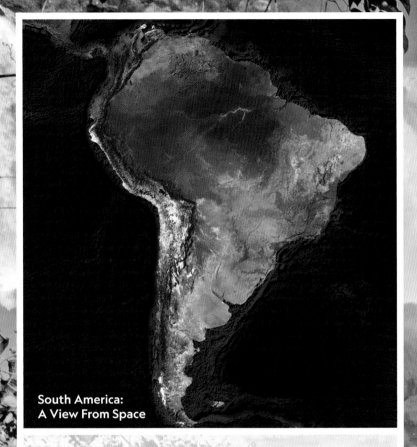

South America:
A View From Space

From the towering, snowcapped Andes in the west to the steamy rainforest of the Amazon Basin in the north, and from the fertile grasslands of the Pampas to the arid Atacama Desert along the Pacific coast, South America is a continent of extremes. North to south, the continent extends from the tropical waters of the Caribbean Sea to the wind-swept islands of Tierra del Fuego. Its longest river, the Amazon, carries more water than any other river in the world.

Tourists take in the stunning Iguazú Falls, which spans the border between Argentina and Brazil.

SOUTH AMERICA

PHYSICAL			POLITICAL		
Land area 6,880,000 sq mi (17,819,000 sq km)	**Lowest point** **Laguna del Carbón,** **Argentina** -344 ft (-105 m)	**Largest lake** **Lake Titicaca,** **Bolivia-Peru** 3,200 sq mi (8,300 sq km)	**Population** 430,173,000 **Number of** **independent** **countries** 12	**Largest country** **Brazil** 3,287,956 sq mi (8,515,770 sq km)	**Most populous country** **Brazil** Pop. 213,445,000
Highest point **Cerro Aconcagua,** **Argentina** 22,831 ft (6,959 m)	**Longest river** **Amazon** 4,150 mi (6,679 km)			**Smallest country** **Suriname** 63,251 sq mi (163,820 sq km)	**Least populous country** **Suriname** Pop. 615,000

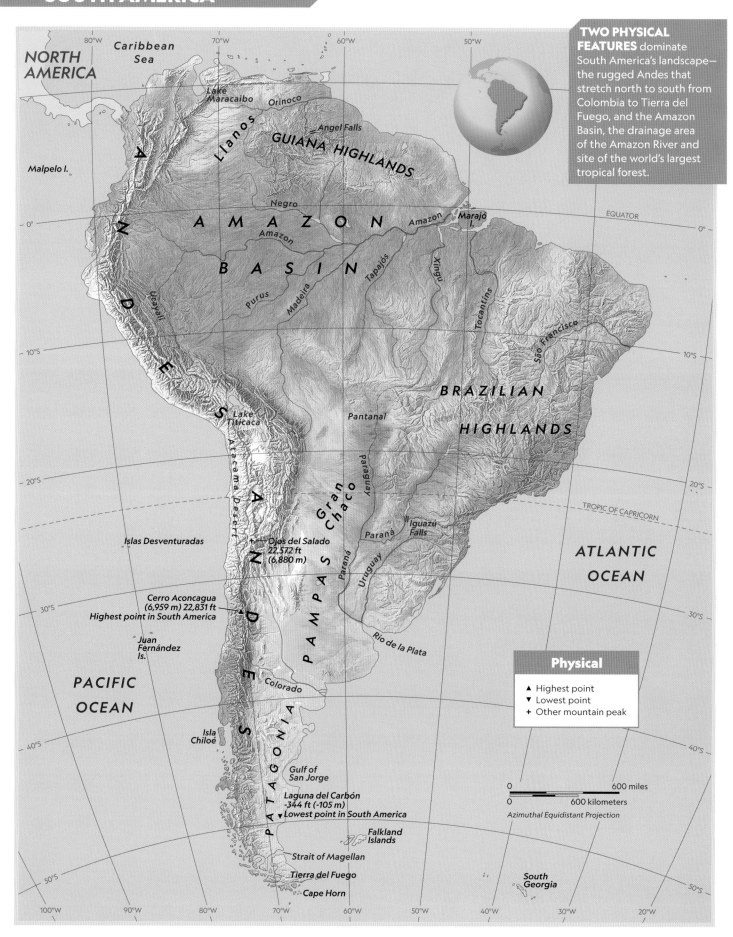

TWO PHYSICAL FEATURES dominate South America's landscape—the rugged Andes that stretch north to south from Colombia to Tierra del Fuego, and the Amazon Basin, the drainage area of the Amazon River and site of the world's largest tropical forest.

NORTH AMERICA

Caribbean Sea

Malpelo I.

Lake Maracaibo

Orinoco

Llanos

Angel Falls

GUIANA HIGHLANDS

A N D E S

Negro

A M A Z O N

Amazon

Marajó I.

EQUATOR

B A S I N

Amazon

Purus

Madeira

Tapajós

Xingu

Tocantins

São Francisco

Ucayali

Lake Titicaca

BRAZILIAN

Pantanal

HIGHLANDS

Atacama Desert

Paraguay

Gran Chaco

PAMPAS

Iguazú Falls

Islas Desventuradas

Ojos del Salado
22,572 ft
(6,880 m)

Paraná

Uruguay

TROPIC OF CAPRICORN

Cerro Aconcagua
(6,959 m) 22,831 ft
Highest point in South America

Paraná

ATLANTIC OCEAN

Juan Fernández Is.

PACIFIC OCEAN

A N D E S

Colorado

Rio de la Plata

Physical

▲ Highest point
▼ Lowest point
+ Other mountain peak

Isla Chiloé

P A T A G O N I A

Gulf of San Jorge

Laguna del Carbón
-344 ft (-105 m)
▼ Lowest point in South America

0 — 600 miles
0 — 600 kilometers
Azimuthal Equidistant Projection

Falkland Islands

Strait of Magellan

Tierra del Fuego

Cape Horn

South Georgia

TWELVE COUNTRIES make up South America. The pre-colonial Inca Empire, the largest in the Americas, consisted of more than 12 million people from 100 ethnic groups. Spanish colonial influence is still evident in the use of the Spanish and Portuguese languages and in the widespread presence of the Roman Catholic church.

NORTH AMERICA

Caribbean Sea

Barranquilla
Maracaibo
Caracas
Barquisimeto
Valencia

VENEZUELA

Georgetown
Paramaribo
Cayenne
French Guiana (France)

GUYANA

SURINAME

Medellín
Bogotá
Cali

COLOMBIA

EQUATOR

Quito

ECUADOR

Guayaquil

Manaus

Belém

Fortaleza

P E R U

Natal

Trujillo

Recife

Lima

B R A Z I L

Salvador (Bahia)

Cusco

BOLIVIA

Goiânia
Brasília

La Paz

Santa Cruz

Belo Horizonte

Sucre

PARAGUAY

Nova Iguaçu
São Paulo
Rio de Janeiro
Santos

San Miguel de Tucumán

Asunción

Curitiba

TROPIC OF CAPRICORN

ATLANTIC OCEAN

C H I L E

Porto Alegre

Córdoba
Santa Fe
Rosario

URUGUAY

A R G E N T I N A

Valparaíso
Santiago

PACIFIC OCEAN

Buenos Aires
La Plata
Montevideo

Mar del Plata

Political

⊛ National capital
⊙ Other capital
● Large city
• Other city

0   600 miles
0   600 kilometers
Azimuthal Equidistant Projection

Stanley
Falkland Islands *(Islas Malvinas)* (U.K.)

Punta Arenas

South Georgia (U.K.)

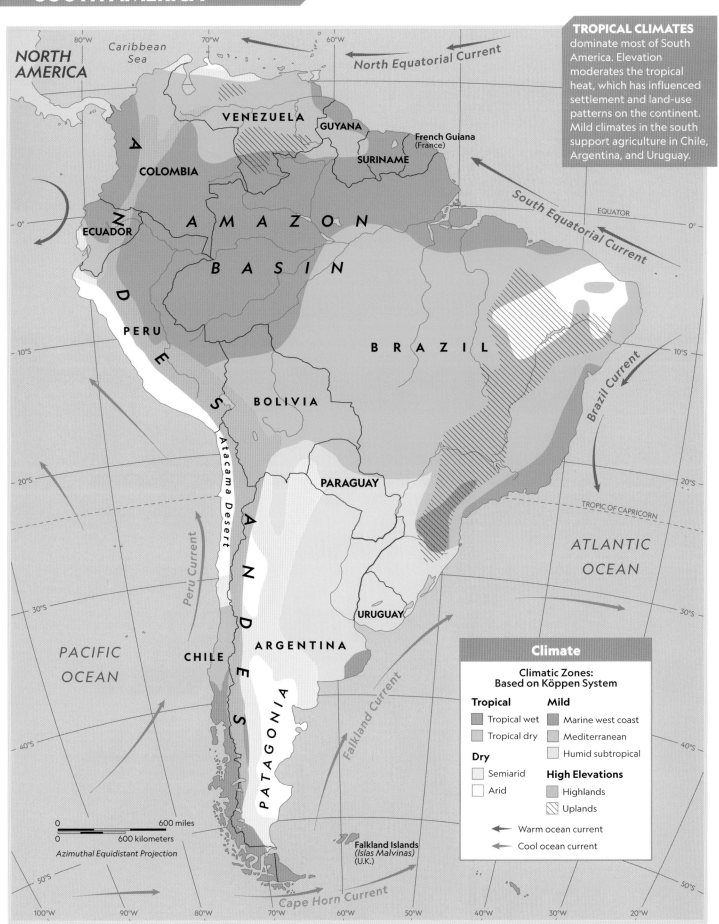

NORTH AMERICA

Caribbean Sea

80°W

70°W

60°W

North Equatorial Current

VENEZUELA

GUYANA

French Guiana (France)

COLOMBIA

SURINAME

South Equatorial Current

EQUATOR

0°

ECUADOR

0°

A M A Z O N

B A S I N

PERU

10°S

A

N

D

E

S

BRAZIL

Brazil Current

10°S

Atacama Desert

BOLIVIA

Peru Current

20°S

PARAGUAY

TROPIC OF CAPRICORN

20°S

ATLANTIC OCEAN

30°S

URUGUAY

30°S

PACIFIC OCEAN

CHILE

ARGENTINA

Falkland Current

40°S

40°S

P A T A G O N I A

0   600 miles
0   600 kilometers

Azimuthal Equidistant Projection

50°S

Falkland Islands
(Islas Malvinas)
(U.K.)

Cape Horn Current

50°S

100°W   90°W   80°W   70°W   60°W   50°W   40°W   30°W   20°W

TROPICAL CLIMATES dominate most of South America. Elevation moderates the tropical heat, which has influenced settlement and land-use patterns on the continent. Mild climates in the south support agriculture in Chile, Argentina, and Uruguay.

Climate

Climatic Zones: Based on Köppen System

Tropical
- Tropical wet
- Tropical dry

Dry
- Semiarid
- Arid

Mild
- Marine west coast
- Mediterranean
- Humid subtropical

High Elevations
- Highlands
- Uplands

→ Warm ocean current
→ Cool ocean current

THE CONTINENT:
SOUTH AMERICA

NORTH
AMERICA

Caribbean
Sea

80°W   70°W   60°W   50°W

VENEZUELA

GUYANA

SURINAME

French Guiana
(France)

COLOMBIA

EQUATOR

0°

A M A Z O N

ECUADOR

0°

B A S I N

PERU

B R A Z I L

10°S

10°S

A
N
D
E
S

BOLIVIA

Arica, Chile
*Driest place in
the world*

Atacama Desert

PARAGUAY

20°S

20°S

TROPIC OF CAPRICORN

CHILE

ATLANTIC
OCEAN

30°S

ARGENTINA

30°S

URUGUAY

PACIFIC
OCEAN

40°S

40°S

PATAGONIA

0   600 miles
0   600 kilometers
Azimuthal Equidistant Projection

Falkland Islands
(Islas Malvinas)
(U.K.)

50°S

50°S

100°W   90°W   80°W   70°W   60°W   50°W   40°W   30°W   20°W

WARM AIR RISING
rapidly over the Equator
triggers daily rainfall, which
supports the rainforest
vegetation of the Amazon
Basin. In contrast, the
combined effects of rain
shadow and cold ocean
currents along the western
coast create the Atacama
Desert, parts of which have
never recorded rainfall.

Precipitation

Average Precipitation per Year

More than 39 inches	More than 99 cm
20–39 inches	50–99 cm
10–19 inches	25–49 cm
Less than 10 inches	Less than 25 cm

Map Source: NOAA

NORTH AMERICA

Caribbean Sea

MOST PEOPLE in South America are concentrated in urban areas along the coastal margins, where mainly European influences are evident. But in the Andean countries, European influences mingle with remnants of the ancient Inca civilization.

Caracas

VENEZUELA

Medellín

Bogotá

GUYANA

SURINAME

French Guiana (France)

Cali **COLOMBIA**

ECUADOR

Guayaquil

EQUATOR

Fortaleza

PERU

B R A Z I L

Recife

Lima

Salvador

BOLIVIA

Brasília

Goiânia

Belo Horizonte

PARAGUAY

Campinas

Rio de Janeiro

Asunción

Curitiba

São Paulo

TROPIC OF CAPRICORN

CHILE

Porto Alegre

ATLANTIC OCEAN

URUGUAY

Santiago

Buenos Aires

ARGENTINA

PACIFIC OCEAN

0 — 600 miles
0 — 600 kilometers

Azimuthal Equidistant Projection

Falkland Islands
(Islas Malvinas)
(U.K.)

Population

People per Square Mile	People per Square Km
More than 500	More than 195
150–500	60–195
25–149	10–59
1–24	1–9
Less than 1	Less than 1

Urban Area Population

■ More than 10 million

▲ 5 million–10 million

• 2.5 million–4.9 million

Map Source: LandScan 2018 High Resolution Global Population Data Set, UN Population Division

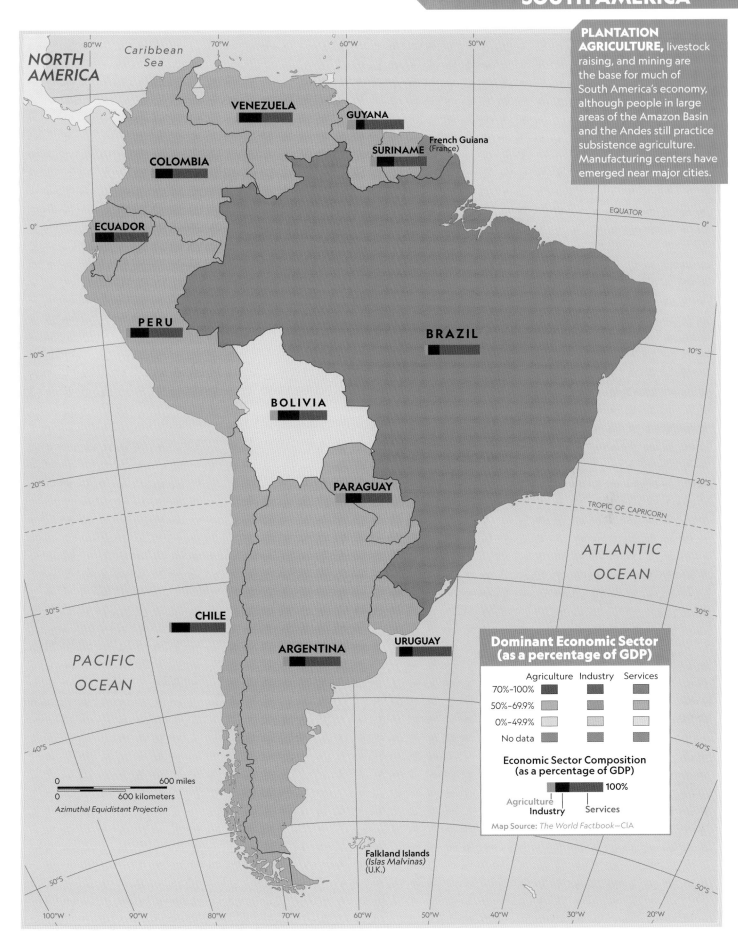

PLANTATION AGRICULTURE, livestock raising, and mining are the base for much of South America's economy, although people in large areas of the Amazon Basin and the Andes still practice subsistence agriculture. Manufacturing centers have emerged near major cities.

NORTH AMERICA

Caribbean Sea

VENEZUELA

GUYANA

COLOMBIA

SURINAME

French Guiana *(France)*

ECUADOR

EQUATOR

PERU

BRAZIL

BOLIVIA

PARAGUAY

TROPIC OF CAPRICORN

ATLANTIC OCEAN

CHILE

ARGENTINA

URUGUAY

PACIFIC OCEAN

Dominant Economic Sector (as a percentage of GDP)

	Agriculture	Industry	Services
70%–100%			
50%–69.9%			
0%–49.9%			
No data			

Economic Sector Composition (as a percentage of GDP)

100%

Agriculture Industry Services

Map Source: *The World Factbook—CIA*

0   600 miles
0   600 kilometers
Azimuthal Equidistant Projection

Falkland Islands
(Islas Malvinas)
(U.K.)

While the digital world may be partly to blame for the loss of Indigenous languages, some organizations are using technology to try to reverse the harm done. Check out these examples of technology being used to save languages that are at risk of dying out.

O **The Living Tongues Institute for Endangered Languages:** This organization supports Indigenous speakers who are saving their languages through political activism, education, and technology. One such technology tool is Living Dictionaries, an online dictionary with words, phrases, and multimedia collected by dozens of language activists in South America.

O **Wikitongues:** Anyone can add to or listen in on Wikitongues's online database of language documentation. This organization's goal is to collect oral history videos and a dictionary for every language in the world.

O **Duolingo:** This app teaches languages with short lessons where users can earn points. There are listening exercises, flash cards, and quizzes to help you learn.

Cultural Languages

South America has an array of Indigenous languages that, for a number of reasons, are in danger of being lost forever. Education is part of the picture, as instruction in these languages does not always continue past the elementary grades. Poverty, political conflict, and the deterioration of oral traditions in an ever-increasing digital world also lead to the loss of languages.

Indigenous languages contain rich cultural stories about a people's ancestors, their place in the world, and how they interact with the land they inhabit. Once a language is gone, so are many ways of seeing the world through that specific culture. One way to preserve Indigenous languages is through living dictionaries, a digital interactive database that includes thousands of written entries for words and phrases paired with audio and images (see sidebar). Another strategy is for elders of a community to teach language classes in their native tongue to adults and children.

⬆ **THE KOGI,** an Indigenous people whose mountain villages are located in the Sierra Nevada de Santa Marta on Colombia's Caribbean coast, speak their ancestral language.

◑ **A TEACHER** in Asunción, Paraguay, explains the Guarani Indigenous alphabet. Guarani is spoken by more than 80 percent of the country's population.

◉ **KIDS WATCH** a television program in Loreto, Peru, that is broadcast in Quechua, the language of the Inca Empire.

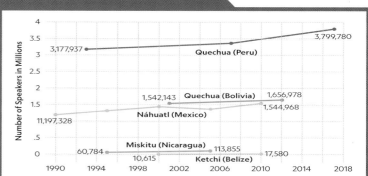

A RISE IN NATIVE SPEAKERS

Number of Speakers in Millions

3,177,937 — Quechua (Peru) — 3,799,780

1,542,143 — Quechua (Bolivia) — 1,656,978
1,544,968
11,197,328 — Náhuatl (Mexico)

Miskitu (Nicaragua)
60,784 — 113,855
10,615 — Ketchi (Belize) — 17,580

1990 1994 1998 2002 2006 2010 2014 2018

Although it's estimated that about one-fifth of Indigenous languages have disappeared, the number of speakers of the most commonly spoken Indigenous languages has increased.

NORTH
AMERICA

Caribbean
Sea

VENEZUELA

GUYANA

SURINAME

French Guiana
(France)

COLOMBIA

A
N
D
E
S

ECUADOR

A M A Z O N

B A S I N

PERU

BRAZIL

BOLIVIA

Atacama Desert

PARAGUAY

TROPIC OF CAPRICORN

ATLANTIC
OCEAN

CHILE

URUGUAY

PACIFIC
OCEAN

ARGENTINA

A
N
D
E
S

PATAGONIA

0   600 miles
0   600 kilometers
Azimuthal Equidistant Projection

Falkland Islands
(Islas Malvinas)
(U.K.)

EQUATOR

**Language Location and
Endangerment Level**

×   Extinct

●   High

●   Medium

    Language hot spot
    (Regions with high linguistic
    density, severe endangerment
    and lack of documentation)

Map Source: H. Hammarström, et al.

Europe:
A View From Space

Smaller than every other continent except Australia, Europe is a mosaic of islands and peninsulas. In fact, Europe itself is one big peninsula, jutting westward from the huge landmass of Asia and nearly touching Africa to the south. Europe's ragged coastline measures more than one and a half times the length of Earth's Equator and provides 32 of the continent's 46 countries direct access to the sea.

St. Vitus Cathedral rises above the historic buildings of Prague, the capital of Czechia (Czech Republic), along the Vltava River.

EUROPE

PHYSICAL

Land area*
**3,841,000 sq mi
(9,947,000 sq km)**

*Land area includes
European Russia, the
area west of the Ural
Mountains; population
includes all of Russia, as
most of its people live in
European Russia.*

**Highest point
El'brus, Russia
18,510 ft (5,642 m)**

**Lowest point
Caspian Sea
-92 ft (-28 m)**

**Longest river
Volga, Russia
2,294 mi (3,692 km)**

**Largest lake
entirely in Europe
Ladoga, Russia
6,900 sq mi (17,872 sq km)**

POLITICAL

Population*
746,318,000
**Number of
independent
countries
46 (including
Russia)**

**Largest country
entirely in Europe
Ukraine
222,607 sq mi (576,550 sq km)**

**Smallest country
Vatican City
0.2 sq mi (0.4 sq km)**

**Most populous country
entirely in Europe
Germany
Pop. 79,903,000**

**Least populous country
Vatican City
Pop. 1,000**

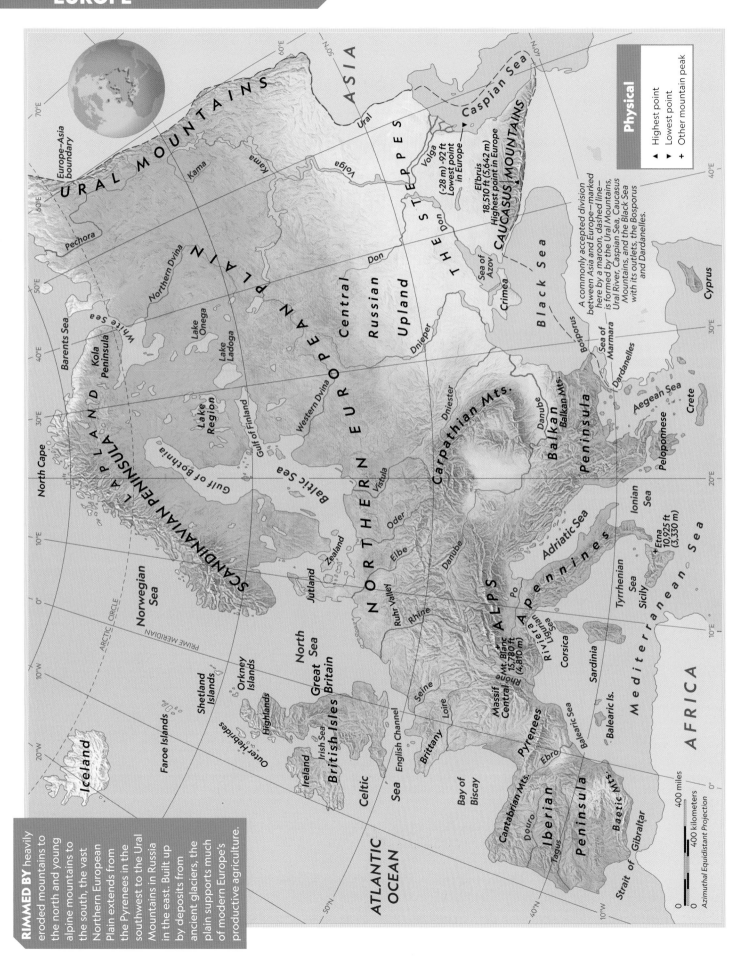

Physical

◄ Highest point
▼ Lowest point
+ Other mountain peak

ASIA

URAL MOUNTAINS

Europe-Asia boundary

70°E
60°E
50°E
40°E
30°E
10°E
0°
10°W
20°W

60°N
50°N
40°N

Pechora

Kama
Kama

Ural
Ural

Volga
Volga

Caspian Sea

(-28 m) -92 ft
Lowest point
in Europe

El'brus
18,510 ft (5,642 m)
Highest point in Europe
CAUCASUS MOUNTAINS

Black Sea

Bosporus

Sea of
Marmara

Dardanelles

Cyprus

A commonly accepted division
between Asia and Europe—marked
here by a maroon, dashed line—
is formed by the Ural Mountains,
Ural River, Caspian Sea, Caucasus
Mountains, and the Black Sea
with its outlets, the Bosporus
and Dardanelles.

NORTHERN EUROPEAN PLAIN

Central
Russian
Upland

THE STEPPES

Don
Don

Dnieper

Sea of
Azov

Crimea

Barents Sea

Northern Dvina

Kola
Peninsula

White Sea

Lake
Onega

Lake
Ladoga

Western Dvina

Lake
Region

Gulf of Finland

Dniester

Carpathian Mts.

Danube

Balkan Mts.

Balkan
Peninsula

Aegean Sea

Crete

Peloponnese

North Cape

LAPLAND

SCANDINAVIAN PENINSULA

Gulf of Bothnia

Baltic Sea

Vistula

Oder

Elbe

Danube

Adriatic Sea

Ionian
Sea

+ Etna
10,925 ft
(3,330 m)

Norwegian
Sea

Zealand

Jutland

Ruhr Valley

Rhine

ALPS

Po

APENNINES

Tyrrhenian
Sea

Sicily

Mediterranean Sea

AFRICA

ARCTIC CIRCLE
PRIME MERIDIAN

Iceland

Faroe Islands

Shetland
Islands

Orkney
Islands

Outer Hebrides

Highlands

North
Sea

Great
Britain

British Isles

Ireland

Irish Sea

Celtic
Sea

English Channel

Brittany

Seine

Loire

Bay of
Biscay

Massif
Central

Mt. Blanc
15,780 ft
(4,810 m)

Rhône

Riviera

Ligurian
Sea

Corsica

Sardinia

Balearic Sea

Balearic Is.

Pyrenees

Cantabrian Mts.

Douro

Tagus

Ebro

Iberian
Peninsula

Baetic Mts.

Strait of
Gibraltar

ATLANTIC
OCEAN

50°N
40°N

10°W

400 miles
0

400 kilometers
0

Azimuthal Equidistant Projection

RIMMED BY heavily
eroded mountains to
the north and young
alpine mountains to
the south, the vast
Northern European
Plain extends from
the Pyrenees in the
southwest to the Ural
Mountains in Russia
in the east. Built up
by deposits from
ancient glaciers, the
plain supports much
of modern Europe's
productive agriculture.

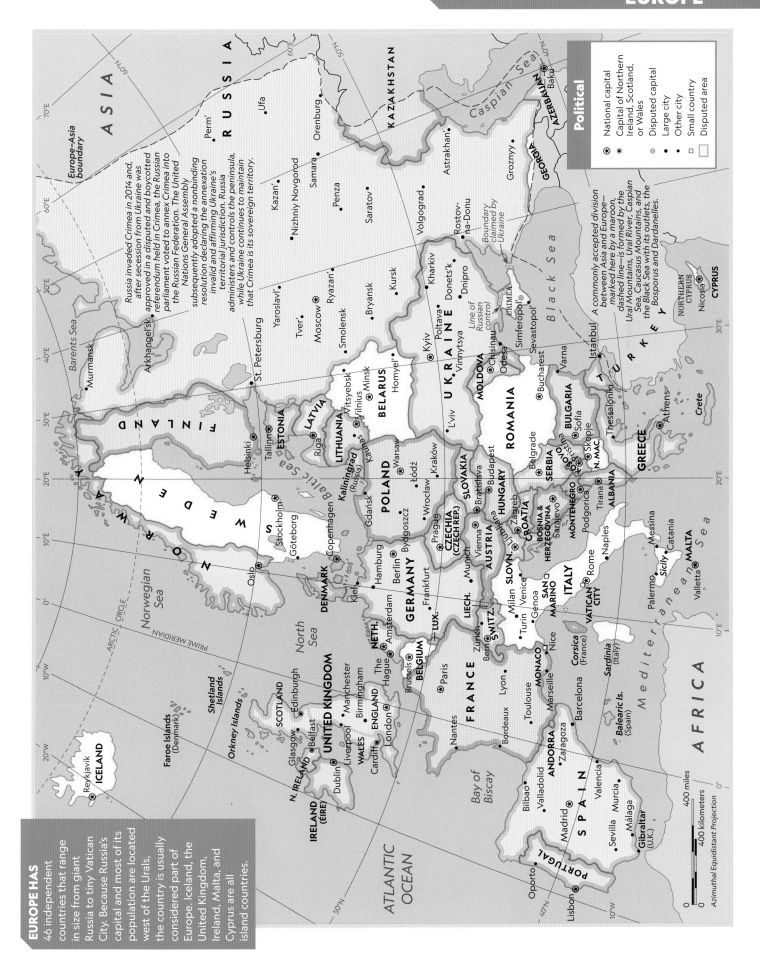

Political

- ⊛ National capital
- ⊛ Capital of Northern Ireland, Scotland, or Wales
- ◎ Disputed capital
- ◎ Large city
- • Other city
- ▫ Small country
- ☐ Disputed area

EUROPE HAS
46 independent countries that range in size from giant Russia to tiny Vatican City. Because Russia's capital and most of its population are located west of the Urals, the country is usually considered part of Europe. Iceland, the United Kingdom, Ireland, Malta, and Cyprus are all island countries.

Russia invaded Crimea in 2014 and, after secession from Ukraine was approved in a disputed and boycotted referendum held in Crimea, the Russian parliament voted to annex Crimea into the Russian Federation. The United Nations General Assembly subsequently adopted a nonbinding resolution declaring the annexation invalid and affirming Ukraine's territorial jurisdiction. Russia administers and controls the peninsula, while Ukraine continues to maintain that Crimea is its sovereign territory.

A commonly accepted division between Asia and Europe—marked here by a maroon, dashed line—is formed by the Ural Mountains, Ural River, Caspian Sea, Caucasus Mountains, and the Black Sea with its outlets, the Bosporus and Dardanelles.

ASIA

RUSSIA

KAZAKHSTAN

Europe-Asia boundary

Ufa
Perm'
Orenburg
Samara
Kazan'
Nizhniy Novgorod
Penza
Saratov
Astrakhan'
Volgograd
Rostov-na-Donu
Groznyy

Caspian Sea

AZERBAIJAN
Baku
GEORGIA

Boundary claimed by Ukraine

Black Sea

Barents Sea
Murmansk
Arkhangel'sk

St. Petersburg
Yaroslavl'
Tver'
Moscow ⊛
Ryazan'
Smolensk
Bryansk
Kursk

Kharkiv
Poltava
Donets'k
Dnipro

UKRAINE
Kyiv ⊛
Vinnytsya
Line of Russian control
CRIMEA ◎
Simferopol'
Sevastopol'

MOLDOVA
Chisinau ⊛
Odesa

Istanbul
Varna
Bucharest ⊛
ROMANIA

BULGARIA
Sofia ⊛

Thessaloníki

TURKEY

NORTHERN CYPRUS
Nicosia ◎
CYPRUS

FINLAND
Helsinki ⊛

SWEDEN
Stockholm ⊛
Göteborg

NORWAY

Oslo ⊛

Baltic Sea

ESTONIA
Tallinn ⊛
LATVIA
Riga ⊛
LITHUANIA
Vilnius ⊛
Kaunas
Kaliningrad (Russia)

BELARUS
Minsk ⊛
Vitsyebsk
Homyel'

POLAND
Warsaw ⊛
Łódź
Kraków
Gdańsk
Wrocław
Bydgoszcz

Lviv

SERBIA
Belgrade ⊛

KOSOVO
Pristina ⊛
N. MAC.
Skopje ⊛

MONTENEGRO
Podgorica ⊛
ALBANIA
Tirana ⊛

GREECE
Athens ⊛
Crete

Copenhagen ⊛
DENMARK
Kiel
Hamburg

GERMANY
Berlin ⊛
Frankfurt
Munich

CZECHIA (CZECH REP.)
Prague ⊛

SLOVAKIA
Bratislava ⊛
Vienna ⊛
AUSTRIA
HUNGARY
Budapest ⊛

SLOVN.
Ljubljana ⊛
Zagreb ⊛
CROATIA
BOSNIA & HERZEGOVINA
Sarajevo ⊛

LIECH.
SWITZ.
Zürich
Bern ⊛

Milan
Venice
Turin
Genoa

SAN MARINO
ITALY
Rome ⊛
VATICAN CITY
Naples

Messina
Sicily
Catania
Palermo

MALTA
Valletta ⊛

Mediterranean Sea

Shetland Islands
Orkney Islands
Faroe Islands (Denmark)

SCOTLAND
Edinburgh ⊛
Glasgow
N. IRELAND
Belfast ⊛
Dublin ⊛
IRELAND (ÉIRE)

UNITED KINGDOM
Manchester
Liverpool
Birmingham
WALES
Cardiff ⊛
ENGLAND
London ⊛

NETH.
Amsterdam ⊛
The Hague
Brussels ⊛
BELGIUM
LUX.

FRANCE
Paris ⊛
Nantes
Lyon
Bordeaux
Toulouse
Marseille
Nice
MONACO

ANDORRA
Barcelona
Zaragoza

SPAIN
Madrid ⊛
Valladolid
Bilbao
Valencia
Murcia
Sevilla
Málaga
Gibraltar (U.K.)

PORTUGAL
Oporto
Lisbon ⊛

Bay of Biscay

Corsica (France)
Sardinia (Italy)
Balearic Is. (Spain)

ATLANTIC OCEAN

AFRICA

Reykjavik ⊛
ICELAND

North Sea

Norwegian Sea

ARCTIC CIRCLE
PRIME MERIDIAN

400 miles
400 kilometers
Azimuthal Equidistant Projection

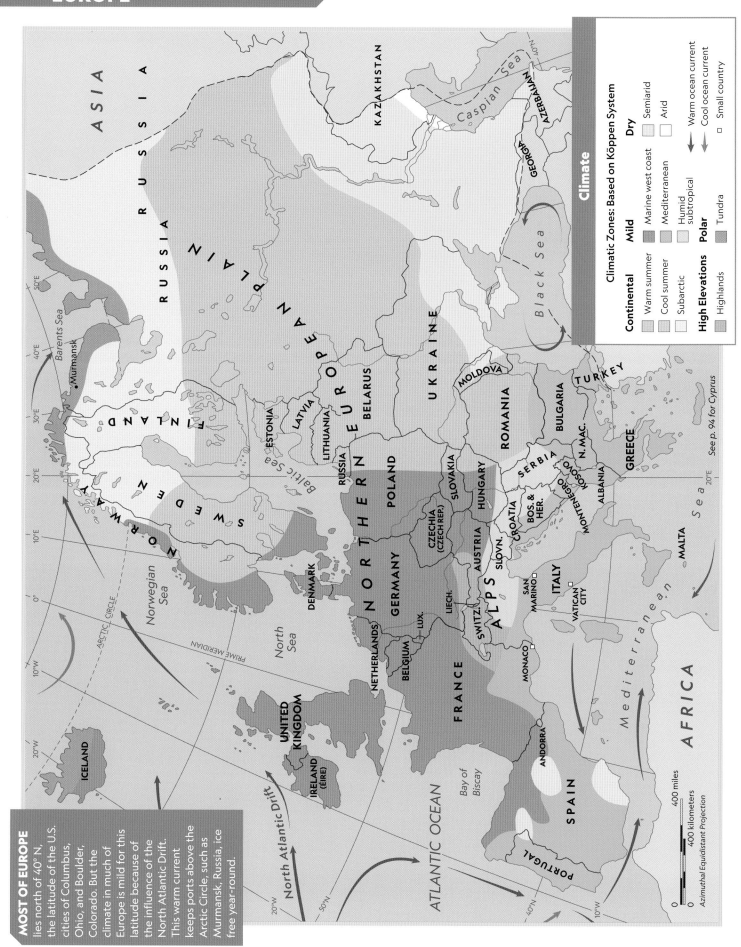

MOST OF EUROPE lies north of 40° N, the latitude of the U.S. cities of Columbus, Ohio, and Boulder, Colorado. But the climate is mild for much of Europe is mild for this latitude because of the influence of the North Atlantic Drift. This warm current keeps ports above the Arctic Circle, such as Murmansk, Russia, ice free year-round.

Climate

Climatic Zones: Based on Köppen System

Continental
- Warm summer
- Cool summer
- Subarctic

High Elevations
- Highlands

Mild
- Marine west coast
- Mediterranean
- Humid subtropical

Polar
- Tundra

Dry
- Semiarid
- Arid

→ Warm ocean current
→ Cool ocean current
□ Small country

See p. 94 for Cyprus

400 miles
400 kilometers
Azimuthal Equidistant Projection

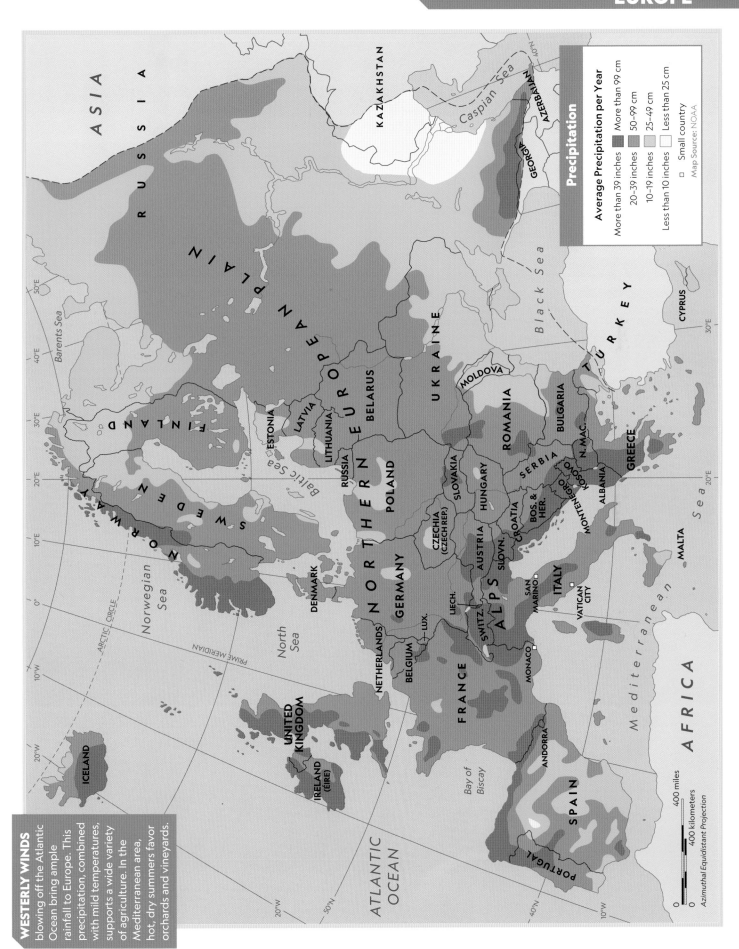

Precipitation

Average Precipitation per Year

More than 39 inches — More than 99 cm
20-39 inches — 50-99 cm
10-19 inches — 25-49 cm
Less than 10 inches — Less than 25 cm
□ Small country

Map Source: NOAA

WESTERLY WINDS
blowing off the Atlantic Ocean bring ample rainfall to Europe. This precipitation, combined with mild temperatures, supports a wide variety of agriculture. In the Mediterranean area, hot, dry summers favor orchards and vineyards.

ASIA

RUSSIA

KAZAKHSTAN

Caspian Sea

AZERBAIJAN

GEORGIA

Barents Sea

EUROPEAN PLAIN

TURKEY

CYPRUS

Black Sea

FINLAND

UKRAINE

MOLDOVA

BULGARIA

N. MAC.

GREECE

Sea

ESTONIA

LATVIA

LITHUANIA

BELARUS

ROMANIA

SERBIA

KOSOVO

ALBANIA

MONTENEGRO

SWEDEN

NORWAY

RUSSIA

POLAND

SLOVAKIA

HUNGARY

CROATIA

BOS. & HER.

Baltic Sea

NORTHERN EUROPE

CZECHIA
(CZECH REP.)

AUSTRIA

SLOVN.

ITALY

SAN MARINO

VATICAN CITY

MALTA

DENMARK

GERMANY

LIECH.

SWITZ.

ALPS

MONACO

Mediterranean

AFRICA

North Sea

NETHERLANDS

BELGIUM

LUX.

FRANCE

ANDORRA

Norwegian Sea

ARCTIC CIRCLE

PRIME MERIDIAN

UNITED KINGDOM

IRELAND
(ÉIRE)

Bay of Biscay

SPAIN

PORTUGAL

ICELAND

ATLANTIC OCEAN

400 miles

400 kilometers

Azimuthal Equidistant Projection

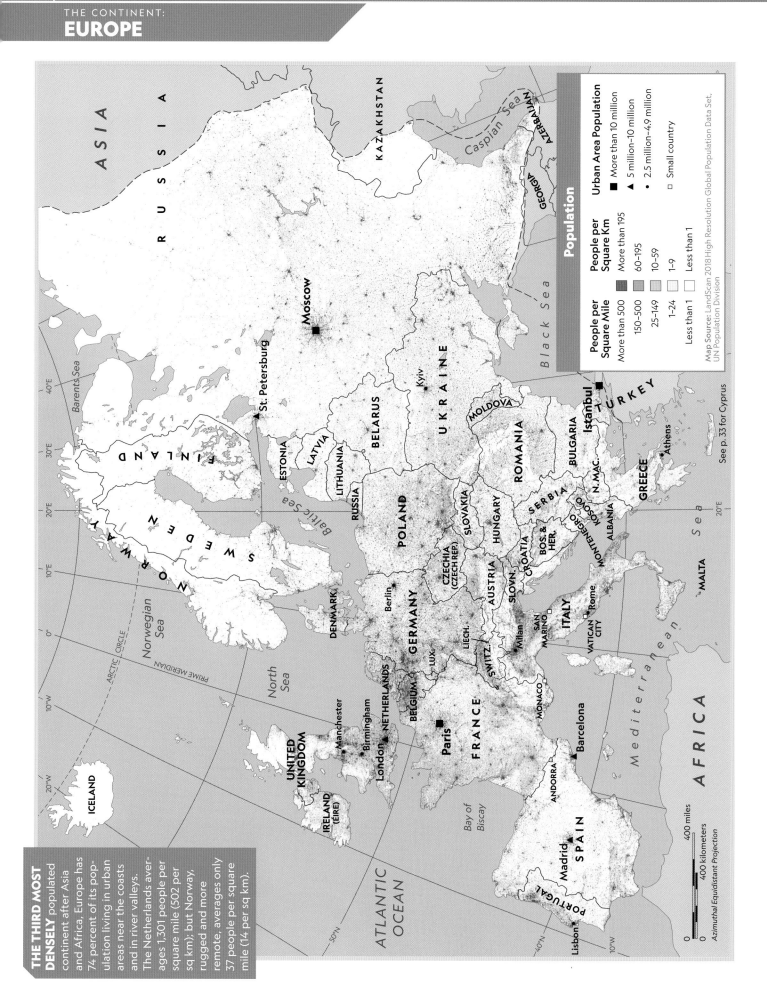

THE THIRD MOST DENSELY populated continent after Asia and Africa, Europe has 74 percent of its population living in urban areas near the coasts and in river valleys. The Netherlands averages 1,301 people per square mile (502 per sq km); but Norway, rugged and more remote, averages only 37 people per square mile (14 per sq km).

Population

People per Square Mile	People per Square Km
More than 500	More than 195
150–500	60–195
25–149	10–59
1–24	1–9
Less than 1	Less than 1

Urban Area Population

■ More than 10 million

▲ 5 million–10 million

• 2.5 million–4.9 million

□ Small country

Map Source: LandScan 2018 High Resolution Global Population Data Set, UN Population Division

See p. 33 for Cyprus

0 — 400 miles
0 — 400 kilometers
Azimuthal Equidistant Projection

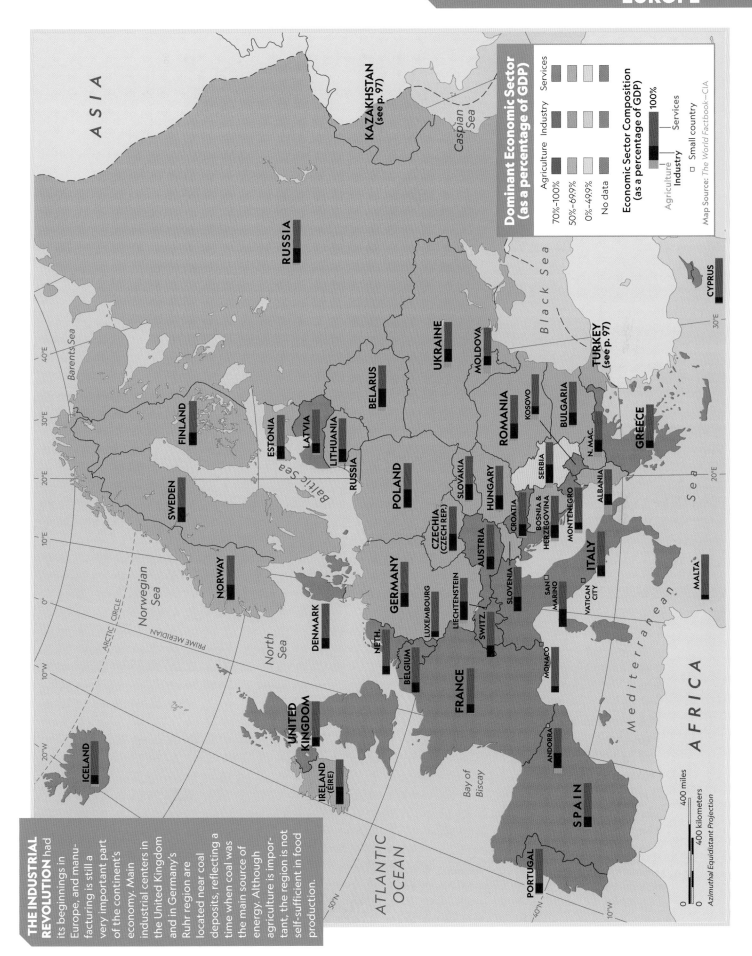

**Dominant Economic Sector
(as a percentage of GDP)**

Agriculture Industry Services

70%–100%

50%–69.9%

0%–49.9%

No data

**Economic Sector Composition
(as a percentage of GDP)**

100%

Services

Agriculture

Industry

□ Small country

Map Source: *The World Factbook*—CIA

THE INDUSTRIAL REVOLUTION had its beginnings in Europe, and manufacturing is still a very important part of the continent's economy. Main industrial centers in the United Kingdom and in Germany's Ruhr region are located near coal deposits, reflecting a time when coal was the main source of energy. Although agriculture is important, the region is not self-sufficient in food production.

400 miles

400 kilometers

Azimuthal Equidistant Projection

KEY TO A HEALTHY FOREST

The Eurasian wolf is considered a keystone species, which means that other animals and plants in an ecosystem largely depend on it. If the number of Eurasian wolves declines, the ecosystem changes drastically. Here are just some ways the Eurasian wolf impacts its ecosystem:

O The wolf's leftovers serve as food for scavenger animals, such as the carrion crow, cinereous vulture, white-tailed eagle, and red kite.

O Wolf packs hunt animals such as roe deer that graze on plants, which helps keep the deer population in check.

O The grazing animals are constantly on the move to avoid wolves, which helps prevent overgrazing in one area.

O Wolves hunt weaker prey that might be injured or sick. This means that the stronger prey animals survive and pass on their genes.

O Deer avoid grazing near wolf dens, so trees in those areas are more likely to survive and grow.

O Ecotourism driven by wolves helps local economies.

Wolf Population

Wolves, bison, lynx, and other big animals were once common in Europe. But from the 1600s to the early 1900s, many of them were hunted almost to extinction. In the past 20 years, apex predators such as the Eurasian wolf have been making a comeback. Wolf packs have returned to Germany, Italy, France, Austria, and Switzerland and have even been spotted in the Netherlands and Belgium as their territory has slowly expanded.

In Europe today, it's estimated there are more than 12,000 wolves in 28 countries. Researchers believe they have benefitted from protected conservation status and the slow exodus of people from rural areas and Alpine valleys. Thanks to the efforts of conservationists throughout Europe, many of these animals are once again living in the ecosystems they used to call home.

AS WOLF POPULATIONS recover, farm animals have become prey for this apex predator. Portugal instituted programs in which guard dogs protect livestock herds from wolves.

IN ROMANIA'S southern Carpathian Mountains, a reintroduction program increased the European bison population from zero in 2012 to more than 60 in 2021.

MANY PLACES IN EUROPE and around the world have created wildlife corridors, a human-made or natural passageway that allows a particular species to travel safely from one part of their habitat to another.

IN 2002, fewer than 100 Iberian lynx roamed Spain, and the species was declared extinct in Portugal. By 2021, an estimated 1,000 of the wild cats were counted on the peninsula, with about 150 in Portugal.

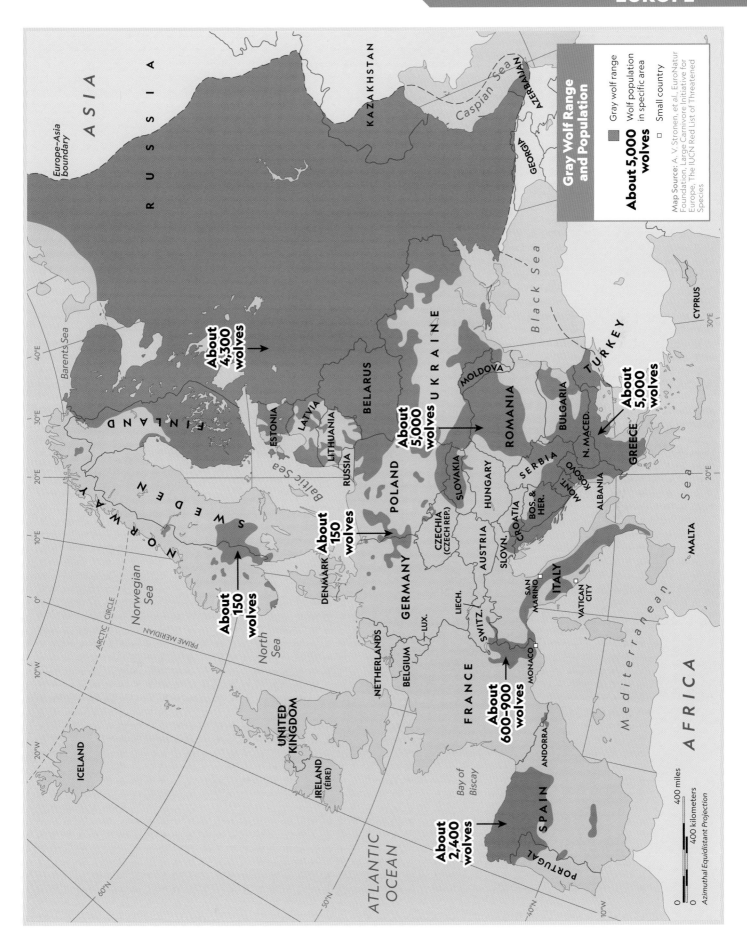

Gray Wolf Range and Population

Gray wolf range

Wolf population in specific area

□ Small country

About 5,000 wolves

Map Source: A. V. Stronen, et al., EuroNatur Foundation, Large Carnivore Initiative for Europe, The IUCN Red List of Threatened Species

About 4,300 wolves

About 5,000 wolves

About 5,000 wolves

About 150 wolves

About 150 wolves

About 600–900 wolves

About 2,400 wolves

Asia:
A View From Space

From the frozen shores of the Arctic Ocean to the equatorial islands of Indonesia, Asia stretches across 90 degrees of latitude. From the Ural Mountains to the Pacific Ocean, it covers more than 150 degrees of longitude. Here, three of history's great culture hearths emerged in the valleys of the Tigris and Euphrates, the Indus, and the Yellow (Huang) Rivers. Today, Asia is home to about 60 percent of Earth's people and some of the world's fastest growing economies.

A fishing village sits amid the towering limestone pillars of Ha Long Bay in Vietnam.

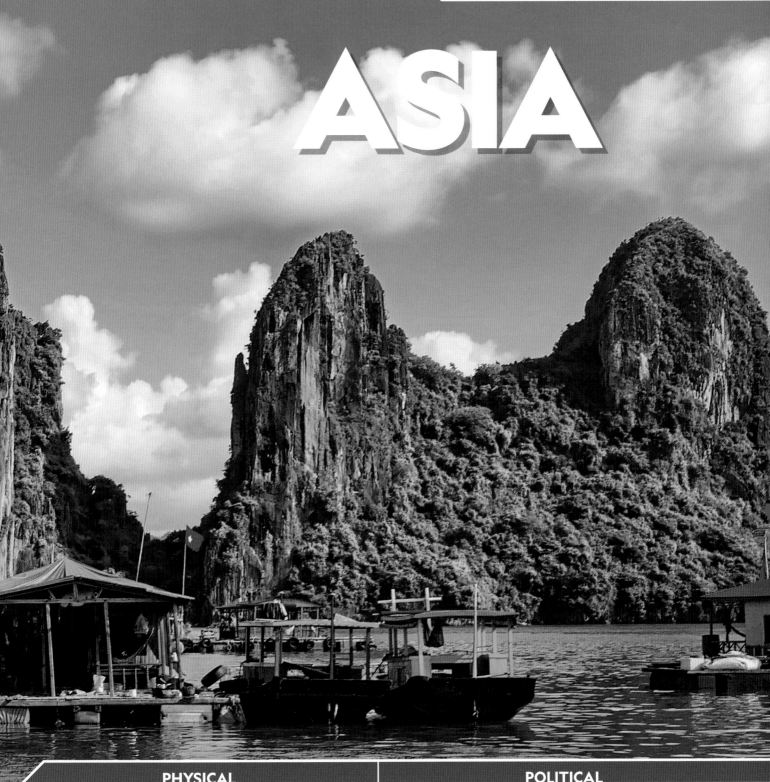

ASIA

PHYSICAL

Land area*
**17,208,000 sq mi
(44,570,000 sq km)**

Land area includes Asian Russia, the area east of the Ural Mountains; population excludes Russia as its population is included in Europe, where most of its people live (see page 81).

**Highest point
Mount Everest,
China-Nepal
29,032 ft (8,849 m)**

**Lowest point
Dead Sea, Israel-Jordan
-1,424 ft (-434 m)**

**Longest river
Yangtze, China
3,880 mi (6,244 km)**

**Largest lake entirely
in Asia
Lake Baikal
12,200 sq mi
(31,500 sq km)**

POLITICAL

Population*
4,582,970,000

**Number of
independent
countries
46 (excluding
Russia)**

**Largest country
entirely in Asia
China
3,705,405 sq mi (9,596,960 sq km)**

**Smallest country
Maldives
115 sq mi (298 sq km)**

**Most populous country
China
Pop. 1,397,898,000**

**Least populous country
Maldives
Pop. 391,000**

ASIA'S PHYSICAL characteristics are impressive. It boasts the world's highest peak (Mount Everest), the deepest lake (Lake Baikal), and 30 percent of Earth's land area. Diversity also marks the Asian landscape, from the dry deserts of the Arabian Peninsula to the frozen tundra of Siberia to steamy rainforests in Borneo.

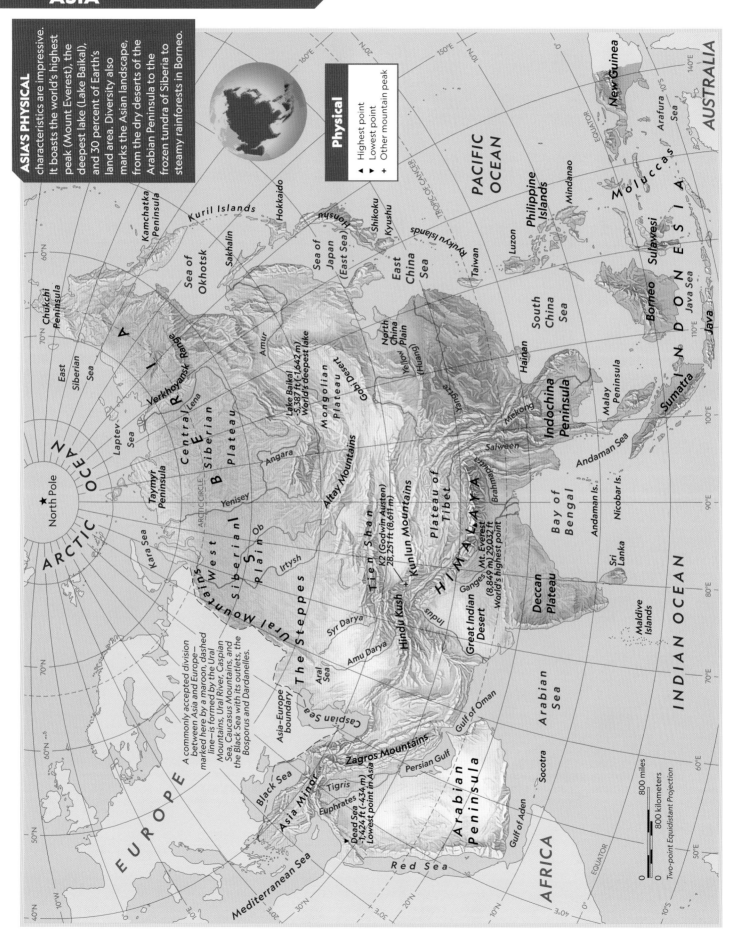

Physical

◄ Highest point
► Lowest point
+ Other mountain peak

A commonly accepted division between Asia and Europe—marked here by a maroon, dashed line—is formed by the Ural Mountains, Ural River, Caspian Sea, Caucasus Mountains, and the Black Sea with its outlets, the Bosporus and Dardanelles.

PACIFIC OCEAN

INDIAN OCEAN

ARCTIC OCEAN

EUROPE

AFRICA

AUSTRALIA

INDONESIA

North Pole

Chukchi Peninsula
Kamchatka Peninsula
Kuril Islands
Hokkaido
Sakhalin
Sea of Okhotsk
East Siberian Sea
Laptev Sea
Taymyr Peninsula
Verkhoyansk Range
Central Siberian Plateau
Lena
Yenisey
Angara
West Siberian Plain
Ob
Irtysh
Kara Sea
The Steppes
Ural Mountains
Syr Darya
Amu Darya
Aral Sea
Caspian Sea
Black Sea
Asia Minor
Asia–Europe boundary
Mediterranean Sea
Tigris
Euphrates
Dead Sea
-1,424 ft (-434 m)
Lowest point in Asia
Red Sea
Gulf of Aden
Zagros Mountains
Persian Gulf
Gulf of Oman
Arabian Peninsula
Socotra
Arabian Sea
Maldive Islands
Sri Lanka
Deccan Plateau
Great Indian Desert
Indus
Ganges
Hindu Kush
Kunlun Mountains
Tien Shan
K2 (Godwin Austen)
28,251 ft (8,611 m)
Altay Mountains
Mongolian Plateau
Gobi Desert
Lake Baikal
-5,387 ft (-1,642 m)
World's deepest lake
Amur
Honshu
Sea of Japan
(East Sea)
Shikoku
Kyushu
East China Sea
Ryukyu Islands
Taiwan
Hainan
South China Sea
North China Plain
Yellow (Huang)
Yangtze
Mekong
Salween
Brahmaputra
Plateau of Tibet
HIMALAYA
Mt. Everest
(8,849 m) 29,032 ft
World's highest point
Bay of Bengal
Andaman Is.
Andaman Sea
Nicobar Is.
Indochina Peninsula
Malay Peninsula
Sumatra
Borneo
Sulawesi
Moluccas
Java
Java Sea
Arafura Sea
New Guinea
Philippine Islands
Luzon
Mindanao

TROPIC OF CANCER

EQUATOR

ARCTIC CIRCLE

800 miles
800 kilometers
Two-point Equidistant Projection

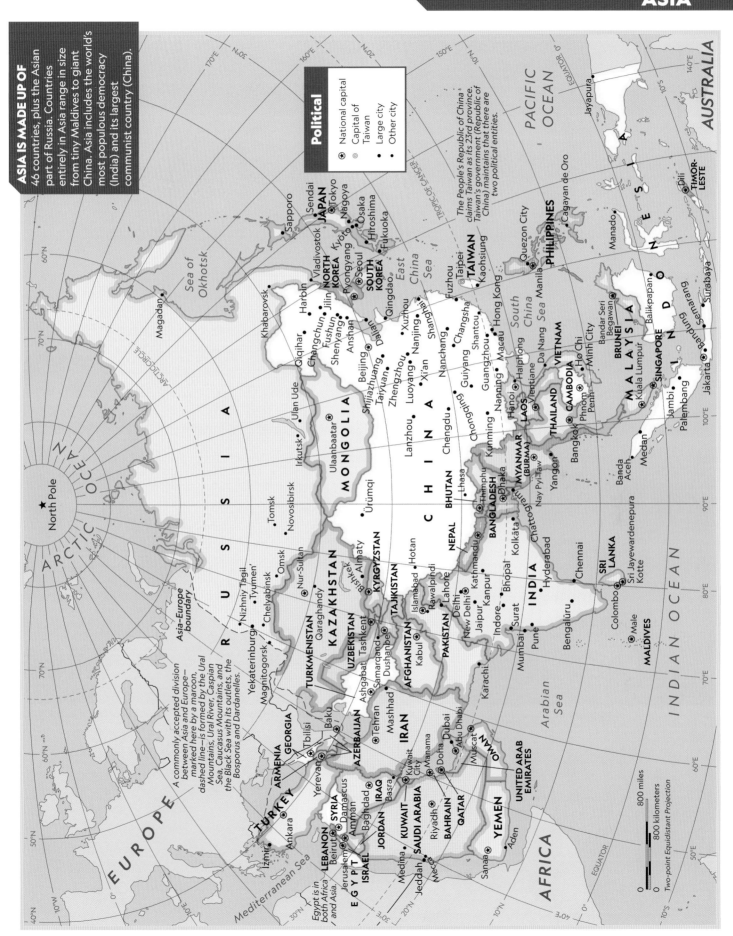

ASIA IS MADE UP OF
46 countries, plus the Asian part of Russia. Countries entirely in Asia range in size from tiny Maldives to giant China. Asia includes the world's most populous democracy (India) and its largest communist country (China).

Political
- ⊛ National capital
- ◎ Capital of Taiwan
- • Large city
- • Other city

The People's Republic of China claims Taiwan as its 23rd province. Taiwan's government (Republic of China) maintains that there are two political entities.

A commonly accepted division between Asia and Europe—marked here by a maroon, dashed line—is formed by the Ural Mountains, Ural River, Caspian Sea, Caucasus Mountains, and the Black Sea with its outlets, the Bosporus and Dardanelles.

Egypt is in both Africa and Asia.

800 miles
800 kilometers
Two-point Equidistant Projection

WET AND DRY extremes characterize Asia's climate. From Mongolia to Saudi Arabia, a dry belt dominates. But the summer monsoon brings heavy rains and sometimes destructive floods in the south. Elevation is the key to climate for the region of the Plateau of Tibet in southwestern China.

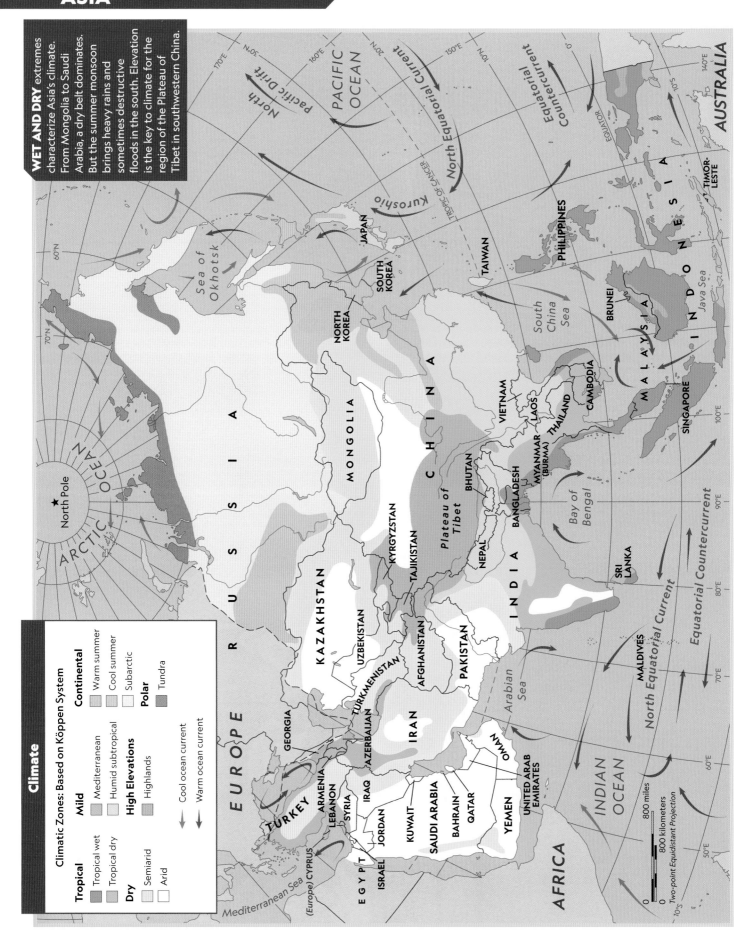

Climate

Climatic Zones: Based on Köppen System

Tropical
- Tropical wet
- Tropical dry

Dry
- Semiarid
- Arid

Mild
- Mediterranean
- Humid subtropical

High Elevations
- Highlands

Continental
- Warm summer
- Cool summer
- Subarctic

Polar
- Tundra

→ Cool ocean current
→ Warm ocean current

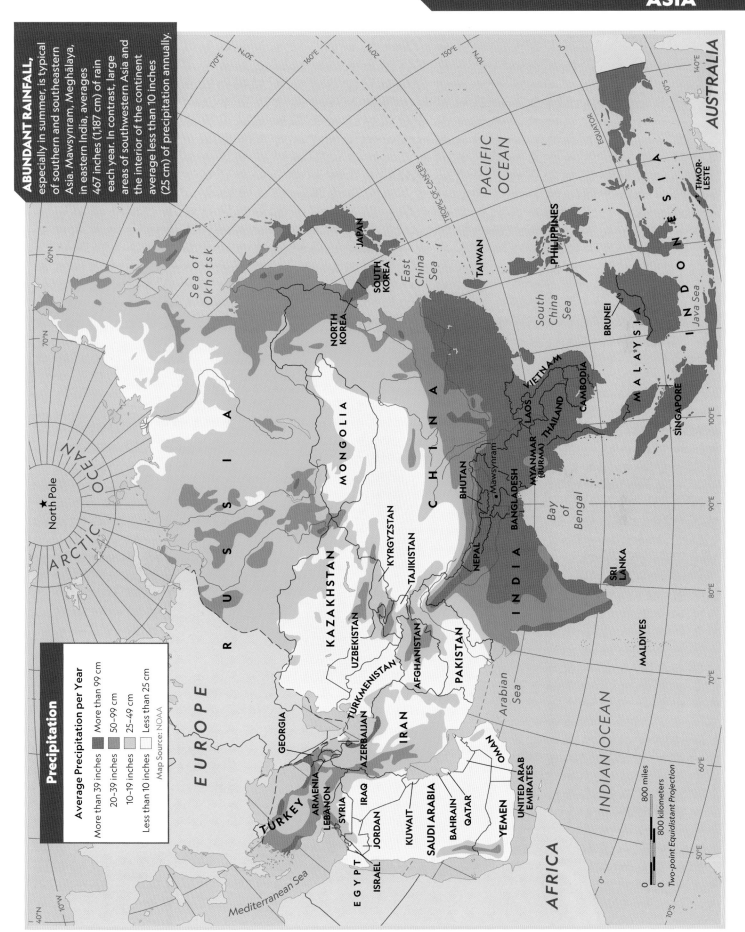

ABUNDANT RAINFALL, especially in summer, is typical of southern and southeastern Asia. Mawsynram, Meghālaya, in eastern India, averages 467 inches (1,187 cm) of rain each year. In contrast, large areas of southwestern Asia and the interior of the continent average less than 10 inches (25 cm) of precipitation annually.

Precipitation

Average Precipitation per Year

- More than 39 inches — More than 99 cm
- 20–39 inches — 50–99 cm
- 10–19 inches — 25–49 cm
- Less than 10 inches — Less than 25 cm

Map Source: NOAA

800 miles

800 kilometers

Two-point Equidistant Projection

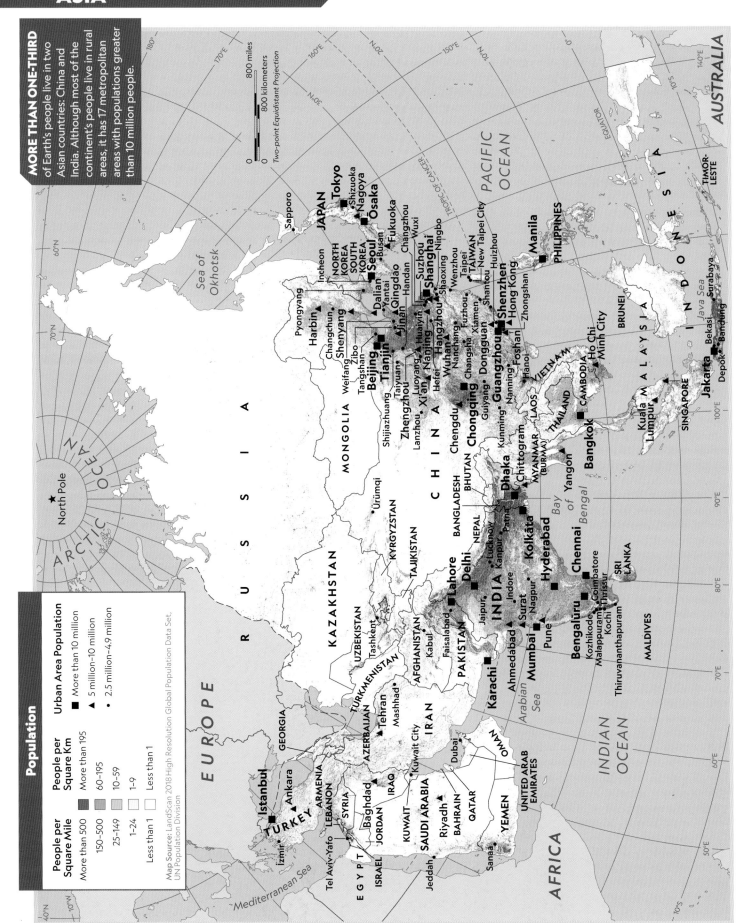

MORE THAN ONE-THIRD of Earth's people live in two Asian countries: China and India. Although most of the continent's people live in rural areas, it has 17 metropolitan areas with populations greater than 10 million people.

800 miles
800 kilometers
Two-point Equidistant Projection

Population

People per Square Mile
- More than 500
- 150–500
- 25–149
- 1–24
- Less than 1

People per Square Km
- More than 195
- 60–195
- 10–59
- 1–9
- Less than 1

Urban Area Population
- ■ More than 10 million
- ▲ 5 million–10 million
- • 2.5 million–4.9 million

Map Source: LandScan 2018 High Resolution Global Population Data Set, UN Population Division

North Pole
ARCTIC OCEAN

EUROPE
AFRICA
AUSTRALIA

RUSSIA
KAZAKHSTAN
MONGOLIA
CHINA
INDIA

PACIFIC OCEAN
INDIAN OCEAN

Sea of Okhotsk
Mediterranean Sea
Arabian Sea
Bay of Bengal
Java Sea

JAPAN
Tokyo
Shizuoka
Nagoya
Osaka
Fukuoka
Sapporo

NORTH KOREA
SOUTH KOREA
Seoul
Incheon
Busan
Pyongyang

Harbin
Changchun
Shenyang
Dalian
Yantai
Qingdao
Jinan
Changzhou
Wuxi
Suzhou
Shanghai
Shaoxing
Ningbo
Wenzhou
Hangzhou
Fuzhou
Xiamen
Shantou
Shenzhen
Hong Kong
Zhongshan
Dongguan
Guangzhou
Foshan
Huizhou
New Taipei City
Taipei
TAIWAN

Beijing
Tianjin
Weifang
Tangshan
Tianjin
Zibo
Shijiazhuang
Taiyuan
Zhengzhou
Luoyang
Xi'an
Lanzhou
Handan
Huaiyin
Nanjing
Hefei
Wuhan
Nanchang
Changsha
Chengdu
Chongqing
Guiyang
Kunming
Nanning

Hanoi
VIETNAM
LAOS
Ho Chi Minh City
CAMBODIA
THAILAND
Bangkok
Yangon
MYANMAR (BURMA)
BRUNEI
MALAYSIA
Kuala Lumpur
SINGAPORE
INDONESIA
Jakarta
Bekasi
Depok
Bandung
Surabaya
TIMOR-LESTE
PHILIPPINES
Manila

Ürümqi
KYRGYZSTAN
TAJIKISTAN
UZBEKISTAN
Tashkent
TURKMENISTAN
AFGHANISTAN
Kabul
PAKISTAN
Faisalabad
Lahore
Karachi
NEPAL
Delhi
Lucknow
Kanpur
Patna
BHUTAN
BANGLADESH
Dhaka
Chittogram
Kolkata
Ahmedabad
Indore
Surat
Nagpur
Mumbai
Pune
Hyderabad
Bengaluru
Chennai
Coimbatore
Kozhikode
Malappuram
Thrissur
Kochi
Thiruvananthapuram
SRI LANKA
MALDIVES
Jaipur
INDIA

IRAN
Tehran
Mashhad
Baghdad
IRAQ
SYRIA
LEBANON
Tel Aviv-Yafo
ISRAEL
JORDAN
SAUDI ARABIA
Riyadh
KUWAIT
Kuwait City
BAHRAIN
QATAR
UNITED ARAB EMIRATES
Dubai
OMAN
YEMEN
Sanaa
Jeddah
EGYPT

GEORGIA
ARMENIA
AZERBAIJAN
Baku
TURKEY
Istanbul
Ankara
İzmir

Tropic of Cancer
Equator

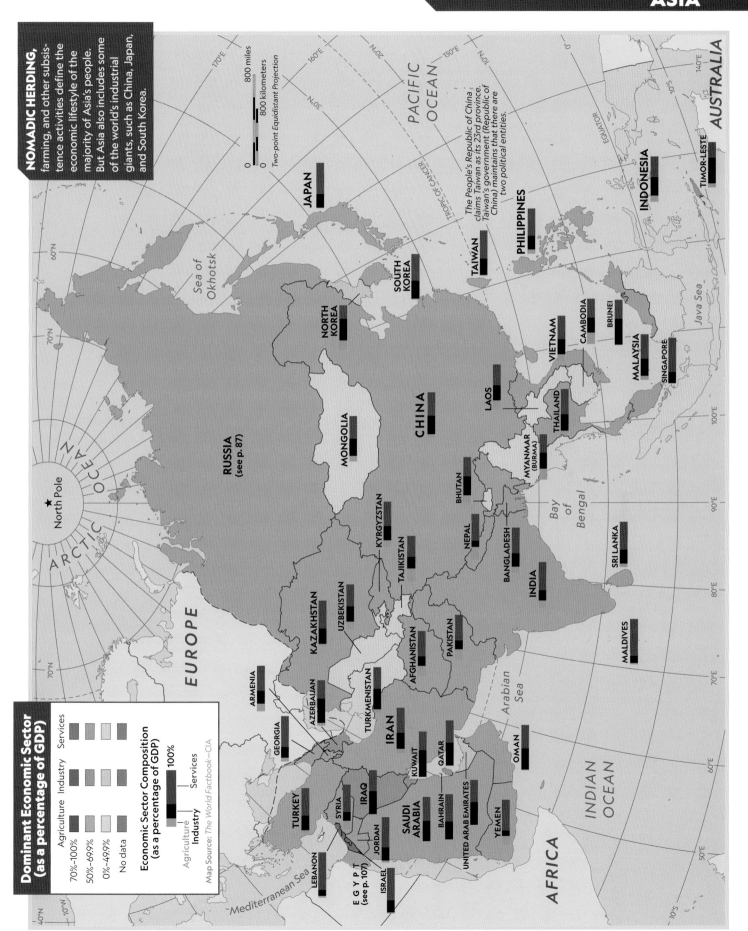

NOMADIC HERDING, farming, and other subsistence activities define the economic lifestyle of the majority of Asia's people. But Asia also includes some of the world's industrial giants, such as China, Japan, and South Korea.

Dominant Economic Sector (as a percentage of GDP)

	Agriculture	Industry	Services
70%-100%			
50%-69.9%			
0%-49.9%			
No data			

Economic Sector Composition (as a percentage of GDP)

100%

Services

Industry

Agriculture

Map Source: *The World Factbook*—CIA

AUSTRALIA

PACIFIC OCEAN

JAPAN

SOUTH KOREA

NORTH KOREA

TAIWAN

PHILIPPINES

INDONESIA

TIMOR-LESTE

Java Sea

Sea of Okhotsk

CAMBODIA

BRUNEI

VIETNAM

MALAYSIA

SINGAPORE

RUSSIA (see p. 87)

MONGOLIA

CHINA

LAOS

THAILAND

MYANMAR (BURMA)

BHUTAN

NEPAL

BANGLADESH

Bay of Bengal

SRI LANKA

KYRGYZSTAN

TAJIKISTAN

INDIA

North Pole

ARCTIC OCEAN

KAZAKHSTAN

UZBEKISTAN

PAKISTAN

AFGHANISTAN

MALDIVES

EUROPE

ARMENIA

AZERBAIJAN

TURKMENISTAN

IRAN

GEORGIA

KUWAIT

QATAR

OMAN

Arabian Sea

INDIAN OCEAN

TURKEY

SYRIA

IRAQ

SAUDI ARABIA

BAHRAIN

UNITED ARAB EMIRATES

YEMEN

JORDAN

LEBANON

ISRAEL

E G Y P T (see p. 107)

Mediterranean Sea

AFRICA

The People's Republic of China claims Taiwan as its 23rd province. Taiwan's government (Republic of China) maintains that there are two political entities.

800 miles

800 kilometers

Two-point Equidistant Projection

TROPIC OF CANCER

EQUATOR

HOW GOVERNMENT TYPE INFLUENCES FREEDOM

This chart displays how a country's Global Freedom Score (0–100) correlates to its freedom type (Free, Not Free, Partly Free) and government type.

NORTH KOREA

Global Freedom Score	3/100
Freedom Type	Not Free
Government Type	Dictatorship, single-party state

BHUTAN

Global Freedom Score	61/100
Freedom Type	Partly Free
Government Type	Constitutional monarchy

MONGOLIA

Global Freedom Score	84/100
Freedom Type	Free
Government Type	Semi-presidential republic

DEFINITIONS OF GOVERNMENT TYPE

Dictatorship, single-party state: All land and businesses are government-owned and individual freedom is limited. A single authoritarian party holds power.

Constitutional monarchy: A king or queen is head of state but power mostly resides in parliament.

Semi-presidential republic: The leader of the majority party is usually elected prime minister.

Global Freedom in Asia

Asia is home to about 60 percent of the world's total population. This continent is also home to an array of different political systems that afford citizens various levels of freedom. For example, China is a Communist-led state, while Thailand is a constitutional monarchy.

In 1948, the United Nations adopted the Universal Declaration of Human Rights. This landmark document agreed that all people should have the same rights, liberties, and freedoms. This map of Asia shows the global freedom status for each country, which is a measurement of how well countries meet the basic tenets of freedom as set forth in the Declaration. The status is determined from multiple scores tallied by a variety of governmental and non-governmental research organizations around the world. Each score is awarded to a specific country based on the categories of political rights, civil liberties, functioning government, and rule of law. The combination of scores awarded for political rights and civil liberties determine whether a country is listed as Free, Partly Free, or Not Free.

⬡ **BEIJING'S IMPOSITION** of a national securi[ty] law for Hong Kong in 2020 resulted in arrests [of] pro-democracy activists. Under the new law, a protester could be held up to six months in ja[il] without being charged for a crime.

⬡ **DEMOCRATIC ELECTIONS** are a hallmark of freedom in Asia and across the globe. Here, a woman casts a vote during the parliamentary elections at a polling station in Seoul, South Korea.

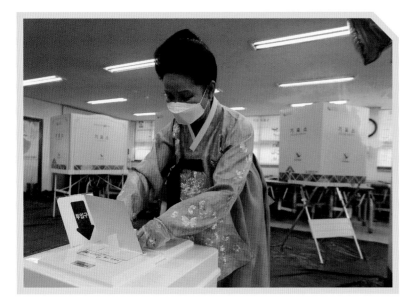

INTERNET FREEDOM DECLINES IN ASIA

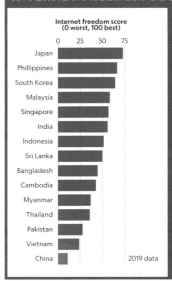

Internet freedom score
(0 worst, 100 best)

0   25   50   75

Japan
Phillippines
South Korea
Malaysia
Singapore
India
Indonesia
Sri Lanka
Bangladesh
Cambodia
Myanmar
Thailand
Pakistan
Vietnam
China

2019 data

In 2019, a variety of different governments in Asia, democratic and non-democratic, added restrictions to internet access and online space to prevent civic expression and activism. Fearful of what people can do when they gather to protest, many political leaders chose to limit civilians' ability to communicate and organize online.

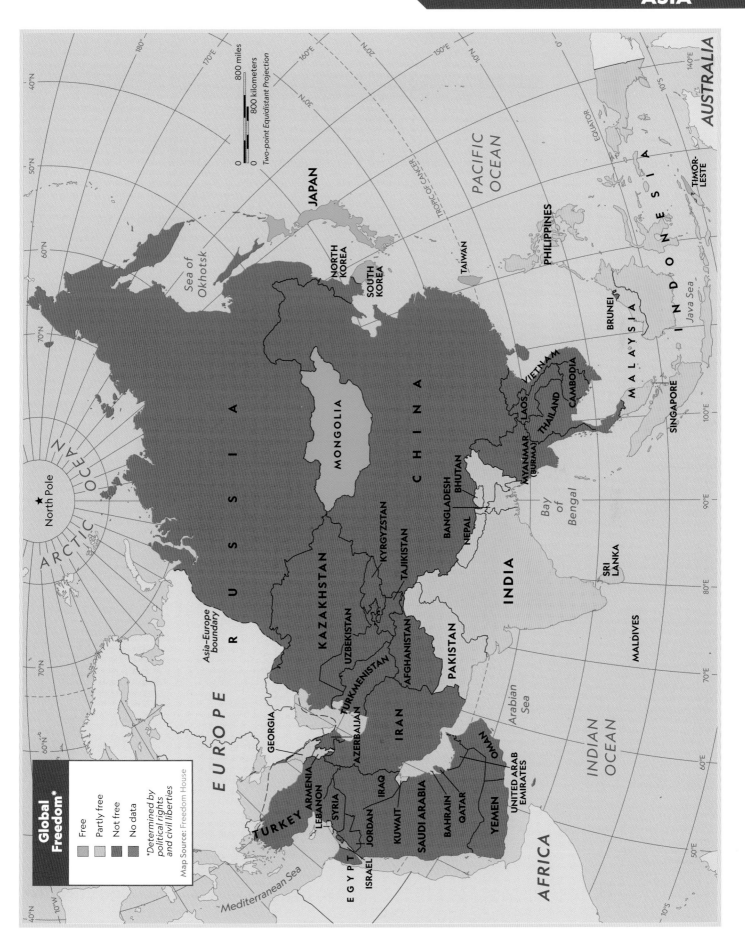

Global Freedom*

Free
Partly free
Not free
No data

*Determined by
political rights
and civil liberties

Map Source: Freedom House

800 miles
800 kilometers
Two-point Equidistant Projection

ARCTIC OCEAN
North Pole

EUROPE

Asia–Europe
boundary

R U S S I A

Sea of
Okhotsk

JAPAN

NORTH
KOREA

SOUTH
KOREA

MONGOLIA

C H I N A

TAIWAN

PACIFIC
OCEAN

PHILIPPINES

KAZAKHSTAN

KYRGYZSTAN

TAJIKISTAN

UZBEKISTAN

TURKMENISTAN

AFGHANISTAN

PAKISTAN

NEPAL

BHUTAN

BANGLADESH

MYANMAR
(BURMA)

LAOS

VIETNAM

THAILAND

CAMBODIA

MALAYSIA

BRUNEI

SINGAPORE

I N D O N E S I A

TIMOR-
LESTE

AUSTRALIA

GEORGIA

AZERBAIJAN

ARMENIA

IRAN

OMAN

UNITED ARAB
EMIRATES

TURKEY

LEBANON

SYRIA

IRAQ

JORDAN

KUWAIT

SAUDI ARABIA

BAHRAIN

QATAR

YEMEN

EGYPT

ISRAEL

I N D I A

SRI
LANKA

MALDIVES

Bay
of
Bengal

Arabian
Sea

INDIAN
OCEAN

AFRICA

Mediterranean Sea

Java Sea

EQUATOR

TROPIC OF CANCER

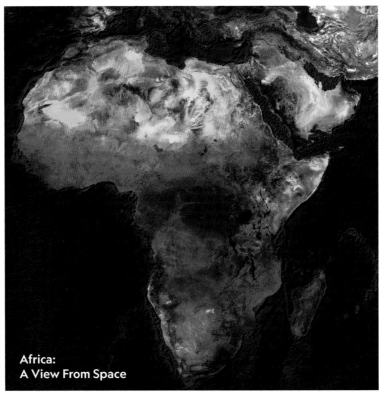

Africa:
A View From Space

F rom space, Africa appears to be divided into three regions: the north, dominated by the Sahara, the largest hot desert in the world; central bands of tropical grasslands and rainforests; and more dry land to the south. The Great Rift Valley may be slowly splitting Africa apart. The valley runs from the Red Sea through the Afar Triangle to the southern lake district.

PHYSICAL

Land area*	Highest point	Longest river
11,608,000 sq mi (30,065,000 sq km)	Kilimanjaro, Tanzania 19,341 ft (5,895 m)	Nile 4,160 mi (6,695 km)
*Land area includes the Sinai, Egypt, although physically part of Asia; population includes the Sinai	Lowest point Lake Assal, Djibouti -509 mi (-155 km)	Largest lake Victoria 26,800 sq mi (69,500 sq km)

POLITICAL

Population	Largest country	Most populous country
1,375,398,000	Algeria 919,595 sq mi (2,381,740 sq km)	Nigeria Pop. 219,464,000
Number of independent countries 54	Smallest country Seychelles 176 sq mi (455 sq km)	Least populous country Seychelles Pop. 96,000

AFRICA

The Pyramids at Giza rise above Cairo, Egypt, as both ancient and modern landscapes converge.

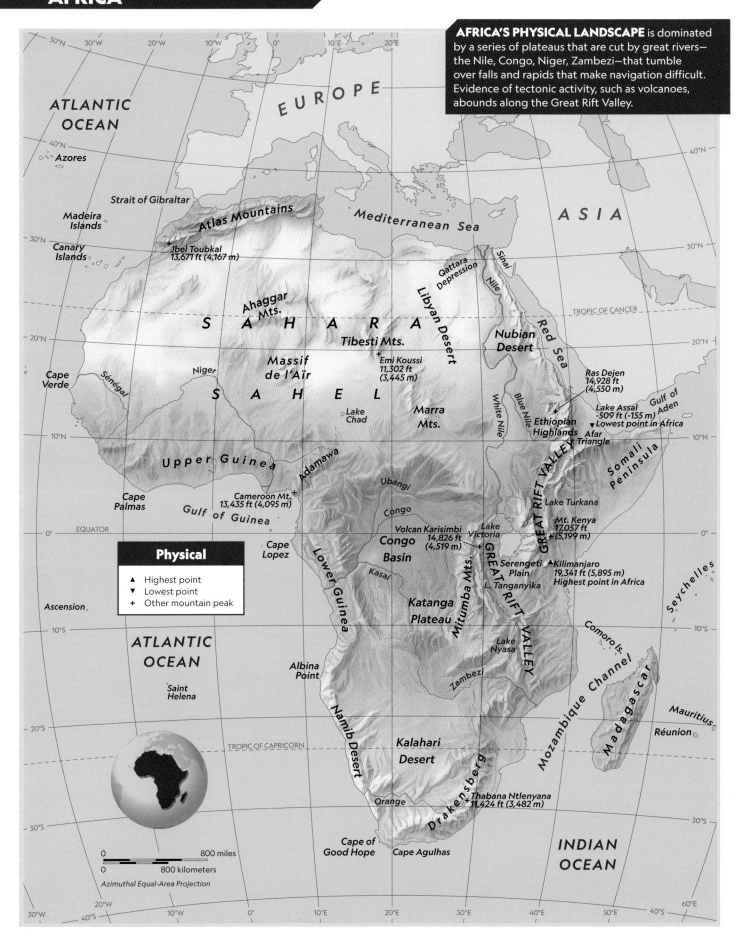

AFRICA'S PHYSICAL LANDSCAPE is dominated by a series of plateaus that are cut by great rivers—the Nile, Congo, Niger, Zambezi—that tumble over falls and rapids that make navigation difficult. Evidence of tectonic activity, such as volcanoes, abounds along the Great Rift Valley.

Physical

- ▲ Highest point
- ▼ Lowest point
- + Other mountain peak

EUROPE

ATLANTIC OCEAN

ASIA

Azores

Strait of Gibraltar

Madeira Islands

Canary Islands

Cape Verde

Atlas Mountains

Jbel Toubkal 13,671 ft (4,167 m)

Mediterranean Sea

Sinai

Qattara Depression

Nile

Red Sea

TROPIC OF CANCER

Ahaggar Mts.

S A H A R A

Libyan Desert

Nubian Desert

Tibesti Mts.

Emi Koussi 11,302 ft (3,445 m)

Massif de l'Aïr

Niger

S A H E L

Lake Chad

Marra Mts.

Sénégal

White Nile

Blue Nile

Ethiopian Highlands

Ras Dejen 14,928 ft (4,550 m)

Lake Assal -509 ft (-155 m) ▼ Lowest point in Africa

Gulf of Aden

Afar Triangle

Somali Peninsula

Upper Guinea

Adamawa

Cape Palmas

Cameroon Mt. 13,435 ft (4,095 m)

Gulf of Guinea

EQUATOR

Ubangi

Congo

Cape Lopez

Volcan Karisimbi 14,826 ft (4,519 m)

Congo Basin

Lake Victoria

Lake Turkana

Mt. Kenya 17,057 ft (5,199 m)

GREAT RIFT VALLEY

Lower Guinea

Kasai

Mitumba Mts.

GREAT RIFT VALLEY

Serengeti Plain

L. Tanganyika

▲ Kilimanjaro 19,341 ft (5,895 m) Highest point in Africa

Seychelles

Ascension

ATLANTIC OCEAN

Katanga Plateau

Lake Nyasa

Saint Helena

Albina Point

Zambezi

Comoro Is.

Mozambique Channel

Madagascar

Mauritius

Réunion

Namib Desert

TROPIC OF CAPRICORN

Kalahari Desert

Drakensberg

Orange

Thabana Ntlenyana 11,424 ft (3,482 m)

Cape of Good Hope

Cape Agulhas

INDIAN OCEAN

0   800 miles
0   800 kilometers

Azimuthal Equal-Area Projection

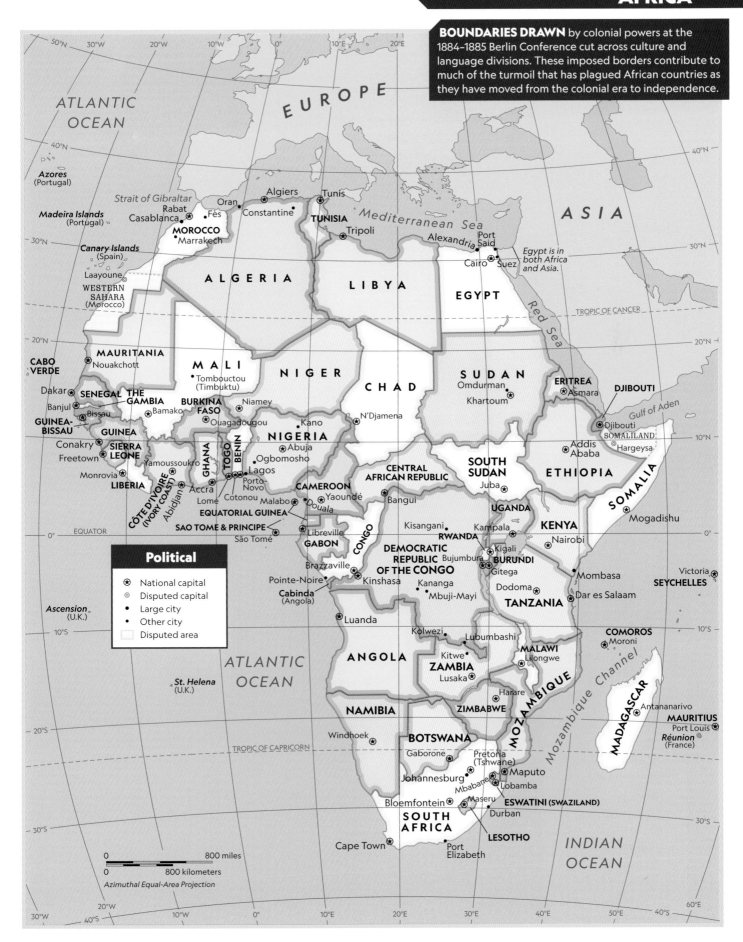

BOUNDARIES DRAWN by colonial powers at the 1884–1885 Berlin Conference cut across culture and language divisions. These imposed borders contribute to much of the turmoil that has plagued African countries as they have moved from the colonial era to independence.

ATLANTIC OCEAN

EUROPE

ASIA

Azores (Portugal)

Madeira Islands (Portugal)

Canary Islands (Spain)

Strait of Gibraltar

Mediterranean Sea

Rabat
Casablanca
Fès
MOROCCO
Marrakech
Oran
Constantine
Algiers
Tunis
TUNISIA
Tripoli
Alexandria
Port Said
Cairo
Suez

Egypt is in both Africa and Asia.

Red Sea

TROPIC OF CANCER

Laayoune
WESTERN SAHARA (Morocco)

ALGERIA
LIBYA
EGYPT

MAURITANIA
Nouakchott

MALI
NIGER
CHAD
SUDAN
Omdurman
Khartoum
ERITREA
Asmara
DJIBOUTI

CABO VERDE

Dakar
SENEGAL
THE GAMBIA
Banjul
Bissau
GUINEA-BISSAU
GUINEA
Conakry
Freetown
SIERRA LEONE
Monrovia
LIBERIA

Tombouctou (Timbuktu)

Niamey

BURKINA FASO
Bamako
Ouagadougou
Kano
NIGERIA
Abuja
Ogbomosho
Lagos
GHANA
TOGO
BENIN
Yamoussoukro
Accra
Porto-Novo
Lomé
Cotonou
CÔTE D'IVOIRE (IVORY COAST)
Abidjan

N'Djamena

CENTRAL AFRICAN REPUBLIC

SOUTH SUDAN
Juba

Gulf of Aden
Djibouti
SOMALILAND
Hargeysa
Addis Ababa
ETHIOPIA
SOMALIA

Mogadishu

CAMEROON
Malabo
Douala
Yaoundé
EQUATORIAL GUINEA
SAO TOME & PRINCIPE
São Tomé
Libreville
GABON
CONGO
Brazzaville
Pointe-Noire
Cabinda (Angola)

Bangui
Kisangani
DEMOCRATIC REPUBLIC OF THE CONGO
Kinshasa
Kananga
Mbuji-Mayi

RWANDA
Kigali
Bujumbura
BURUNDI
Gitega
Dodoma

UGANDA
Kampala
KENYA
Nairobi

Mombasa
Dar es Salaam
TANZANIA

SEYCHELLES
Victoria

EQUATOR

Political

- ⊛ National capital
- ◎ Disputed capital
- ● Large city
- • Other city
- ▢ Disputed area

Ascension (U.K.)

St. Helena (U.K.)

ATLANTIC OCEAN

Luanda
ANGOLA
Kolwezi
Lubumbashi
Kitwe
ZAMBIA
Lusaka

COMOROS
Moroni

MALAWI
Lilongwe

MOZAMBIQUE
Mozambique Channel

MADAGASCAR
Antananarivo

MAURITIUS
Port Louis
Réunion (France)

Harare
ZIMBABWE

TROPIC OF CAPRICORN

NAMIBIA
Windhoek
BOTSWANA
Gaborone
Pretoria (Tshwane)
Johannesburg
Maputo
Mbabane
Lobamba
Maseru
ESWATINI (SWAZILAND)
Bloemfontein
Durban
SOUTH AFRICA
Cape Town
Port Elizabeth
LESOTHO

INDIAN OCEAN

0   800 miles
0   800 kilometers
Azimuthal Equal-Area Projection

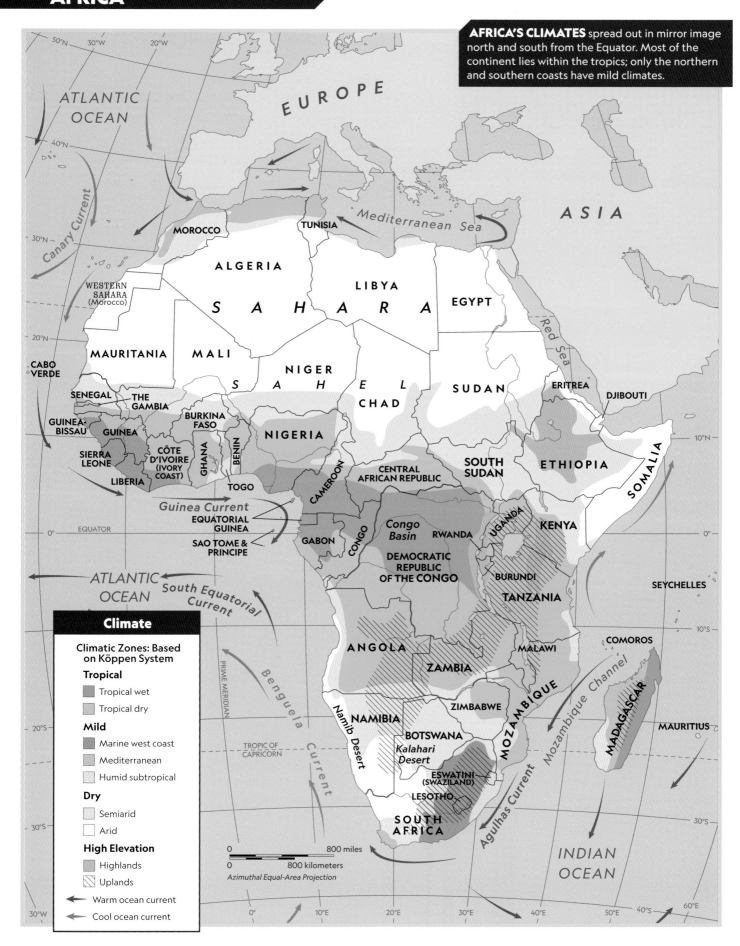

AFRICA'S CLIMATES spread out in mirror image north and south from the Equator. Most of the continent lies within the tropics; only the northern and southern coasts have mild climates.

ATLANTIC OCEAN

EUROPE

ASIA

Mediterranean Sea

Canary Current

Red Sea

WESTERN SAHARA (Morocco)

MOROCCO

TUNISIA

ALGERIA

LIBYA

EGYPT

S A H A R A

MAURITANIA

MALI

NIGER

S A H E L

SUDAN

ERITREA

DJIBOUTI

CHAD

SENEGAL

THE GAMBIA

BURKINA FASO

NIGERIA

CABO VERDE

GUINEA-BISSAU

GUINEA

SIERRA LEONE

CÔTE D'IVOIRE (IVORY COAST)

GHANA

BENIN

TOGO

LIBERIA

CAMEROON

CENTRAL AFRICAN REPUBLIC

SOUTH SUDAN

ETHIOPIA

SOMALIA

Guinea Current

EQUATORIAL GUINEA

SAO TOME & PRINCIPE

GABON

CONGO

Congo Basin

DEMOCRATIC REPUBLIC OF THE CONGO

RWANDA

UGANDA

KENYA

EQUATOR

BURUNDI

TANZANIA

SEYCHELLES

ATLANTIC OCEAN

South Equatorial Current

ANGOLA

ZAMBIA

MALAWI

COMOROS

Mozambique Channel

MADAGASCAR

MAURITIUS

PRIME MERIDIAN

Benguela Current

ZIMBABWE

MOZAMBIQUE

NAMIBIA

Namib Desert

BOTSWANA

Kalahari Desert

ESWATINI (SWAZILAND)

TROPIC OF CAPRICORN

LESOTHO

Agulhas Current

SOUTH AFRICA

INDIAN OCEAN

Climate

Climatic Zones: Based on Köppen System

Tropical
- Tropical wet
- Tropical dry

Mild
- Marine west coast
- Mediterranean
- Humid subtropical

Dry
- Semiarid
- Arid

High Elevation
- Highlands
- Uplands

→ Warm ocean current
→ Cool ocean current

0   800 miles
0   800 kilometers
Azimuthal Equal-Area Projection

50°N, 40°N, 30°N, 20°N, 10°N, 0°, 10°S, 20°S, 30°S

30°W, 20°W, 0°, 10°E, 20°E, 30°E, 40°E, 50°E, 60°E, 40°S

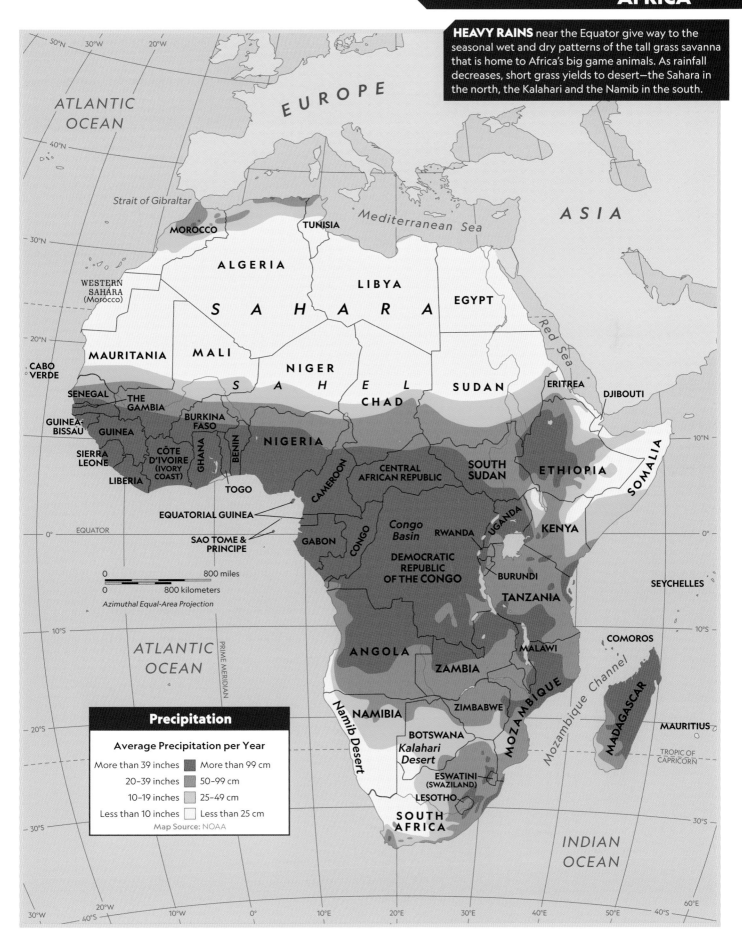

HEAVY RAINS near the Equator give way to the seasonal wet and dry patterns of the tall grass savanna that is home to Africa's big game animals. As rainfall decreases, short grass yields to desert—the Sahara in the north, the Kalahari and the Namib in the south.

ATLANTIC OCEAN

EUROPE

ASIA

Mediterranean Sea

Strait of Gibraltar

MOROCCO

TUNISIA

ALGERIA

LIBYA

EGYPT

WESTERN SAHARA (Morocco)

S A H A R A

Red Sea

MAURITANIA

MALI

NIGER

CABO VERDE

SENEGAL

THE GAMBIA

S A H E L

SUDAN

ERITREA

DJIBOUTI

GUINEA-BISSAU

GUINEA

BURKINA FASO

CHAD

SIERRA LEONE

CÔTE D'IVOIRE (IVORY COAST)

GHANA

BENIN

NIGERIA

CENTRAL AFRICAN REPUBLIC

SOUTH SUDAN

ETHIOPIA

SOMALIA

LIBERIA

TOGO

EQUATORIAL GUINEA

SAO TOME & PRINCIPE

CAMEROON

GABON

CONGO

Congo Basin

RWANDA

UGANDA

KENYA

EQUATOR

DEMOCRATIC REPUBLIC OF THE CONGO

BURUNDI

SEYCHELLES

TANZANIA

0   800 miles
0   800 kilometers

Azimuthal Equal-Area Projection

COMOROS

ATLANTIC OCEAN

PRIME MERIDIAN

ANGOLA

ZAMBIA

MALAWI

MOZAMBIQUE

Mozambique Channel

MADAGASCAR

MAURITIUS

ZIMBABWE

Namib Desert

NAMIBIA

BOTSWANA

Kalahari Desert

TROPIC OF CAPRICORN

Precipitation

Average Precipitation per Year

More than 39 inches	More than 99 cm
20–39 inches	50–99 cm
10–19 inches	25–49 cm
Less than 10 inches	Less than 25 cm

Map Source: NOAA

ESWATINI (SWAZILAND)

LESOTHO

SOUTH AFRICA

INDIAN OCEAN

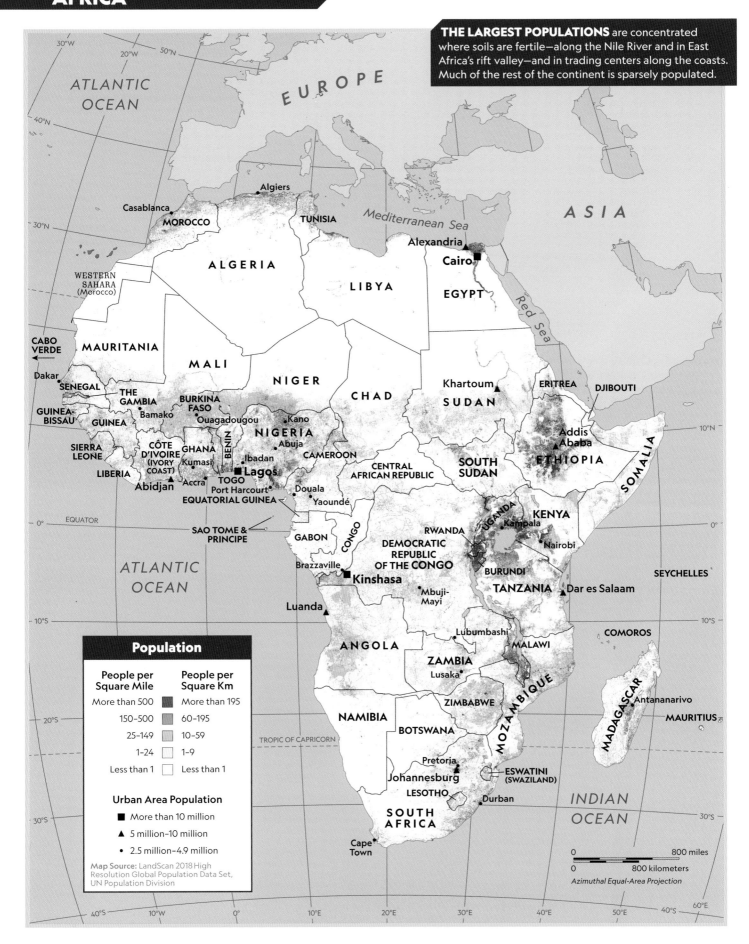

THE LARGEST POPULATIONS are concentrated where soils are fertile—along the Nile River and in East Africa's rift valley—and in trading centers along the coasts. Much of the rest of the continent is sparsely populated.

ATLANTIC OCEAN

EUROPE

ASIA

Mediterranean Sea

Algiers

Casablanca

MOROCCO

TUNISIA

Alexandria

Cairo

ALGERIA

LIBYA

EGYPT

Red Sea

WESTERN SAHARA (Morocco)

CABO VERDE

MAURITANIA

MALI

NIGER

CHAD

Khartoum

SUDAN

ERITREA

DJIBOUTI

Dakar

SENEGAL

THE GAMBIA

BURKINA FASO

Bamako

Ouagadougou

Kano

Addis Ababa

GUINEA-BISSAU

GUINEA

NIGERIA

Abuja

ETHIOPIA

SOMALIA

SIERRA LEONE

CÔTE D'IVOIRE (IVORY COAST)

GHANA

Kumasi

BENIN

Ibadan

CAMEROON

SOUTH SUDAN

10°N

LIBERIA

Accra

TOGO

Lagos

Port Harcourt

Douala

Yaoundé

CENTRAL AFRICAN REPUBLIC

Abidjan

EQUATORIAL GUINEA

SAO TOME & PRINCIPE

GABON

CONGO

KENYA

UGANDA

Kampala

Nairobi

EQUATOR

DEMOCRATIC REPUBLIC OF THE CONGO

RWANDA

Brazzaville

Kinshasa

BURUNDI

SEYCHELLES

0°

Mbuji-Mayi

TANZANIA

Dar es Salaam

Luanda

ATLANTIC OCEAN

10°S

Lubumbashi

COMOROS

ANGOLA

ZAMBIA

Lusaka

MALAWI

ZIMBABWE

MOZAMBIQUE

MADAGASCAR

Antananarivo

NAMIBIA

TROPIC OF CAPRICORN

BOTSWANA

MAURITIUS

Pretoria

ESWATINI (SWAZILAND)

INDIAN OCEAN

Johannesburg

LESOTHO

Durban

SOUTH AFRICA

Cape Town

Population

People per Square Mile
- More than 500
- 150–500
- 25–149
- 1–24
- Less than 1

People per Square Km
- More than 195
- 60–195
- 10–59
- 1–9
- Less than 1

Urban Area Population
- ■ More than 10 million
- ▲ 5 million–10 million
- • 2.5 million–4.9 million

Map Source: LandScan 2018 High Resolution Global Population Data Set, UN Population Division

0   800 miles
0   800 kilometers

Azimuthal Equal-Area Projection

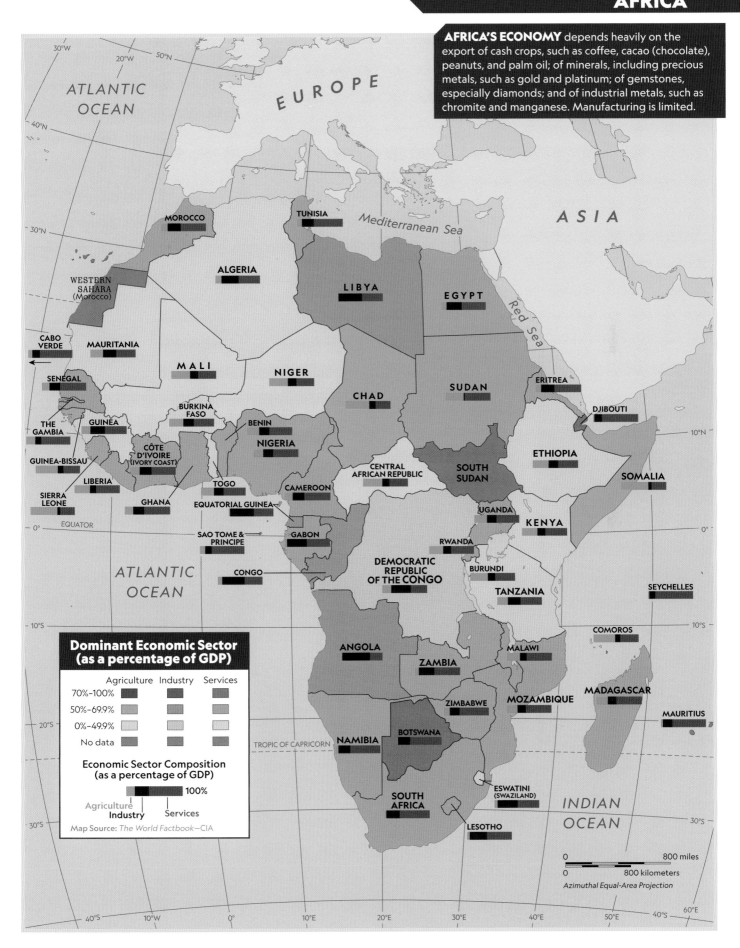

AFRICA'S ECONOMY depends heavily on the export of cash crops, such as coffee, cacao (chocolate), peanuts, and palm oil; of minerals, including precious metals, such as gold and platinum; of gemstones, especially diamonds; and of industrial metals, such as chromite and manganese. Manufacturing is limited.

ATLANTIC OCEAN

EUROPE

Mediterranean Sea

ASIA

Red Sea

MOROCCO

TUNISIA

ALGERIA

LIBYA

EGYPT

WESTERN SAHARA (Morocco)

CABO VERDE

MAURITANIA

MALI

NIGER

SUDAN

ERITREA

SENEGAL

BURKINA FASO

CHAD

DJIBOUTI

THE GAMBIA

GUINEA

BENIN

NIGERIA

ETHIOPIA

GUINEA-BISSAU

CÔTE D'IVOIRE (IVORY COAST)

CENTRAL AFRICAN REPUBLIC

SOUTH SUDAN

SOMALIA

SIERRA LEONE

LIBERIA

TOGO

CAMEROON

GHANA

EQUATORIAL GUINEA

UGANDA

KENYA

SAO TOME & PRINCIPE

GABON

RWANDA

EQUATOR

CONGO

DEMOCRATIC REPUBLIC OF THE CONGO

BURUNDI

TANZANIA

SEYCHELLES

ATLANTIC OCEAN

COMOROS

ANGOLA

ZAMBIA

MALAWI

MADAGASCAR

ZIMBABWE

MOZAMBIQUE

MAURITIUS

BOTSWANA

TROPIC OF CAPRICORN

NAMIBIA

ESWATINI (SWAZILAND)

INDIAN OCEAN

SOUTH AFRICA

LESOTHO

Dominant Economic Sector (as a percentage of GDP)

	Agriculture	Industry	Services
70%–100%			
50%–69.9%			
0%–49.9%			
No data			

Economic Sector Composition (as a percentage of GDP)

100%

Agriculture
Industry
Services

Map Source: *The World Factbook*—CIA

0   800 miles
0   800 kilometers

Azimuthal Equal-Area Projection

GROWING TECH CAPACITY

- In 2020, 397 African companies secured U.S. $701.5 million worth of investment—a record-breaking year for tech start-ups.

- From 2015 to 2020, African tech start-ups grew 46 percent annually in comparison to only 8 percent growth globally.

- Emerging tech start-up sectors include education, health care, transportation, and leisure and travel.

- In 2019, women-led start-up companies around the world received less than 5 percent of the global venture capital (investors who support promising companies for a share of their business). In Africa, 20.1 percent of the total global venture capital invested was for female tech entrepreneurs.

- African women have started initiatives such as African Women in Technology, FirstCheck Africa, #HerFutureAfrica, and Women in Tech Africa that promote and invest in women interested in the tech field.

Innovation in Technology

Africa is becoming a new center for technological innovation. By 2030, estimates show that 230 million jobs on the continent will require some level of digital skills. With a population expected to increase some 2.5 billion by 2050, having jobs for people is essential to Africa's economic success.

Companies are establishing business centers in areas such as mobile phone service, aircraft production, biotechnology, 3D printing, artificial intelligence, and software. To encourage these businesses and to develop new ideas, "tech hubs" are springing up across the continent. Fueled by the financing of digital entrepreneurs, tech hubs are organizations with physical addresses that provide space, training, and support for individuals who want to turn an idea into reality.

Ten cities are home to some 250 tech hubs that make up more than 40 percent of the total number of tech hubs in Africa. As the map illustrates, many of these hubs are along the coast.

CHIPPER, one example of a mobile app that allows users to send and receive money across Africa, operates in seven African countries: Ghana, Uganda, Nigeria, Tanzania, Rwanda, South Africa, and Kenya.

LAGOS, NIGERIA (below), is home to 54gene, a start-up founded by a Nigerian scientist. 54gene builds genomic, or DNA, data sets to help target and develop better medicines for Africa. Currently, less than 3 percent of genomic data is from African populations.

CIRA V03

AN EGYPTIAN ENGINEER developed this robot prototype to assist physicians at a hospital in Tanta, Egypt.

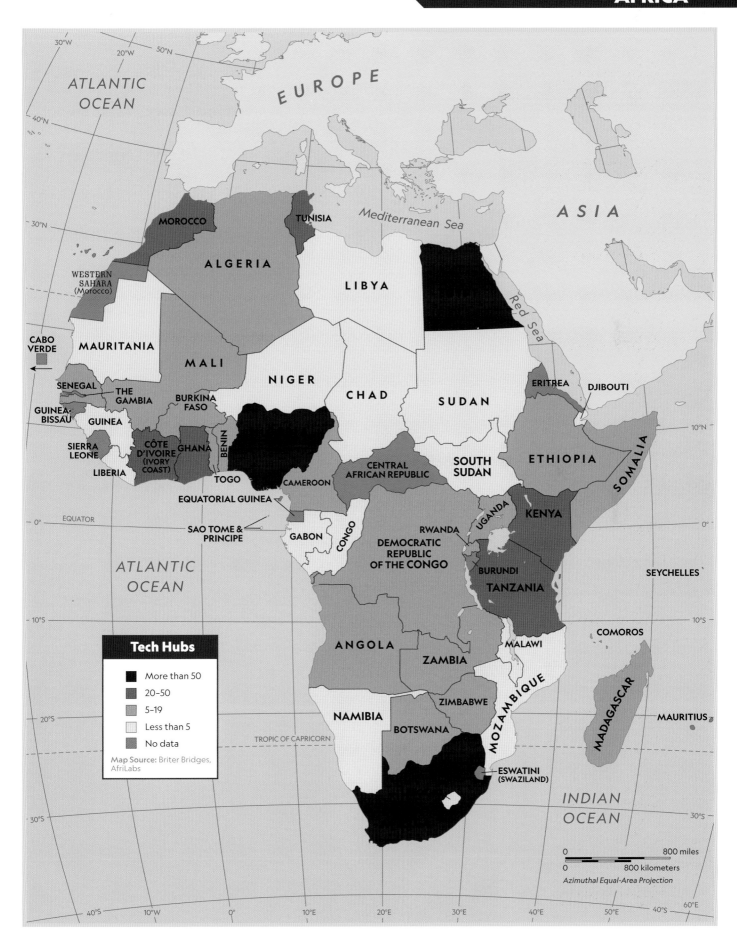

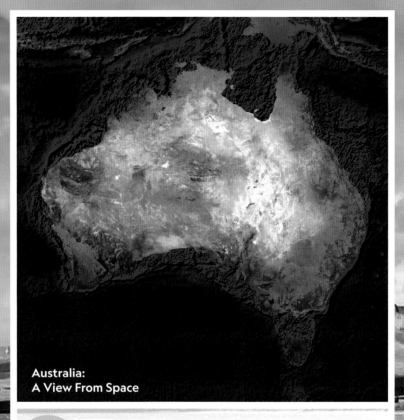

Australia:
A View From Space

Smallest of Earth's great landmasses, Australia is the only one that is both a continent and a country. It is part of the greater region of Oceania, which includes New Zealand, the eastern part of New Guinea, and hundreds of smaller islands scattered across the Pacific Ocean. Although Hawai'i is politically part of the United States, geographically and culturally it is part of Oceania.

The turquoise water of Lake Tekapo in New Zealand gets its bright color from rock dust ground up by glaciers.

AUSTRALIA
& OCEANIA

PHYSICAL

Land area 3,297,000 sq mi (8,538,000 sq km)	**Lowest point** **Lake Eyre, Australia** -49 ft (-15 m)	**Largest lake** **Lake Eyre,** **Australia** 3,741 sq mi (9,690 sq km)
Highest point **Mount Wilhelm,** **Papua New Guinea** 14,793 ft (4,509 m)	**Longest river** **Murray, Australia** 1,558 mi (2,508 km)	

POLITICAL

Population 41,668,000	**Largest country** **Australia** 2,988,902 sq mi (7,741,220 sq km)	**Most populous country** **Australia** Pop. 25,810,000
Number of **independent** **countries** 14	**Smallest country** **Nauru** 8 sq mi (21 sq km)	**Least populous country** **Nauru** Pop. 10,000

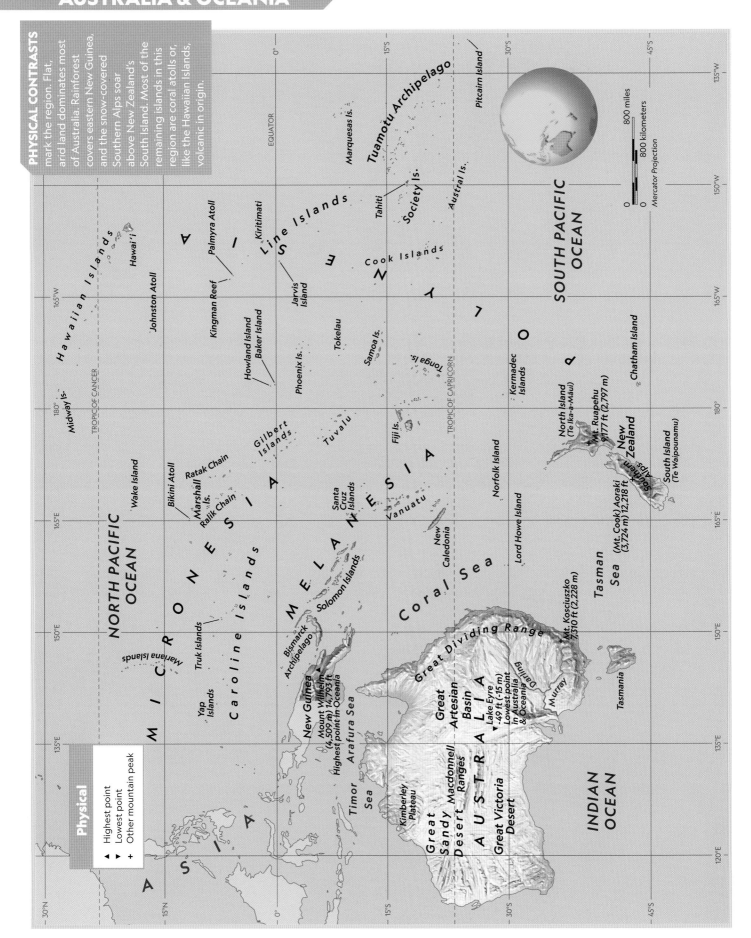

PHYSICAL CONTRASTS mark the region. Flat, arid land dominates most of Australia. Rainforest covers eastern New Guinea, and the snow-covered Southern Alps soar above New Zealand's South Island. Most of the remaining islands in this region are coral atolls or, like the Hawaiian Islands, volcanic in origin.

Physical
◄ Highest point
► Lowest point
+ Other mountain peak

800 miles
800 kilometers
Mercator Projection

EQUATOR

TROPIC OF CANCER

TROPIC OF CAPRICORN

NORTH PACIFIC OCEAN

SOUTH PACIFIC OCEAN

INDIAN OCEAN

Coral Sea

Tasman Sea

Timor Sea

Arafura Sea

MICRONESIA

MELANESIA

POLYNESIA

ASIA

AUSTRALIA

New Guinea
Mount Wilhelm
(4,509 m) 14,793 ft
Highest point in Oceania

Great Dividing Range

Great Artesian Basin

Great Sandy Desert

Macdonnell Ranges

Great Victoria Desert

Kimberley Plateau

Lake Eyre
-49 ft (-15 m)
Lowest point in Australia & Oceania ►

Mt. Kosciuszko
7,310 ft (2,228 m)

Murray
Darling

Tasmania

New Zealand
North Island
(Te Ika-a-Māui)
South Island
(Te Waipounamu)
Southern Alps
Mt. Ruapehu
9,177 ft (2,797 m)
Aoraki (Mt. Cook) 12,218 ft
(3,724 m)

Chatham Island

Norfolk Island

Lord Howe Island

New Caledonia

Kermadec Islands

Vanuatu

Fiji Is.

Tonga Is.

Samoa Is.

Tokelau

Tuvalu

Santa Cruz Islands

Solomon Islands

Bismarck Archipelago

Caroline Islands

Truk Islands

Yap Islands

Mariana Islands

Wake Island

Bikini Atoll
Ratak Chain
Marshall Is.
Ralik Chain

Gilbert Islands

Phoenix Is.

Howland Island
Baker Island

Kingman Reef

Palmyra Atoll

Line Islands

Kiritimati

Jarvis Island

Cook Islands

Society Is.
Tahiti

Austral Is.

Tuamotu Archipelago

Marquesas Is.

Pitcairn Island

Hawaiian Islands
Hawai'i
Midway Is.
Johnston Atoll

30°N
15°N
0°
15°S
30°S
45°S

120°E
135°E
150°E
165°E
180°
165°W
150°W
135°W

0°
15°S
30°S
45°S

THE REGION is made up of more than two dozen countries and dependencies. In the early years of the 20th century, most of the islands were under the control of the United Kingdom, France, or the United States. Independence has been a slow and sometimes difficult process.

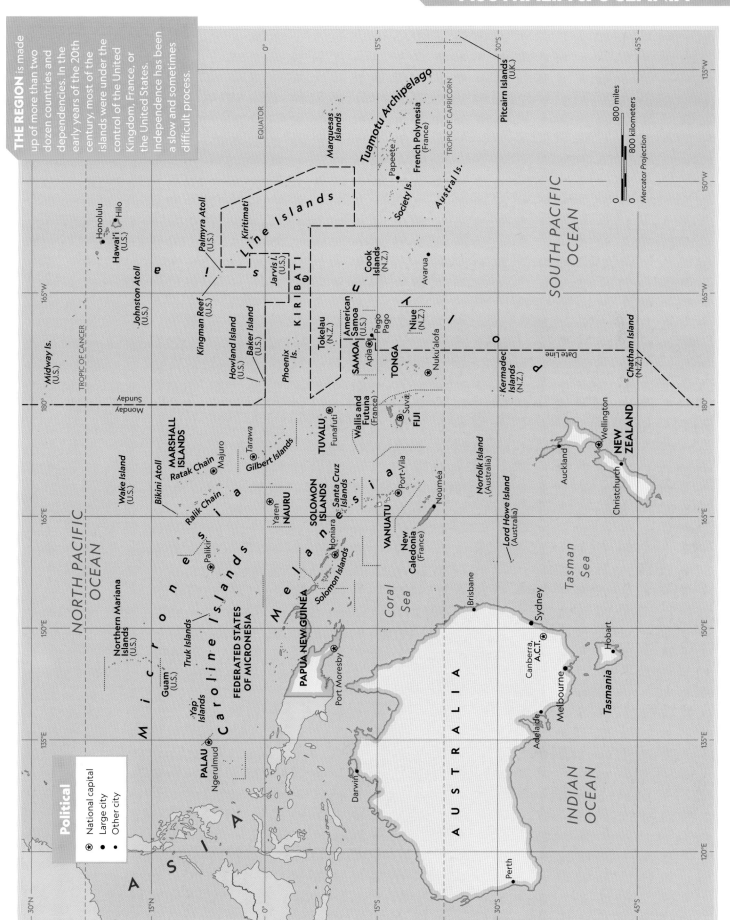

Honolulu
Hilo
Hawai'i (U.S.)

Johnston Atoll (U.S.)

Midway Is. (U.S.)

TROPIC OF CANCER

Palmyra Atoll (U.S.)
Kiritimati
Line Islands
Jarvis I. (U.S.)
Kingman Reef (U.S.)

Marquesas Islands

Tuamotu Archipelago
Papeete
French Polynesia (France)
Society Is.
Austral Is.
TROPIC OF CAPRICORN

Pitcairn Islands (U.K.)

EQUATOR

KIRIBATI

Cook Islands (N.Z.)
Avarua

Tokelau (N.Z.)
American Samoa (U.S.)
Pago Pago
Niue (N.Z.)

Howland Island (U.S.)
Baker Island (U.S.)
Phoenix Is.

SAMOA
Apia
TONGA
Nuku'alofa

SOUTH PACIFIC OCEAN

800 miles
800 kilometers
Mercator Projection

Sunday
Monday

Wake Island (U.S.)

MARSHALL ISLANDS
Ratak Chain
Majuro
Ralik Chain
Bikini Atoll

Tarawa

Gilbert Islands

TUVALU
Funafuti

Wallis and Futuna (France)

Suva
FIJI

Kermadec Islands (N.Z.)

Chatham Island (N.Z.)

Date Line

Wellington
NEW ZEALAND
Auckland
Christchurch

NORTH PACIFIC OCEAN

Northern Mariana Islands (U.S.)

Guam (U.S.)
Yap Islands
Truk Islands

FEDERATED STATES OF MICRONESIA
Palikir
Caroline Islands

Micronesia

Yaren
NAURU

SOLOMON ISLANDS
Honiara
Santa Cruz Islands
Solomon Islands

Melanesia

VANUATU
Port-Vila
New Caledonia (France)
Nouméa

Norfolk Island (Australia)

Lord Howe Island (Australia)

Tasman Sea

PALAU
Ngerulmud

PAPUA NEW GUINEA
Port Moresby

ASIA

Darwin

AUSTRALIA

Perth

Adelaide

Coral Sea

Brisbane

Sydney
Canberra, A.C.T.
Melbourne

Hobart
Tasmania

INDIAN OCEAN

Polynesia

Political
⊛ National capital
● Large city
• Other city

30°N
15°N
0°
15°S
30°S
45°S

120°E
135°E
150°E
165°E
180°
165°W
150°W
135°W

AUSTRALIA'S CLIMATES range from tropical-wet along the northeast coast to the dry expanses of the interior, known as the outback. Southern westerly winds give New Zealand a climate similar to that of western Europe. Elevation and local wind patterns influence climate on the region's other islands.

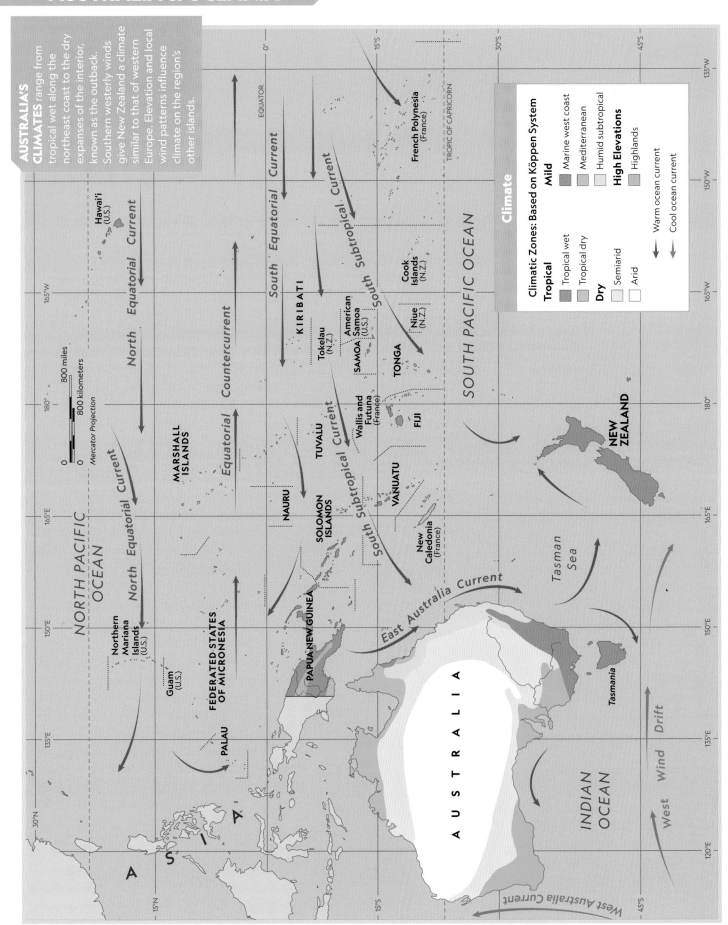

Climate

Climatic Zones: Based on Köppen System

Tropical
- Tropical wet
- Tropical dry

Dry
- Semiarid
- Arid

Mild
- Marine west coast
- Mediterranean
- Humid subtropical

High Elevations
- Highlands

→ Warm ocean current
→ Cool ocean current

ASIA

NORTH PACIFIC OCEAN

North Equatorial Current

Hawai'i (U.S.)

North Equatorial Current

North Equatorial Countercurrent

Equatorial Counter Current

South Equatorial Current

French Polynesia (France)

TROPIC OF CAPRICORN

EQUATOR

Northern Mariana Islands (U.S.)

Guam (U.S.)

PALAU

FEDERATED STATES OF MICRONESIA

MARSHALL ISLANDS

NAURU

KIRIBATI

Tokelau (N.Z.)

American Samoa (U.S.)

SAMOA

Cook Islands (N.Z.)

Niue (N.Z.)

TONGA

TUVALU

Wallis and Futuna (France)

FIJI

South Subtropical Current

South Subtropical Current

SOUTH PACIFIC OCEAN

SOLOMON ISLANDS

PAPUA NEW GUINEA

VANUATU

New Caledonia (France)

East Australia Current

NEW ZEALAND

Tasman Sea

Tasmania

AUSTRALIA

INDIAN OCEAN

West Wind Drift

West Australia Current

0   800 miles
0   800 kilometers
Mercator Projection

NORTH PACIFIC OCEAN

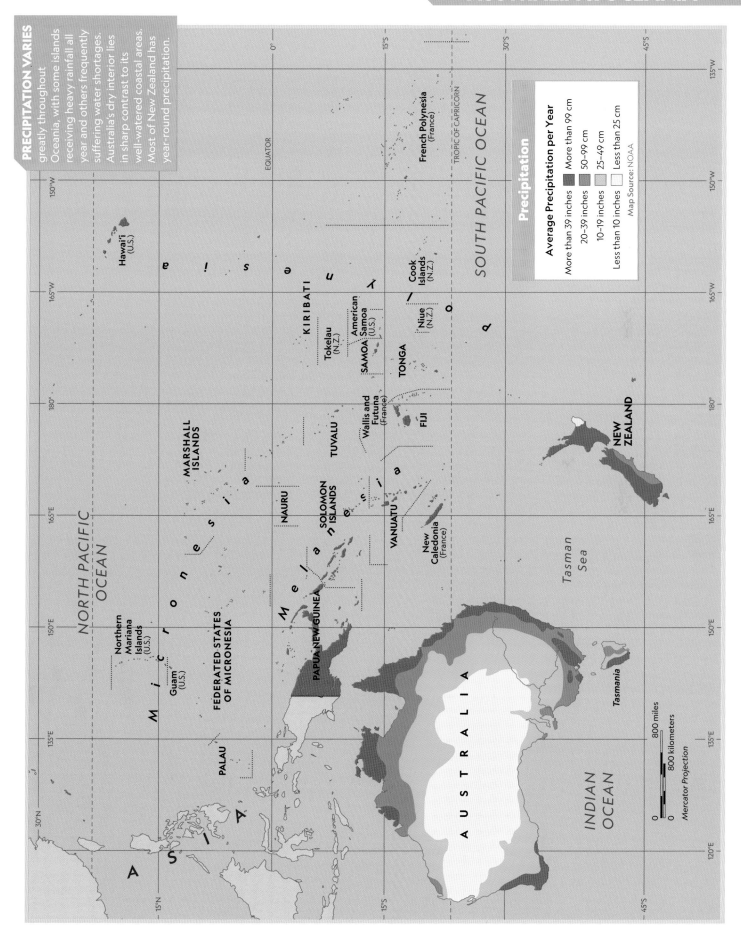

PRECIPITATION VARIES greatly throughout Oceania, with some islands receiving heavy rainfall all year and others frequently suffering water shortages. Australia's dry interior lies in sharp contrast to its well-watered coastal areas. Most of New Zealand has year-round precipitation.

Precipitation

Average Precipitation per Year

More than 39 inches — More than 99 cm
20–39 inches — 50–99 cm
10–19 inches — 25–49 cm
Less than 10 inches — Less than 25 cm

Map Source: NOAA

NORTH PACIFIC OCEAN

SOUTH PACIFIC OCEAN

INDIAN OCEAN

EQUATOR

TROPIC OF CAPRICORN

Hawai'i (U.S.)

French Polynesia (France)

KIRIBATI

Tokelau (N.Z.)

American Samoa (U.S.)

SAMOA

TONGA

Niue (N.Z.)

Cook Islands (N.Z.)

MARSHALL ISLANDS

TUVALU

Wallis and Futuna (France)

FIJI

NAURU

SOLOMON ISLANDS

VANUATU

New Caledonia (France)

Northern Mariana Islands (U.S.)

Guam (U.S.)

FEDERATED STATES OF MICRONESIA

PALAU

PAPUA NEW GUINEA

Micronesia

Melanesia

Polynesia

ASIA

AUSTRALIA

Tasmania

Tasman Sea

NEW ZEALAND

800 miles
800 kilometers

Mercator Projection

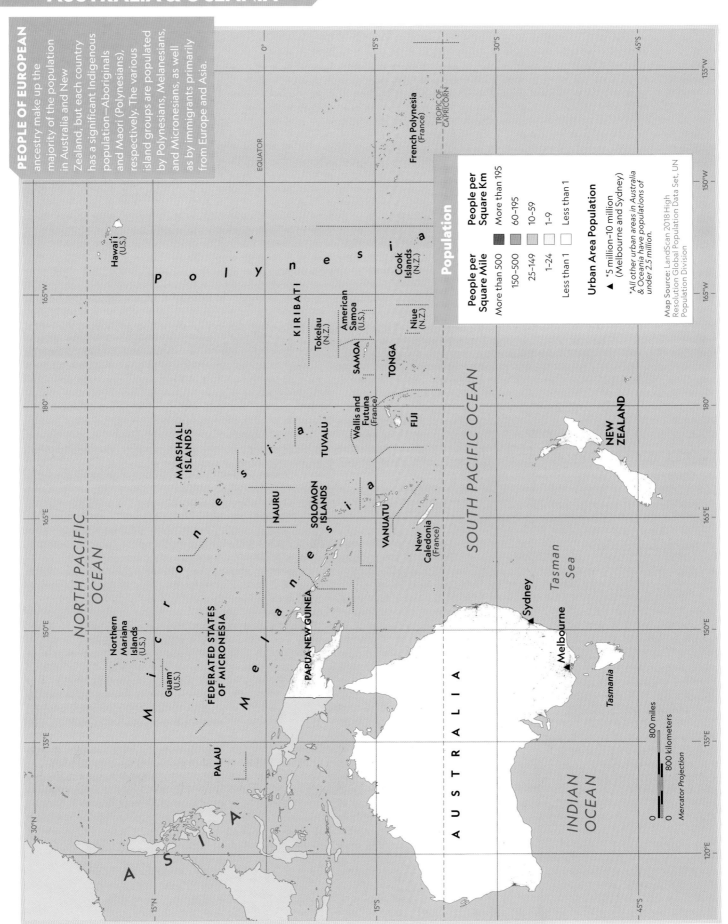

PEOPLE OF EUROPEAN ancestry make up the majority of the population in Australia and New Zealand, but each country has a significant Indigenous population—Aboriginals and Maori (Polynesians), respectively. The various island groups are populated by Polynesians, Melanesians, and Micronesians, as well as by immigrants primarily from Europe and Asia.

Population

People per Square Mile
More than 500
150–500
25–149
1–24
Less than 1

People per Square Km
More than 195
60–195
10–59
1–9
Less than 1

Urban Area Population
▲ *5 million–10 million (Melbourne and Sydney)

*All other urban areas in Australia & Oceania have populations of under 2.5 million.

Map Source: LandScan 2018 High Resolution Global Population Data Set, UN Population Division

PRIMARY ECONOMIC

products make up much of the economic base in Australia and Oceania. New Zealand and Australia account for more than two-thirds of world wool exports and almost one-fifth of beef exports. Plantation agriculture, fishing, tourism, or mining form the economic base in most of the small island countries. For example, exports of fish are important for Tuvalu, and Fiji is a major exporter of sugar and bottled water.

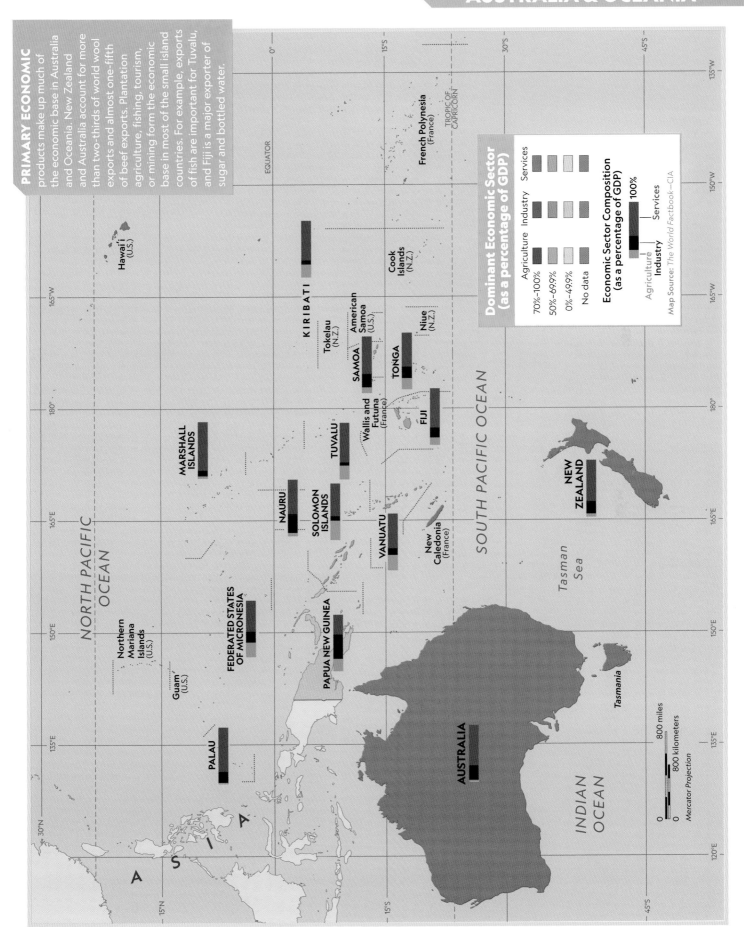

Dominant Economic Sector (as a percentage of GDP)

Agriculture | Industry | Services

70%–100%
50%–69.9%
0%–49.9%
No data

Economic Sector Composition (as a percentage of GDP)

Agriculture
Industry
Services

100%

Map Source: *The World Factbook*—CIA

NORTH PACIFIC OCEAN

SOUTH PACIFIC OCEAN

INDIAN OCEAN

Tasman Sea

ASIA

Hawai'i (U.S.)

KIRIBATI

Tokelau (N.Z.)

American Samoa (U.S.)

SAMOA

Niue (N.Z.)

TONGA

Cook Islands (N.Z.)

French Polynesia (France)

TROPIC OF CAPRICORN

EQUATOR

MARSHALL ISLANDS

TUVALU

Wallis and Futuna (France)

FIJI

NAURU

SOLOMON ISLANDS

VANUATU

New Caledonia (France)

NEW ZEALAND

Northern Mariana Islands (U.S.)

Guam (U.S.)

FEDERATED STATES OF MICRONESIA

PAPUA NEW GUINEA

PALAU

AUSTRALIA

Tasmania

Mercator Projection

800 miles
800 kilometers
0
0

Forest Extent

Australia's forests are extremely diverse with more than eight different types of forest coverage (see map at right). These include rainforest, callitris, casuarina, mangrove, melaleuca, acacia, and various kinds of eucalypt woodlands.

Each forest type is found in a unique geography. High rainfall in Australia's rainforests produces lush forest growth. Callitris trees grow in small patches of drier land, in sandy soils or rocky areas. Casuarina forests typically occur along riverbanks and some coastal areas. Mangrove trees have exposed roots that climb stilt-like above water. Melaleuca forests mainly occur in northern coastal or near-coastal areas. Eucalypt evolved from rainforest trees to adapt to drought-prone, nutrient-poor soils. Almost 1,000 species of the flowering acacia plant are found throughout Australia, the second most common forest type after eucalypt. As the map illustrates, the continent's interior does not have a lot of forest coverage. It is an arid and semi-arid region, and forests are unable to thrive there.

Australia's forests support a wide array of animals, including kookaburras, red kangaroos, koalas, sugar gliders, wombats, and brush turkeys.

BUSHFIRES

In late 2019 through early 2020, bushfires in Australia burned nearly 47 million acres (19 million ha)—the size of more than 35 million American football fields—and impacted almost three billion animals.

According to Global Forest Watch, more than 70 percent of the fires occurred in forests, mainly forests of eucalypts, which are more flammable than other species of forest trees.

Australia's flora and fauna have spent millennia adapting to dry, hot conditions and frequent bushfires. However, global climate change has increased the threat of bushfires.

THE KOALA'S diet consists of only eucalyptus leaves. These leaves are poisonous to most animals, but the koala's unique digestive system breaks down the chemicals.

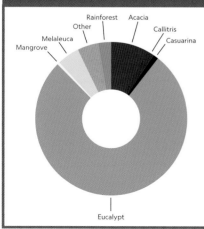

THE WATER MOUSE is one of the few mammals in Australia that lives year-round in the mangroves, building mud nests inside hollow trunks. Equipped with water-repellent fur, these tiny rodents feed on small crabs and worms.

AUSTRALIA FOREST TYPES

Pie chart showing forest types: Rainforest, Acacia, Callitris, Casuarina, Other, Melaleuca, Mangrove, Eucalypt

Eucalypt trees make up over 75 percent of Australia's forests. The rainforest accounts for less than 3 percent, but it contains 60 percent of Australia's plant species and provides habitat for 40 percent of the country's bird species and 35 percent of its mammalian species.

THE RED KANGAROO lives in the dry inland and grasslands where daytime temperatures can reach more than 105°F (40°C). To stay cool, these large marsupials take shelter under scattered trees and lick their chest and forearms.

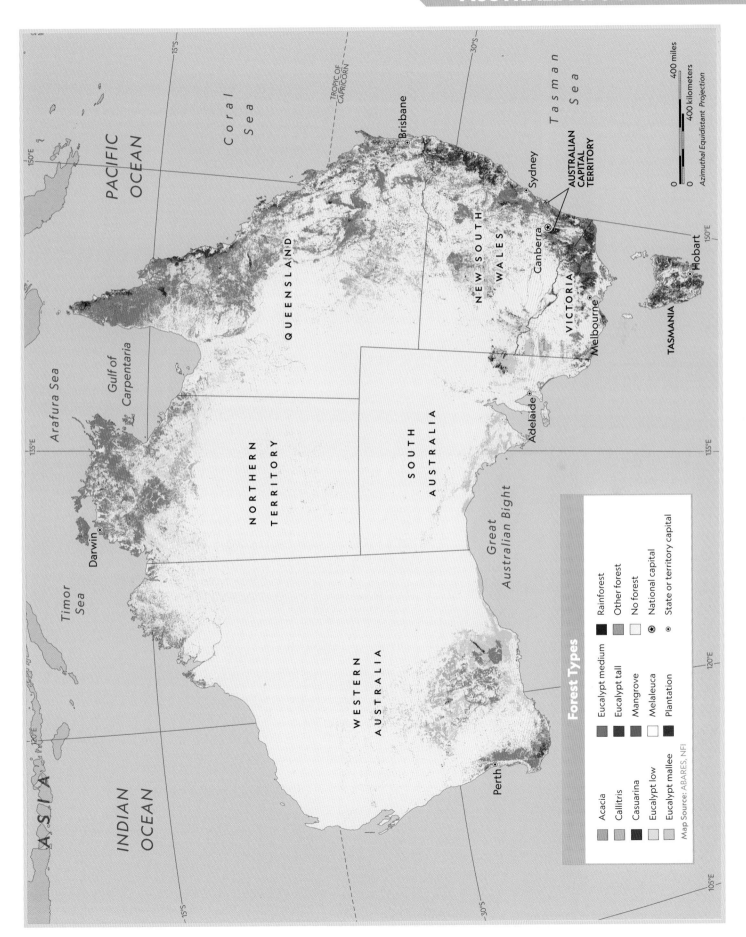

PACIFIC
OCEAN

Coral
Sea

TROPIC OF
CAPRICORN

Tasman
Sea

Brisbane

Sydney

AUSTRALIAN
CAPITAL
TERRITORY

Canberra

NEW SOUTH
WALES

VICTORIA

Melbourne

Hobart

TASMANIA

Gulf of
Carpentaria

Arafura Sea

QUEENSLAND

NORTHERN
TERRITORY

SOUTH
AUSTRALIA

Adelaide

Great
Australian Bight

Timor
Sea

Darwin

WESTERN
AUSTRALIA

Perth

INDIAN
OCEAN

ASIA

400 miles
400 kilometers
Azimuthal Equidistant Projection

Forest Types

Acacia	Eucalypt medium	Rainforest
Callitris	Eucalypt tall	Other forest
Casuarina	Mangrove	No forest
Eucalypt low	Melaleuca	⊛ National capital
Eucalypt mallee	Plantation	⊙ State or territory capital

Map Source: ABARES, NFI

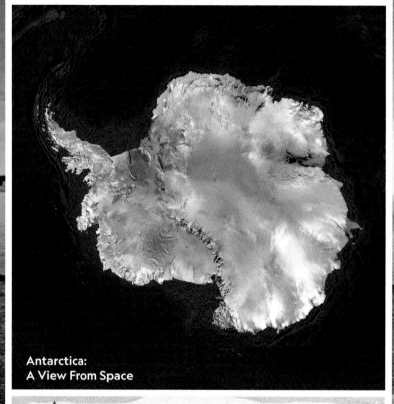

Antarctica:
A View From Space

About 180 million years ago, Antarctica broke away from the ancient super-continent Gondwana (see page 16). Slowly the continent drifted to its present location at Earth's southernmost point. Antarctica has no permanent human population, but it does have many types of wildlife. Seals, whales, and birds such as penguins, albatrosses, petrels, and terns have adapted to the continent's bitter-cold climate and long, dark winters.

A Weddell seal lies on the shore of the Weddell Sea in Antarctica.

ANTARCTICA

PHYSICAL			POLITICAL		
Land area 5,100,000 sq mi (13,209,000 sq km)	Lowest point Byrd Glacier (depression) -9,416 ft (-2,870 m)	Average precipitation on the polar plateau Less than 2 in (5 cm) per year	Population **There are no permanent inhabitants, but there are staff at both year-round and summer-only research stations.**	Number of independent countries 0	Number of countries operating year-round research stations 20
Highest point Vinson Massif 16,067 ft (4,897 m)	Coldest place Annual average temperature Ridge A -94°F (-70°C)			Number of countries claiming land 7	Number of year-round research stations 40

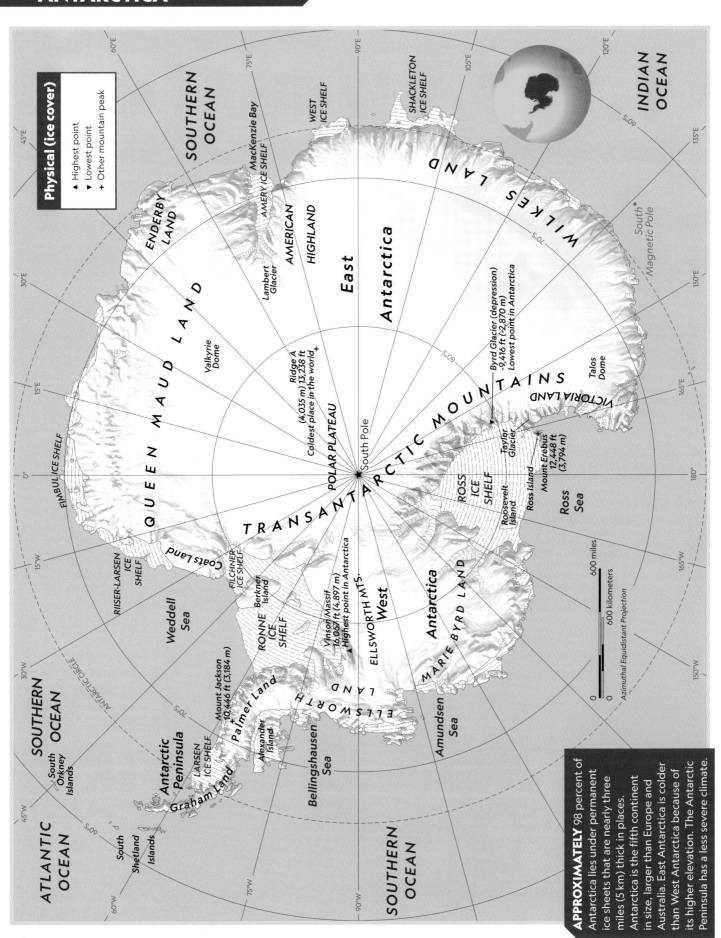

Physical (ice cover)
- ▲ Highest point
- ▼ Lowest point
- + Other mountain peak

SOUTHERN OCEAN

INDIAN OCEAN

60°E
75°E
90°E
105°E
120°E
135°E
150°E
165°E
45°E
30°E
15°E
0°
15°W
30°W
45°W
60°W
75°W
90°W
180°
165°W
150°W

60°S
70°S
80°S

MacKenzie Bay
AMERY ICE SHELF
WEST ICE SHELF
SHACKLETON ICE SHELF
ENDERBY LAND
AMERICAN HIGHLAND
Lambert Glacier
WILKES LAND

QUEEN MAUD LAND

East Antarctica

South Magnetic Pole

Valkyrie Dome

Ridge A (4,035 m) 13,238 ft
Coldest place in the world +

POLAR PLATEAU

South Pole

Byrd Glacier (depression) -9,416 ft (-2,870 m) Lowest point in Antarctica

VICTORIA LAND

Talos Dome

FIMBUL ICE SHELF

Coats Land

TRANSANTARCTIC MOUNTAINS

ROSS ICE SHELF

Taylor Glacier

▲ Mount Erebus 12,448 ft (3,794 m)

Roosevelt Island

Ross Island

Ross Sea

RIISER-LARSEN ICE SHELF

FILCHNER ICE SHELF

Berkner Island

RONNE ICE SHELF

Vinson Massif 16,067 ft (4,897 m) ▲ Highest point in Antarctica

ELLSWORTH MTS.

West Antarctica

MARIE BYRD LAND

Weddell Sea

ANTARCTIC CIRCLE

SOUTHERN OCEAN

South Orkney Islands

+ Mount Jackson 10,446 ft (3,184 m)

Palmer Land

Alexandre Island

ELLSWORTH LAND

Amundsen Sea

ATLANTIC OCEAN

South Shetland Islands

Antarctic Peninsula

Graham Land

LARSEN ICE SHELF

Bellingshausen Sea

SOUTHERN OCEAN

600 miles
600 kilometers
Azimuthal Equidistant Projection

APPROXIMATELY 98 percent of Antarctica lies under permanent ice sheets that are nearly three miles (5 km) thick in places. Antarctica is the fifth continent in size, larger than Europe and Australia. East Antarctica is colder than West Antarctica because of its higher elevation. The Antarctic Peninsula has a less severe climate.

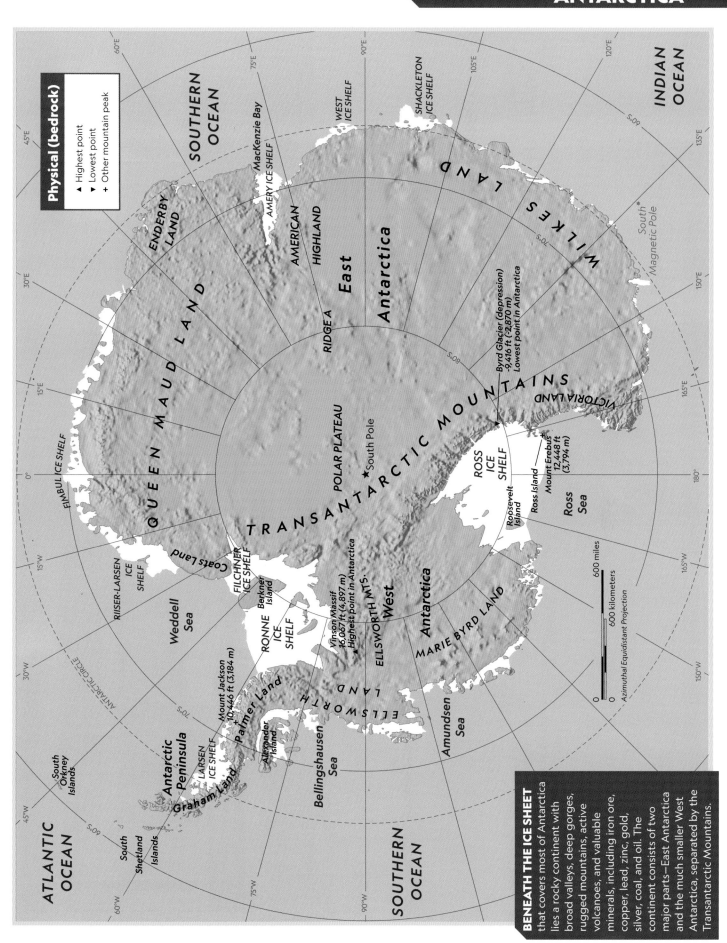

Physical (bedrock)
- ▲ Highest point
- ▼ Lowest point
- + Other mountain peak

SOUTHERN OCEAN

INDIAN OCEAN

ATLANTIC OCEAN

MacKenzie Bay

AMERY ICE SHELF

ENDERBY LAND

WEST ICE SHELF

SHACKLETON ICE SHELF

AMERICAN HIGHLAND

East Antarctica

WILKES LAND

QUEEN MAUD LAND

RIDGE A

South Magnetic Pole

VICTORIA LAND

FIMBUL ICE SHELF

POLAR PLATEAU

★ South Pole

Byrd Glacier (depression)
-9,416 ft (-2,870 m)
Lowest point in Antarctica

TRANSANTARCTIC MOUNTAINS

ROSS ICE SHELF

Mount Erebus
12,448 ft
(3,794 m)

Ross Island

Ross Sea

Roosevelt Island

RIISER-LARSEN ICE SHELF

Coats Land

FILCHNER ICE SHELF

Berkner Island

RONNE ICE SHELF

Weddell Sea

Vinson Massif
16,067 ft (4,897 m)
▲ Highest point in Antarctica

ELLSWORTH MTS.

West Antarctica

MARIE BYRD LAND

Mount Jackson
10,446 ft (3,184 m)

LARSEN ICE SHELF

Alexander Island

Palmer Land

ELLSWORTH LAND

Amundsen Sea

Antarctic Peninsula

Graham Land

Bellingshausen Sea

South Orkney Islands

South Shetland Islands

ANTARCTIC CIRCLE

SOUTHERN OCEAN

600 miles
600 kilometers
Azimuthal Equidistant Projection

BENEATH THE ICE SHEET
that covers most of Antarctica lies a rocky continent with broad valleys, deep gorges, rugged mountains, active volcanoes, and valuable minerals, including iron ore, copper, lead, zinc, gold, silver, coal, and oil. The continent consists of two major parts—East Antarctica and the much smaller West Antarctica, separated by the Transantarctic Mountains.

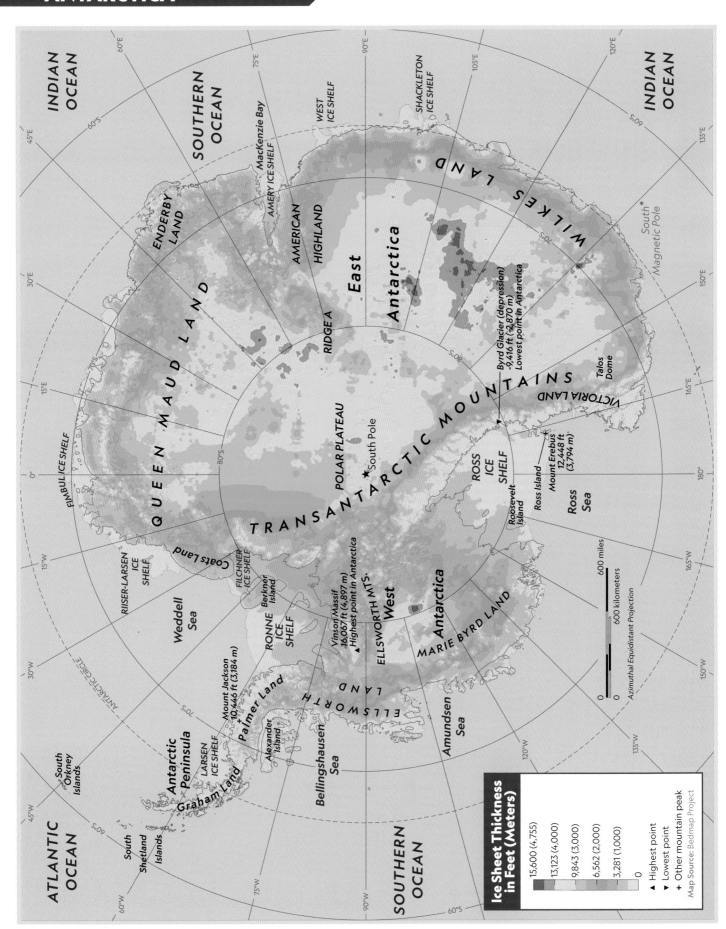

LAND OF ICE AND SNOW

○ At almost 5.4 million square miles (14 million sq km), the Antarctic ice sheet is about the area of the contiguous United States and Mexico. The ice sheet contains 60 percent of Earth's total freshwater, and 90 percent of its ice.

○ Antarctica holds the record for being the coldest, driest, highest, windiest, and remotest continent on the planet.

○ About five million penguins call Antarctica home, but the most abundant land animal is the tiny nematode worm.

○ No permanent populations live in Antarctica, but 21 countries operate year-round scientific research stations.

○ Antarctica contains unique ice core records that provide details about the causes and results of climate change over time.

Ice Sheet Thickness

Antarctica is a continent capped by an ice sheet that is between one and four miles (1.6 and 6.4 km) thick. An ice sheet is a mass of glacial ice at least 20,000 square miles (50,000 sq km) in size. It is formed over time as snow accumulates, melts, refreezes, gets compressed, and becomes more dense. The Antarctic ice sheet is so heavy that it has pushed the land below sea level in some locations on the continent.

The size and extent of Antarctica's icy surface is a major component of our planet's climate system. The white reflective snow and ice help to regulate regional and global climate. The bright surface reflects the solar energy in sunlight back into the atmosphere and into space, which helps keep Earth's poles cooler. When warming temperatures melt sea ice, fewer surfaces are left to reflect the light, which then causes the water to warm. This slow warming causes more ice to melt and sea levels to slowly rise.

◗ **SOUTHERN ELEPHANT SEALS** have thick layers of blubber, or fat, that keep body heat from escaping. They can live off their fat reserves for weeks.

◖ **WHEN FOOD IS HARD TO FIND** in the cold, dark Southern Ocean, Antarctic krill can shrink their body size and use their own body proteins as an energy source.

◖ **THE EMPEROR PENGUIN** has four layers of overlapping feathers that protect it from Antarctica's icy winds. These birds huddle together to reduce heat loss, switching positions so that each penguin gets a turn in the warm center.

SHRINKING ICE MASS

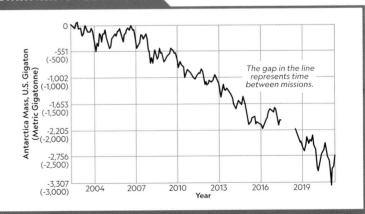

The gap in the line represents time between missions.

Antarctica Mass, U.S. Gigaton (Metric Gigatonne)

0
-551 (-500)
-1,002 (-1,000)
-1,653 (-1,500)
-2,205 (-2,000)
-2,756 (-2,500)
-3,307 (-3,000)

2004   2007   2010   2013   2016   2019
Year

In 2002, NASA launched its Gravity Recovery and Climate Experiment (GRACE) satellites to record Antarctica's ice thickness every year. Data has shown that Antarctica has been losing 166 billion tons (151 billion t) of mass annually due to melting.

Flags & Stats

These flags and factoids represent the world's 195 independent countries—those with national governments that are recognized as having the highest legal authority over the land and people within their boundaries. Capital city populations (2021) are from the United Nations Population Division and sometimes include the surrounding area. All other data are based on the CIA's 2021 *World Factbook*.

All flags are national flags recognized by the United Nations. Area figures include land and water bodies. Languages are those most commonly spoken within a country or official languages, which are marked with an asterisk (*).

Argentina
CONTINENT: South America
AREA: 1,073,518 sq mi (2,780,400 sq km)
POPULATION: 45,865,000
CAPITAL: Buenos Aires 15,258,000
LANGUAGE: Spanish*, Italian, English, German, French

Bahamas, The
CONTINENT: North America
AREA: 5,359 sq mi (13,880 sq km)
POPULATION: 353,000
CAPITAL: Nassau 280,000
LANGUAGE: English*, Creole

Belgium
CONTINENT: Europe
AREA: 11,787 sq mi (30,528 sq km)
POPULATION: 11,779,000
CAPITAL: Brussels 2,096,000
LANGUAGE: Dutch*, French*, German*

Armenia
CONTINENT: Asia
AREA: 11,484 sq mi (29,743 sq km)
POPULATION: 3,012,000
CAPITAL: Yerevan 1,089,000
LANGUAGE: Armenian*, Russian

Bahrain
CONTINENT: Asia
AREA: 293 sq mi (760 sq km)
POPULATION: 1,527,000
CAPITAL: Manama 664,000
LANGUAGE: Arabic*, English, Farsi, Urdu

Belize
CONTINENT: North America
AREA: 8,867 sq mi (22,966 sq km)
POPULATION: 406,000
CAPITAL: Belmopan 23,000
LANGUAGE: English*, Spanish, Creole, Maya

Afghanistan
CONTINENT: Asia
AREA: 251,827 sq mi (652,230 sq km)
POPULATION: 37,466,000
CAPITAL: Kabul 4,336,000
LANGUAGE: Afghan Persian (Dari)*, Pashto*, Uzbek, English

Andorra
CONTINENT: Europe
AREA: 181 sq mi (468 sq km)
POPULATION: 86,000
CAPITAL: Andorra la Vella 23,000
LANGUAGE: Catalan*, French, Castilian, Portuguese

Australia
REGION: Australia & Oceania
AREA: 2,988,902 sq mi (7,741,220 sq km)
POPULATION: 25,810,000
CAPITAL: Canberra, A.C.T. 462,000
LANGUAGE: English

Bangladesh
CONTINENT: Asia
AREA: 57,321 sq mi (148,460 sq km)
POPULATION: 164,099,000
CAPITAL: Dhaka 21,741,000
LANGUAGE: Bangla (Bengali)*

Benin
CONTINENT: Africa
AREA: 43,484 sq mi (112,622 sq km)
POPULATION: 13,302,000
CAPITAL: Porto-Novo (official capital) 285,000; Cotonou (administrative) 699,000
LANGUAGE: French*, Fon, Yoruba, tribal languages

Albania
CONTINENT: Europe
AREA: 11,100 sq mi (28,748 sq km)
POPULATION: 3,088,000
CAPITAL: Tirana 503,000
LANGUAGE: Albanian*

Angola
CONTINENT: Africa
AREA: 481,353 sq mi (1,246,700 sq km)
POPULATION: 33,643,000
CAPITAL: Luanda 8,632,000
LANGUAGE: Portuguese*, Umbundu, other African languages

Austria
CONTINENT: Europe
AREA: 32,383 sq mi (83,871 sq km)
POPULATION: 8,885,000
CAPITAL: Vienna 1,945,000
LANGUAGE: German*, Croatian (official in Burgenland)*

Barbados
CONTINENT: North America
AREA: 166 sq mi (430 sq km)
POPULATION: 302,000
CAPITAL: Bridgetown 89,000
LANGUAGE: English*, Bajan

Bhutan
CONTINENT: Asia
AREA: 14,824 sq mi (38,394 sq km)
POPULATION: 857,000
CAPITAL: Thimphu 203,000
LANGUAGE: Sharchhopka, Dzongkha*, Lhotshamkha

Algeria
CONTINENT: Africa
AREA: 919,595 sq mi (2,381,740 sq km)
POPULATION: 43,577,000
CAPITAL: Algiers 2,809,000
LANGUAGE: Arabic*, French, Berber (Tamazight)*

Antigua and Barbuda
CONTINENT: North America
AREA: 171 sq mi (443 sq km)
POPULATION: 99,000
CAPITAL: St. John's 21,000
LANGUAGE: English*, Antiguan creole

Azerbaijan
CONTINENT: Asia/Europe
AREA: 33,436 sq mi (86,600 sq km)
POPULATION: 10,282,000
CAPITAL: Baku 2,371,000
LANGUAGE: Azerbaijani (Azeri)*, Russian

Belarus
CONTINENT: Europe
AREA: 80,155 sq mi (207,600 sq km)
POPULATION: 9,442,000
CAPITAL: Minsk 2,039,000
LANGUAGE: Russian*, Belarusian*

Bolivia
CONTINENT: South America
AREA: 424,164 sq mi (1,098,581 sq km)
POPULATION: 11,759,000
CAPITAL: La Paz (administrative) 1,882,000; Sucre (constitutional) 278,000
LANGUAGE: Spanish*, Quechua*, Aymara*, Guarani*

Bosnia and Herzegovina
CONTINENT: Europe
AREA: 19,767 sq mi
(51,197 sq km)
POPULATION: 3,825,000
CAPITAL: Sarajevo 344,000
LANGUAGE: Bosnian*, Serbian*, Croatian*

Botswana
CONTINENT: Africa
AREA: 224,607 sq mi
(581,730 sq km)
POPULATION: 2,351,000
CAPITAL: Gaborone 269,000
LANGUAGE: Setswana, Sekalanga, Shekgalagadi, English*

Brazil
CONTINENT: South America
AREA: 3,287,956 sq mi
(8,515,770 sq km)
POPULATION: 213,445,000
CAPITAL: Brasília 4,728,000
LANGUAGE: Portuguese*

Brunei
CONTINENT: Asia
AREA: 2,226 sq mi
(5,765 sq km)
POPULATION: 471,000
CAPITAL: Bandar Seri Begawan 241,000
LANGUAGE: Malay*, English, Chinese

Bulgaria
CONTINENT: Europe
AREA: 42,811 sq mi
(110,879 sq km)
POPULATION: 6,919,000
CAPITAL: Sofia 1,284,000
LANGUAGE: Bulgarian*

Burkina Faso
CONTINENT: Africa
AREA: 105,869 sq mi
(274,200 sq km)
POPULATION: 21,383,000
CAPITAL: Ouagadougou 2,915,000
LANGUAGE: French*, African languages

Burundi
CONTINENT: Africa
AREA: 10,745 sq mi (27,830 sq km)
POPULATION: 12,241,000
CAPITAL: Bujumbura (commercial) 1,075,000; Gitega (official) 135,000
LANGUAGE: Kirundi*, French*, English*, Swahili

Cabo Verde
CONTINENT: Africa
AREA: 1,557 sq mi
(4,033 sq km)
POPULATION: 589,000
CAPITAL: Praia 168,000
LANGUAGE: Portuguese*, Krioulo

Cambodia
CONTINENT: Asia
AREA: 69,898 sq mi
(181,035 sq km)
POPULATION: 17,304,000
CAPITAL: Phnom Penh 2,144,000
LANGUAGE: Khmer*

Cameroon
CONTINENT: Africa
AREA: 183,568 sq mi
(475,440 sq km)
POPULATION: 28,524,000
CAPITAL: Yaoundé 4,164,000
LANGUAGE: African languages, English*, French*

Canada
CONTINENT: North America
AREA: 3,855,103 sq mi
(9,984,670 sq km)
POPULATION: 37,943,000
CAPITAL: Ottawa 1,408,000
LANGUAGE: English*, French*

Central African Republic
CONTINENT: Africa
AREA: 240,535 sq mi
(622,984 sq km)
POPULATION: 5,358,000
CAPITAL: Bangui 910,000
LANGUAGE: French*, Sangho*, tribal languages

Chad
CONTINENT: Africa
AREA: 495,755 sq mi
(1,284,000 sq km)
POPULATION: 17,414,000
CAPITAL: N'Djamena 1,476,000
LANGUAGE: French*, Arabic*, Sara, Indigenous languages

Chile
CONTINENT: South America
AREA: 291,932 sq mi
(756,102 sq km)
POPULATION: 18,308,000
CAPITAL: Santiago 6,812,000
LANGUAGE: Spanish*, English

China
CONTINENT: Asia
AREA: 3,705,405 sq mi
(9,596,960 sq km)
POPULATION: 1,397,898,000
CAPITAL: Beijing 20,897,000
LANGUAGE: Standard Chinese (Mandarin)*, Yue (Cantonese), Wu, Minbei, Minnan, Xiang, Gan, regional official languages

Colombia
CONTINENT: South America
AREA: 439,735 sq mi
(1,138,910 sq km)
POPULATION: 50,356,000
CAPITAL: Bogotá 11,167,000
LANGUAGE: Spanish*

Comoros
CONTINENT: Africa
AREA: 863 sq mi
(2,235 sq km)
POPULATION: 864,000
CAPITAL: Moroni 62,000
LANGUAGE: Arabic*, French*, Shikomoro (Comorian)*

Congo
CONTINENT: Africa
AREA: 132,047 sq mi
(342,000 sq km)
POPULATION: 5,417,000
CAPITAL: Brazzaville 2,470,000
LANGUAGE: French*, Lingala, Monokutuba, Kikongo, local languages

Congo, Democratic Republic of the
CONTINENT: Africa
AREA: 905,354 sq mi
(2,344,858 sq km)
POPULATION: 105,045,000
CAPITAL: Kinshasa 14,970,000
LANGUAGE: French*, Lingala, Kingwana, Kikongo, Tshiluba

Costa Rica
CONTINENT: North America
AREA: 19,730 sq mi
(51,100 sq km)
POPULATION: 5,151,000
CAPITAL: San José 1,421,000
LANGUAGE: Spanish*, English

Côte d'Ivoire (Ivory Coast)
CONTINENT: Africa
AREA: 124,504 sq mi (322,463 sq km)
POPULATION: 28,088,000
CAPITAL: Abidjan (administrative) 5,355,000; Yamoussoukro (legislative) 231,000
LANGUAGE: French*, Diola, Native dialects

Croatia
CONTINENT: Europe
AREA: 21,851 sq mi
(56,594 sq km)
POPULATION: 4,209,000
CAPITAL: Zagreb 685,000
LANGUAGE: Croatian*, Serbian

Cuba
CONTINENT: North America
AREA: 42,803 sq mi
(110,860 sq km)
POPULATION: 11,032,000
CAPITAL: Havana 2,143,000
LANGUAGE: Spanish*

Cyprus
CONTINENT: Europe
AREA: 3,572 sq mi
(9,251 sq km)
POPULATION: 1,282,000
CAPITAL: Nicosia 269,000
LANGUAGE: Greek*, Turkish*, English

Czechia (Czech Republic)
CONTINENT: Europe
AREA: 30,451 sq mi
(78,867 sq km)
POPULATION: 10,703,000
CAPITAL: Prague 1,312,000
LANGUAGE: Czech*, Slovak

Denmark
CONTINENT: Europe
AREA: 16,639 sq mi
(43,094 sq km)
POPULATION: 5,895,000
CAPITAL: Copenhagen 1,359,000
LANGUAGE: Danish, Faroese,
Greenlandic, English

Egypt
CONTINENT: Africa/Asia
AREA: 386,662 sq mi
(1,001,450 sq km)
POPULATION: 106,437,000
CAPITAL: Cairo 21,323,000
LANGUAGE: Arabic*, English,
French

Eswatini (Swaziland)
CONTINENT: Africa
AREA: 6,704 sq mi (17,364 sq km)
POPULATION: 1,113,000
CAPITAL: Mbabane
(administrative) 68,000;
Lobamba (legislative and
royal) 11,000
LANGUAGE: English*, siSwati*

Gabon
CONTINENT: Africa
AREA: 103,347 sq mi
(267,667 sq km)
POPULATION: 2,285,000
CAPITAL: Libreville 845,000
LANGUAGE: French*, Fang,
Myene, Nzebi, Bapounou/
Eschira, Bandjabi

Greece
CONTINENT: Europe
AREA: 50,949 sq mi
(131,957 sq km)
POPULATION: 10,570,000
CAPITAL: Athens 3,153,000
LANGUAGE: Greek*

Djibouti
CONTINENT: Africa
AREA: 8,958 sq mi
(23,200 sq km)
POPULATION: 938,000
CAPITAL: Djibouti 584,000
LANGUAGE: French*, Arabic*,
Somali, Afar

El Salvador
CONTINENT: North America
AREA: 8,124 sq mi
(21,041 sq km)
POPULATION: 6,528,000
CAPITAL: San Salvador 1,107,000
LANGUAGE: Spanish*

Ethiopia
CONTINENT: Africa
AREA: 426,372 sq mi
(1,104,300 sq km)
POPULATION: 110,871,000
CAPITAL: Addis Ababa
5,006,000
LANGUAGE: Oromo, Amharic*,
Somali, Tigrinya, Afar

Gambia, The
CONTINENT: Africa
AREA: 4,363 sq mi
(11,300 sq km)
POPULATION: 2,221,000
CAPITAL: Banjul 459,000
LANGUAGE: English*,
Mandinka, Wolof, Fula

Grenada
CONTINENT: North America
AREA: 133 sq mi (344 sq km)
POPULATION: 114,000
CAPITAL: St. George's 39,000
LANGUAGE: English*, French
patois

Dominica
CONTINENT: North America
AREA: 290 sq mi (751 sq km)
POPULATION: 75,000
CAPITAL: Roseau 15,000
LANGUAGE: English*, French
patois

Equatorial Guinea
CONTINENT: Africa
AREA: 10,831 sq mi
(28,051 sq km)
POPULATION: 857,000
CAPITAL: Malabo 297,000
LANGUAGE: Spanish*,
Portuguese*, French*, Fang,
Bubi

Fiji
REGION: Australia & Oceania
AREA: 7,056 sq mi
(18,274 sq km)
POPULATION: 940,000
CAPITAL: Suva 178,000
LANGUAGE: English*, Fijian*,
Hindustani

Georgia
CONTINENT: Asia/Europe
AREA: 26,911 sq mi
(69,700 sq km)
POPULATION: 4,934,000
CAPITAL: Tbilisi 1,079,000
LANGUAGE: Georgian*

Guatemala
CONTINENT: North America
AREA: 42,042 sq mi
(108,889 sq km)
POPULATION: 17,423,000
CAPITAL: Guatemala City
2,983,000
LANGUAGE: Spanish*,
Maya languages

Dominican
Republic
CONTINENT: North America
AREA: 18,792 sq mi
(48,670 sq km)
POPULATION: 10,597,000
CAPITAL: Santo Domingo
3,389,000
LANGUAGE: Spanish*

Eritrea
CONTINENT: Africa
AREA: 45,406 sq mi
(117,600 sq km)
POPULATION: 6,147,000
CAPITAL: Asmara 998,000
LANGUAGE: Tigrinya*, Arabic*,
English*, Tigre, Kunama, Afar,
other Cushitic languages

Finland
CONTINENT: Europe
AREA: 130,558 sq mi
(338,145 sq km)
POPULATION: 5,587,000
CAPITAL: Helsinki 1,317,000
LANGUAGE: Finnish*, Swedish*

Germany
CONTINENT: Europe
AREA: 137,847 sq mi
(357,022 sq km)
POPULATION: 79,903,000
CAPITAL: Berlin 3,567,000
LANGUAGE: German*

Guinea
CONTINENT: Africa
AREA: 94,926 sq mi
(245,857 sq km)
POPULATION: 12,878,000
CAPITAL: Conakry 1,991,000
LANGUAGE: French*, Afican
languages

Ecuador
CONTINENT: South America
AREA: 109,483 sq mi
(283,561 sq km)
POPULATION: 17,093,000
CAPITAL: Quito 1,901,000
LANGUAGE: Spanish*,
Amerindian languages

Estonia
CONTINENT: Europe
AREA: 17,463 sq mi
(45,228 sq km)
POPULATION: 1,220,000
CAPITAL: Tallinn 449,000
LANGUAGE: Estonian*, Russian

France
CONTINENT: Europe
AREA: 248,573 sq mi
(643,801 sq km)
POPULATION: 68,084,000
CAPITAL: Paris 11,079,000
LANGUAGE: French*

Ghana
CONTINENT: Africa
AREA: 92,098 sq mi
(238,533 sq km)
POPULATION: 32,373,000
CAPITAL: Accra 2,557,000
LANGUAGE: Assanta, Ewe,
Fante, English*

Guinea-Bissau
CONTINENT: Africa
AREA: 13,948 sq mi
(36,125 sq km)
POPULATION: 1,976,000
CAPITAL: Bissau 621,000
LANGUAGE: Crioulo,
Portuguese*, Pular, Mandingo

Guyana
CONTINENT: South America

AREA: 83,000 sq mi
(214,969 sq km)

POPULATION: 788,000

CAPITAL: Georgetown 110,000

LANGUAGE: English*, Guyanese
Creole, Amerindian languages,
Indian languages, Chinese

India
CONTINENT: Asia

AREA: 1,269,219 sq mi
(3,287,263 sq km)

POPULATION: 1,339,331,000

CAPITAL: New Delhi 31,181,000

LANGUAGE: Hindi*, English*

Israel
CONTINENT: Asia

AREA: 8,970 sq mi
(23,232 sq km)

POPULATION: 8,787,000

CAPITAL: Jerusalem 944,000

LANGUAGE: Hebrew*, Arabic,
English

Kazakhstan
CONTINENT: Asia/Europe

AREA: 1,052,089 sq mi
(2,724,900 sq km)

POPULATION: 19,246,000

CAPITAL: Nur-Sultan 1,212,000

LANGUAGE: Kazakh (Qazaq)*,
Russian*, English

Kyrgyzstan
CONTINENT: Asia

AREA: 77,201 sq mi
(199,951 sq km)

POPULATION: 6,019,000

CAPITAL: Bishkek 1,060,000

LANGUAGE: Kyrgyz*, Uzbek,
Russian*

Haiti
CONTINENT: North America

AREA: 10,714 sq mi
(27,750 sq km)

POPULATION: 11,198,000

CAPITAL: Port-au-Prince
2,844,000

LANGUAGE: French*, Creole*

Indonesia
CONTINENT: Asia

AREA: 735,358 sq mi
(1,904,569 sq km)

POPULATION: 275,122,000

CAPITAL: Jakarta 10,915,000

LANGUAGE: Bahasa Indonesia*,
English, Dutch, local dialects

Italy
CONTINENT: Europe

AREA: 116,348 sq mi
(301,340 sq km)

POPULATION: 62,390,000

CAPITAL: Rome 4,278,000

LANGUAGE: Italian*, German,
French, Slovene

Kenya
CONTINENT: Africa

AREA: 224,081 sq mi
(580,367 sq km)

POPULATION: 54,685,000

CAPITAL: Nairobi 4,922,000

LANGUAGE: English*, Kiswahili*,
Indigenous languages

Laos
CONTINENT: Asia

AREA: 91,429 sq mi
(236,800 sq km)

POPULATION: 7,574,000

CAPITAL: Vientiane 694,000

LANGUAGE: Lao*, French,
English, ethnic languages

Honduras
CONTINENT: North America

AREA: 43,278 sq mi
(112,090 sq km)

POPULATION: 9,346,000

CAPITAL: Tegucigalpa 1,485,000

LANGUAGE: Spanish*,
Amerindian dialects

Iran
CONTINENT: Asia

AREA: 636,371 sq mi
(1,648,195 sq km)

POPULATION: 85,889,000

CAPITAL: Tehran 9,259,000

LANGUAGE: Persian (Farsi)*,
Turkic dialects, Kurdish

Jamaica
CONTINENT: North America

AREA: 4,244 sq mi
(10,991 sq km)

POPULATION: 2,817,000

CAPITAL: Kingston 592,000

LANGUAGE: English*, English
patois

Kiribati
REGION: Australia & Oceania

AREA: 313 sq mi (811 sq km)

POPULATION: 113,000

CAPITAL: Tarawa 64,000

LANGUAGE: I-Kiribati, English*

Latvia
CONTINENT: Europe

AREA: 24,938 sq mi
(64,589 sq km)

POPULATION: 1,863,000

CAPITAL: Riga 628,000

LANGUAGE: Latvian*, Russian

Hungary
CONTINENT: Europe

AREA: 35,918 sq mi
(93,028 sq km)

POPULATION: 9,728,000

CAPITAL: Budapest 1,772,000

LANGUAGE: Hungarian*,
English, German

Iraq
CONTINENT: Asia

AREA: 169,235 sq mi
(438,317 sq km)

POPULATION: 39,650,000

CAPITAL: Baghdad 7,323,000

LANGUAGE: Arabic*, Kurdish*,
Turkmen, Syriac, Armenian

Japan
CONTINENT: Asia

AREA: 145,914 sq mi
(377,915 sq km)

POPULATION: 124,687,000

CAPITAL: Tokyo 37,340,000

LANGUAGE: Japanese

Kosovo
CONTINENT: Europe

AREA: 4,203 sq mi
(10,887 sq km)

POPULATION: 1,935,000

CAPITAL: Pristina 217,000

LANGUAGE: Albanian*,
Serbian*, Bosnian

Lebanon
CONTINENT: Asia

AREA: 4,015 sq mi
(10,400 sq km)

POPULATION: 5,261,000

CAPITAL: Beirut 2,435,000

LANGUAGE: Arabic*, French,
English, Armenian

Iceland
CONTINENT: Europe

AREA: 39,769 sq mi
(103,000 sq km)

POPULATION: 354,000

CAPITAL: Reykjavík 216,000

LANGUAGE: Icelandic, English,
Nordic languages, German

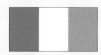

Ireland (Éire)
CONTINENT: Europe

AREA: 27,133 sq mi
(70,273 sq km)

POPULATION: 5,225,000

CAPITAL: Dublin 1,242,000

LANGUAGE: English*, Irish
(Gaelic)*

Jordan
CONTINENT: Asia

AREA: 34,495 sq mi
(89,342 sq km)

POPULATION: 10,910,000

CAPITAL: Amman 2,182,000

LANGUAGE: Arabic*, English

Kuwait
CONTINENT: Asia

AREA: 6,880 sq mi
(17,818 sq km)

POPULATION: 3,177,000

CAPITAL: Kuwait City 3,177,000

LANGUAGE: Arabic*, English

Lesotho
CONTINENT: Africa

AREA: 11,720 sq mi
(30,355 sq km)

POPULATION: 2,178,000

CAPITAL: Maseru 202,000

LANGUAGE: Sesotho*, English*,
Zulu, Xhosa

Liberia
CONTINENT: Africa
AREA: 43,000 sq mi
(111,369 sq km)
POPULATION: 5,214,000
CAPITAL: Monrovia 1,569,000
LANGUAGE: English*,
Indigenous languages

Madagascar
CONTINENT: Africa
AREA: 226,658 sq mi
(587,041 sq km)
POPULATION: 27,534,000
CAPITAL: Antananarivo
3,532,000
LANGUAGE: French*,
Malagasy*, English

Malta
CONTINENT: Europe
AREA: 122 sq mi (316 sq km)
POPULATION: 461,000
CAPITAL: Valletta 213,000
LANGUAGE: Maltese*, English*

Micronesia, Federated States of
REGION: Australia & Oceania
AREA: 271 sq mi (702 sq km)
POPULATION: 102,000
CAPITAL: Palikir 7,000
LANGUAGE: English*,
Chuukese, Kosrean, Pohnpeian,
other Indigenous languages

Morocco
CONTINENT: Africa
AREA: 276,662 sq mi
(716,550 sq km)
POPULATION: 36,562,000
CAPITAL: Rabat 1,907,000
LANGUAGE: Arabic*,
Tamazight*, other Berber
languages, French

Libya
CONTINENT: Africa
AREA: 679,362 sq mi
(1,759,540 sq km)
POPULATION: 7,017,000
CAPITAL: Tripoli 1,170,000
LANGUAGE: Arabic*, Italian,
English, Berber

Malawi
CONTINENT: Africa
AREA: 45,747 sq mi
(118,484 sq km)
POPULATION: 20,309,000
CAPITAL: Lilongwe 1,171,000
LANGUAGE: English*, Chewa,
other Bantu languages

Marshall Islands
REGION: Australia & Oceania
AREA: 70 sq mi (181 sq km)
POPULATION: 79,000
CAPITAL: Majuro 31,000
LANGUAGE: Marshallese*,
English*

Moldova
CONTINENT: Europe
AREA: 13,070 sq mi
(33,851 sq km)
POPULATION: 3,324,000
CAPITAL: Chişinău 494,000
LANGUAGE: Moldovan*,
Romanian*

Mozambique
CONTINENT: Africa
AREA: 308,642 sq mi
(799,380 sq km)
POPULATION: 30,888,000
CAPITAL: Maputo 1,122,000
LANGUAGE: Makhuwa,
Portuguese*, local languages

Liechtenstein
CONTINENT: Europe
AREA: 62 sq mi (160 sq km)
POPULATION: 39,000
CAPITAL: Vaduz 5,000
LANGUAGE: German*

Malaysia
CONTINENT: Asia
AREA: 127,355 sq mi
(329,847 sq km)
POPULATION: 33,519,000
CAPITAL: Kuala Lumpur 8,211,000
LANGUAGE: Bahasa Malaysia
(Malay)*, English, Chinese,
Tamil, Telugu, Malayalam,
Panjabi, Thai

Mauritania
CONTINENT: Africa
AREA: 397,955 sq mi
(1,030,700 sq km)
POPULATION: 4,079,000
CAPITAL: Nouakchott 1,372,000
LANGUAGE: Arabic*, Pulaar,
Soninke, Wolof, French

Monaco
CONTINENT: Europe
AREA: 1 sq mi (2 sq km)
POPULATION: 31,000
CAPITAL: Monaco 31,000
LANGUAGE: French*, English,
Italian, Monegasque

Myanmar (Burma)
CONTINENT: Asia
AREA: 261,228 sq mi
(676,578 sq km)
POPULATION: 57,069,000
CAPITAL: Nay Pyi Taw 640,000
LANGUAGE: Burmese*

Lithuania
CONTINENT: Europe
AREA: 25,212 sq mi
(65,300 sq km)
POPULATION: 2,712,000
CAPITAL: Vilnius 540,000
LANGUAGE: Lithuanian*

Maldives
CONTINENT: Asia
AREA: 115 sq mi (298 sq km)
POPULATION: 391,000
CAPITAL: Male 177,000
LANGUAGE: Dhivehi*, English

Mauritius
CONTINENT: Africa
AREA: 788 sq mi (2,040 sq km)
POPULATION: 1,386,000
CAPITAL: Port Louis 149,000
LANGUAGE: Creole, English*

Mongolia
CONTINENT: Asia
AREA: 603,908 sq mi
(1,564,116 sq km)
POPULATION: 3,199,000
CAPITAL: Ulaanbaatar 1,615,000
LANGUAGE: Mongolian*,
Turkic, Russian

Namibia
CONTINENT: Africa
AREA: 318,261 sq mi
(824,292 sq km)
POPULATION: 2,678,000
CAPITAL: Windhoek 446,000
LANGUAGE: Indigenous
languages, Afrikaans, English*

Luxembourg
CONTINENT: Europe
AREA: 998 sq mi (2,586 sq km)
POPULATION: 640,000
CAPITAL: Luxembourg 120,000
LANGUAGE: Luxembourgish*,
Portuguese, French*, German*

Mali
CONTINENT: Africa
AREA: 478,841 sq mi
(1,240,192 sq km)
POPULATION: 20,138,000
CAPITAL: Bamako 2,713,000
LANGUAGE: French*, Bambara,
African languages

Mexico
CONTINENT: North America
AREA: 758,449 sq mi
(1,964,375 sq km)
POPULATION: 130,207,000
CAPITAL: Mexico City 21,919,000
LANGUAGE: Spanish

Montenegro
CONTINENT: Europe
AREA: 5,333 sq mi
(13,812 sq km)
POPULATION: 607,000
CAPITAL: Podgorica 177,000
LANGUAGE: Serbian,
Montenegrin*

Nauru
REGION: Australia & Oceania
AREA: 8 sq mi (21 sq km)
POPULATION: 10,000
CAPITAL: Yaren 1,000
LANGUAGE: Nauruan*, English

Nepal
CONTINENT: Asia
AREA: 56,827 sq mi
(147,181 sq km)
POPULATION: 30,425,000
CAPITAL: Kathmandu 1,472,000
LANGUAGE: Nepali*, Maithali

Nigeria
CONTINENT: Africa
AREA: 356,669 sq mi
(923,768 sq km)
POPULATION: 219,464,000
CAPITAL: Abuja 3,464,000
LANGUAGE: English*,
Indigenous languages

Pakistan
CONTINENT: Asia
AREA: 307,374 sq mi
(796,095 sq km)
POPULATION: 238,181,000
CAPITAL: Islamabad 1,164,000
LANGUAGE: Punjabi, Sindhi,
Saraiki, Urdu*, English*

Peru
CONTINENT: South America
AREA: 496,224 sq mi
(1,285,216 sq km)
POPULATION: 32,201,000
CAPITAL: Lima 10,883,000
LANGUAGE: Spanish*,
Quechua*, Aymara*

Romania
CONTINENT: Europe
AREA: 92,043 sq mi
(238,391 sq km)
POPULATION: 21,230,000
CAPITAL: Bucharest 1,794,000
LANGUAGE: Romanian*

Netherlands
CONTINENT: Europe
AREA: 16,040 sq mi
(41,543 sq km)
POPULATION: 17,337,000
CAPITAL: Amsterdam (official)
1,158,000; The Hague
(administrative) 704,000
LANGUAGE: Dutch*

North Korea
CONTINENT: Asia
AREA: 46,540 sq mi
(120,538 sq km)
POPULATION: 25,831,000
CAPITAL: Pyongyang 3,108,000
LANGUAGE: Korean

Palau
REGION: Australia & Oceania
AREA: 177 sq mi (459 sq km)
POPULATION: 22,000
CAPITAL: Ngerulmud 277
LANGUAGE: Palauan*, English*,
Filipino

Philippines
CONTINENT: Asia
AREA: 115,831 sq mi
(300,000 sq km)
POPULATION: 110,818,000
CAPITAL: Manila 14,159,000
LANGUAGE: Filipino (Tagalog)*,
English*, Indigenous languages

Russia
CONTINENT: Europe/Asia
AREA: 6,612,093 sq mi
(17,125,242 sq km)
POPULATION: 142,321,000
CAPITAL: Moscow 12,593,000
LANGUAGE: Russian*

New Zealand
REGION: Australia & Oceania
AREA: 103,799 sq mi
(268,838 sq km)
POPULATION: 4,991,000
CAPITAL: Wellington 417,000
LANGUAGE: English*, Maori*

North Macedonia
CONTINENT: Europe
AREA: 9,928 sq mi
(25,713 sq km)
POPULATION: 2,128,000
CAPITAL: Skopje 601,000
LANGUAGE: Macedonian*,
Albanian

Panama
CONTINENT: North America
AREA: 29,120 sq mi
(75,420 sq km)
POPULATION: 3,929,000
CAPITAL: Panama City 1,899,000
LANGUAGE: Spanish*,
Indigenous languages, English

Poland
CONTINENT: Europe
AREA: 120,728 sq mi
(312,685 sq km)
POPULATION: 38,186,000
CAPITAL: Warsaw 1,790,000
LANGUAGE: Polish*

Rwanda
CONTINENT: Africa
AREA: 10,169 sq mi
(26,338 sq km)
POPULATION: 12,943,000
CAPITAL: Kigali 1,170,000
LANGUAGE: Kinyarwanda*,
French*, English*, Kiswahili
(Swahili)*

Nicaragua
CONTINENT: North America
AREA: 50,336 sq mi
(130,370 sq km)
POPULATION: 6,244,000
CAPITAL: Managua 1,073,000
LANGUAGE: Spanish*

Norway
CONTINENT: Europe
AREA: 125,021 sq mi
(323,802 sq km)
POPULATION: 5,510,000
CAPITAL: Oslo 1,056,000
LANGUAGE: Bokmal
Norwegian*, Nynorsk
Norwegian*

Papua New Guinea
REGION: Australia & Oceania
AREA: 178,703 sq mi
(462,840 sq km)
POPULATION: 7,400,000
CAPITAL: Port Moresby 391,000
LANGUAGE: Tok Pisin*, English*,
Hiri Motu*, other Indigenous
languages

Portugal
CONTINENT: Europe
AREA: 35,556 sq mi
(92,090 sq km)
POPULATION: 10,264,000
CAPITAL: Lisbon 2,972,000
LANGUAGE: Portuguese*,
Mirandese*

Samoa
REGION: Australia & Oceania
AREA: 1,093 sq mi
(2,831 sq km)
POPULATION: 205,000
CAPITAL: Apia 36,000
LANGUAGE: Samoan
(Polynesian)*, English*

Niger
CONTINENT: Africa
AREA: 489,191 sq mi
(1,267,000 sq km)
POPULATION: 23,606,000
CAPITAL: Niamey 1,336,000
LANGUAGE: French*, Hausa,
Djerma

Oman
CONTINENT: Asia
AREA: 119,499 sq mi
(309,500 sq km)
POPULATION: 3,695,000
CAPITAL: Muscat 1,590,000
LANGUAGE: Arabic*, English,
Baluchi, Swahili, Urdu, Indian
dialects

Paraguay
CONTINENT: South America
AREA: 157,048 sq mi
(406,752 sq km)
POPULATION: 7,273,000
CAPITAL: Asunción (Paraguay)
3,394,000
LANGUAGE: Spanish*, Guarani*

Qatar
CONTINENT: Asia
AREA: 4,473 sq mi
(11,586 sq km)
POPULATION: 2,480,000
CAPITAL: Doha 646,000
LANGUAGE: Arabic*, English

San Marino
CONTINENT: Europe
AREA: 24 sq mi (61 sq km)
POPULATION: 34,000
CAPITAL: San Marino 4,000
LANGUAGE: Italian

Sao Tome and Principe
CONTINENT: Africa
AREA: 372 sq mi (964 sq km)
POPULATION: 214,000
CAPITAL: São Tomé 80,000
LANGUAGE: Portuguese*, Forro

Sierra Leone
CONTINENT: Africa
AREA: 27,699 sq mi (71,740 sq km)
POPULATION: 6,807,000
CAPITAL: Freetown 1,236,000
LANGUAGE: English*, Mende, Temne, Krio

Somalia
CONTINENT: Africa
AREA: 246,201 sq mi (637,657 sq km)
POPULATION: 12,095,000
CAPITAL: Mogadishu 2,388,000
LANGUAGE: Somali*, Arabic*, Italian, English

Sri Lanka
CONTINENT: Asia
AREA: 25,332 sq mi (65,610 sq km)
POPULATION: 23,044,000
CAPITAL: Colombo (administrative) 619,000; Sri Jayewardenepura Kotte (legislative) 103,000
LANGUAGE: Sinhala*, Tamil*, English

Suriname
CONTINENT: South America
AREA: 63,251 sq mi (163,820 sq km)
POPULATION: 615,000
CAPITAL: Paramaribo 239,000
LANGUAGE: Dutch*, English, Sranang Tongo, Caribbean Hindustani, Javanese

Saudi Arabia
CONTINENT: Asia
AREA: 830,000 sq mi (2,149,690 sq km)
POPULATION: 34,784,000
CAPITAL: Riyadh 7,388,000
LANGUAGE: Arabic*

Singapore
CONTINENT: Asia
AREA: 278 sq mi (719 sq km)
POPULATION: 5,866,000
CAPITAL: Singapore 5,866,000
LANGUAGE: English*, Mandarin*, other Chinese dialects, Malay*, Tamil*

South Africa
CONTINENT: Africa
AREA: 470,693 sq mi (1,219,090 sq km)
POPULATION: 56,979,000
CAPITAL: Pretoria (Tshwane) (administrative) 2,655,000; Cape Town (legislative) 4,710,000; Bloemfontein (judicial) 578,000
LANGUAGE: isiZulu*, isiXhosa*, other Indigenous languages*, Afrikaans*, English*

St. Kitts and Nevis
CONTINENT: North America
AREA: 101 sq mi (261 sq km)
POPULATION: 54,000
CAPITAL: Basseterre 14,000
LANGUAGE: English*

Sweden
CONTINENT: Europe
AREA: 173,860 sq mi (450,295 sq km)
POPULATION: 10,262,000
CAPITAL: Stockholm 1,657,000
LANGUAGE: Swedish*

Senegal
CONTINENT: Africa
AREA: 75,955 sq mi (196,722 sq km)
POPULATION: 16,082,000
CAPITAL: Dakar 3,230,000
LANGUAGE: French*, Wolof, other Indigenous languages

Slovakia
CONTINENT: Europe
AREA: 18,933 sq mi (49,035 sq km)
POPULATION: 5,436,000
CAPITAL: Bratislava 437,000
LANGUAGE: Slovak*

South Korea
CONTINENT: Asia
AREA: 38,502 sq mi (99,720 sq km)
POPULATION: 51,715,000
CAPITAL: Seoul 9,968,000
LANGUAGE: Korean, English

St. Lucia
CONTINENT: North America
AREA: 238 sq mi (616 sq km)
POPULATION: 167,000
CAPITAL: Castries 22,000
LANGUAGE: English*, French patois

Switzerland
CONTINENT: Europe
AREA: 15,937 sq mi (41,277 sq km)
POPULATION: 8,454,000
CAPITAL: Bern 434,000
LANGUAGE: German (Swiss German)*, French*, Italian*, Romansch*

Serbia
CONTINENT: Europe
AREA: 29,913 sq mi (77,474 sq km)
POPULATION: 6,974,000
CAPITAL: Belgrade 1,402,000
LANGUAGE: Serbian*

Slovenia
CONTINENT: Europe
AREA: 7,827 sq mi (20,273 sq km)
POPULATION: 2,102,000
CAPITAL: Ljubljana 286,000
LANGUAGE: Slovenian*

South Sudan
CONTINENT: Africa
AREA: 248,777 sq mi (644,329 sq km)
POPULATION: 10,984,000
CAPITAL: Juba 421,000
LANGUAGE: English*, Arabic, Dinka, Nuer, Bari, Zande, Shilluk

St. Vincent and the Grenadines
CONTINENT: North America
AREA: 150 sq mi (389 sq km)
POPULATION: 101,000
CAPITAL: Kingstown 27,000
LANGUAGE: English*, Vincentian Creole English, French patois

Syria
CONTINENT: Asia
AREA: 71,870 sq mi (186,142 sq km)
POPULATION: 20,384,000
CAPITAL: Damascus 2,440,000
LANGUAGE: Arabic*, Kurdish, Armenian, Aramaic, Circassian, French, English

Seychelles
CONTINENT: Africa
AREA: 176 sq mi (455 sq km)
POPULATION: 96,000
CAPITAL: Victoria 28,000
LANGUAGE: Seychellois Creole*, English*, French*

Solomon Islands
REGION: Australia & Oceania
AREA: 11,157 sq mi (28,896 sq km)
POPULATION: 691,000
CAPITAL: Honiara 82,000
LANGUAGE: Melanesian pidgin, English*, Indigenous languages

Spain
CONTINENT: Europe
AREA: 195,124 sq mi (505,370 sq km)
POPULATION: 47,261,000
CAPITAL: Madrid 6,669,000
LANGUAGE: Castilian Spanish*, Catalan, Galician*, Basque*

Sudan
CONTINENT: Africa
AREA: 718,723 sq mi (1,861,484 sq km)
POPULATION: 46,751,000
CAPITAL: Khartoum 5,989,000
LANGUAGE: Arabic*, English*, Nubian, Ta Bedawie, Fur

Tajikistan
CONTINENT: Asia
AREA: 55,637 sq mi (144,100 sq km)
POPULATION: 8,991,000
CAPITAL: Dushanbe 938,000
LANGUAGE: Tajik*, Uzbek

Tanzania
CONTINENT: Africa
AREA: 365,754 sq mi (947,300 sq km)
POPULATION: 62,093,000
CAPITAL: Dar es Salaam (administrative) 7,047,000; Dodoma (official) 262,000
LANGUAGE: Kiswahili (Swahili)*, Kiunguja, English*, Arabic, local languages

Trinidad and Tobago
CONTINENT: North America
AREA: 1,980 sq mi (5,128 sq km)
POPULATION: 1,221,000
CAPITAL: Port of Spain 544,000
LANGUAGE: English*, Creole, Caribbean Hindustani, Spanish, Chinese

Uganda
CONTINENT: Africa
AREA: 93,065 sq mi (241,038 sq km)
POPULATION: 44,712,000
CAPITAL: Kampala 3,470,000
LANGUAGE: English*, Ganda (Luganda), local languages, Swahili*, Arabic

Uruguay
CONTINENT: South America
AREA: 68,037 sq mi (176,215 sq km)
POPULATION: 3,398,000
CAPITAL: Montevideo 1,760,000
LANGUAGE: Spanish*

Vietnam
CONTINENT: Asia
AREA: 127,881 sq mi (331,210 sq km)
POPULATION: 102,790,000
CAPITAL: Hanoi 4,875,000
LANGUAGE: Vietnamese*, English, French, Chinese, Khmer, Mon-Khmer, Malayo-Polynesian

Thailand
CONTINENT: Asia
AREA: 198,117 sq mi (513,120 sq km)
POPULATION: 69,481,000
CAPITAL: Bangkok 10,723,000
LANGUAGE: Thai*, English

Tunisia
CONTINENT: Africa
AREA: 63,170 sq mi (163,610 sq km)
POPULATION: 11,811,000
CAPITAL: Tunis 2,403,000
LANGUAGE: Arabic*, French, Berber

Ukraine
CONTINENT: Europe
AREA: 222,607 sq mi (576,550 sq km)
POPULATION: 43,746,000
CAPITAL: Kyiv 3,001,000
LANGUAGE: Ukrainian*, Russian

Uzbekistan
CONTINENT: Asia
AREA: 172,742 sq mi (447,400 sq km)
POPULATION: 30,843,000
CAPITAL: Tashkent 2,545,000
LANGUAGE: Uzbek*, Russian, Tajik

Yemen
CONTINENT: Asia
AREA: 203,850 sq mi (527,968 sq km)
POPULATION: 30,399,000
CAPITAL: Sanaa 3,075,000
LANGUAGE: Arabic*

Timor-Leste
CONTINENT: Asia
AREA: 5,743 sq mi (14,874 sq km)
POPULATION: 1,414,000
CAPITAL: Dili 281,000
LANGUAGE: Tetun*, Mambai, Makasai, Portuguese*, Indonesian, English

Turkey
CONTINENT: Asia/Europe
AREA: 302,535 sq mi (783,562 sq km)
POPULATION: 82,482,000
CAPITAL: Ankara 5,216,000
LANGUAGE: Turkish*, Kurdish

United Arab Emirates
CONTINENT: Asia
AREA: 32,278 sq mi (83,600 sq km)
POPULATION: 9,857,000
CAPITAL: Abu Dhabi 1,512,000
LANGUAGE: Arabic*, English, Hindi, Malayam, Urdu, Pashto, Tagalog, Persian

Vanuatu
REGION: Australia & Oceania
AREA: 4,706 sq mi (12,189 sq km)
POPULATION: 303,000
CAPITAL: Port-Vila 53,000
LANGUAGE: Local languages, Bislama*, English*, French*

Zambia
CONTINENT: Africa
AREA: 290,587 sq mi (752,618 sq km)
POPULATION: 19,078,000
CAPITAL: Lusaka 2,906,000
LANGUAGE: Bembe, Nyanja, Tonga, other Indigenous languages, English*

Togo
CONTINENT: Africa
AREA: 21,925 sq mi (56,785 sq km)
POPULATION: 8,283,000
CAPITAL: Lomé 1,874,000
LANGUAGE: French*, Ewe, Mina, Kabye, Dagomba

Turkmenistan
CONTINENT: Asia
AREA: 188,456 sq mi (488,100 sq km)
POPULATION: 5,580,000
CAPITAL: Ashgabat 865,000
LANGUAGE: Turkmen*, Russian, Uzbek

United Kingdom
CONTINENT: Europe
AREA: 94,058 sq mi (243,610 sq km)
POPULATION: 66,052,000
CAPITAL: London 9,426,000
LANGUAGE: English, Scots, Scottish Gailic, Welsh, Irish, Cornish

Vatican City
CONTINENT: Europe
AREA: 0.2 sq mi (0.4 sq km)
POPULATION: 1,000
CAPITAL: Vatican City 1,000
LANGUAGE: Italian, Latin, French

Zimbabwe
CONTINENT: Africa
AREA: 150,872 sq mi (390,757 sq km)
POPULATION: 14,830,000
CAPITAL: Harare 1,542,000
LANGUAGE: Shona*, Ndebele*, English*, Indigenous languages*

Tonga
REGION: Australia & Oceania
AREA: 288 sq mi (747 sq km)
POPULATION: 106,000
CAPITAL: Nuku'alofa 23,000
LANGUAGE: Tongan*, English*

Tuvalu
REGION: Australia & Oceania
AREA: 10 sq mi (26 sq km)
POPULATION: 11,000
CAPITAL: Funafuti 7,000
LANGUAGE: Tuvaluan*, English*, Samoan, Kiribati

United States
CONTINENT: North America
AREA: 3,796,741 sq mi (9,833,517 sq km)
POPULATION: 334,998,000
CAPITAL: Washington, D.C. 5,378,000
LANGUAGE: English, Spanish, Native American languages

Venezuela
CONTINENT: South America
AREA: 352,144 sq mi (912,050 sq km)
POPULATION: 29,069,000
CAPITAL: Caracas 2,946,000
LANGUAGE: Spanish*, Indigenous languages

METRIC CONVERSION TABLES
CONVERSION TO METRIC MEASURES

SYMBOL	WHEN YOU KNOW	MULTIPLY BY	TO FIND	SYMBOL
LENGTH				
in	inches	2.54	centimeters	cm
ft	feet	0.30	meters	m
yd	yards	0.91	meters	m
mi	miles	1.61	kilometers	km
AREA				
in²	square inches	6.45	square centimeters	cm²
ft²	square feet	0.09	square meters	m²
yd²	square yards	0.84	square meters	m²
mi²	square miles	2.59	square kilometers	km²
—	acres	0.40	hectares	ha
MASS				
oz	ounces	28.35	grams	g
lb	pounds	0.45	kilograms	kg
—	short tons	0.91	metric tons	t
VOLUME				
in³	cubic inches	16.39	milliliters	mL
liq oz	liquid ounces	29.57	milliliters	mL
pt	pints	0.47	liters	L
qt	quarts	0.95	liters	L
gal	gallons	3.79	liters	L
ft³	cubic feet	0.03	cubic meters	m³
yd³	cubic yards	0.76	cubic meters	m³
TEMPERATURE				
°F	degrees Fahrenheit	5/9 after subtracting 32	degrees Celsius (centigrade)	°C

CONVERSION FROM METRIC MEASURES

SYMBOL	WHEN YOU KNOW	MULTIPLY BY	TO FIND	SYMBOL
LENGTH				
cm	centimeters	0.39	inches	in
m	meters	3.28	feet	ft
m	meters	1.09	yards	yd
km	kilometers	0.62	miles	mi
AREA				
cm²	square centimeters	0.16	square inches	in²
m²	square meters	10.76	square feet	ft²
m²	square meters	1.20	square yards	yd²
km²	square kilometers	0.39	square miles	mi²
ha	hectares	2.47	acres	—
MASS				
g	grams	0.04	ounces	oz
kg	kilograms	2.20	pounds	lb
t	metric tons	1.10	short tons	—
VOLUME				
mL	milliliters	0.06	cubic inches	in³
mL	milliliters	0.03	liquid ounces	liq oz
L	liters	2.11	pints	pt
L	liters	1.06	quarts	qt
L	liters	0.26	gallons	gal
m³	cubic meters	35.31	cubic feet	ft³
m³	cubic meters	1.31	cubic yards	yd³
TEMPERATURE				
°C	degrees Celsius (centigrade)	9/5 then add 32	degrees Fahrenheit	°F

ABBREVIATIONS
COUNTRY NAMES

ARM. ....Armenia
AZER. ....Azerbaijan
B. & H.; BOS. & HER. .... Bosnia and Herzegovina
BELG. ....Belgium
EST. ....Estonia
HUNG. ....Hungary
KOS. ....Kosovo
LATV. ....Latvia
LIECH. ....Liechtenstein
LITH. ....Lithuania
LUX. ....Luxembourg
MOLD. .... Moldova
N. MAC. ....Macedonia
N.Z. ....New Zealand
NETH. ....Netherlands
SLOVN. ....Slovenia
SWITZ. ....Switzerland
U.A.E. ....United Arab Emirates
U.K. ....United Kingdom
U.S. .... United States

PHYSICAL FEATURES

I.-s. ....Island-s
L. .... Lake
Mt.-s. .... Mont, Mount-ain-s

OTHER

AFR. ....African
DEM. ....Democratic
D.C. ....District of Columbia
EQ. ....Equatorial
Hts. .... Heights
INT'L. ....International
OKLA. ....Oklahoma
REP. ....Republic
S. ....South
St. .... Saint
TENN. .... Tennessee
& .... and

SELECTED WORLD FACTS

THE EARTH

AREA: 196,940,000 sq mi (510,072,000 sq km)

LAND: 57,506,000 sq mi (148,940,000 sq km)— 29.1%

WATER: 139,434,000 sq mi (361,132,000 sq km)— 70.9%

POPULATION: 7,800,000,000 people

DEEPEST POINT IN EACH OCEAN

	FEET	METERS
Challenger Deep, Mariana Trench, Pacific	-36,037	-10,984
Puerto Rico Trench, Atlantic	-28,232	-8,605
South Sandwich Trench, Southern	-24,390	-7,434
Java Trench, Indian	-23,376	-7,125
Molloy Deep, Arctic	-18,599	-5,669

THE OCEANS

	AREA		PERCENTAGE OF EARTH'S OCEANS
	SQ MI	SQ KM	
Pacific	65,100,000	168,600,000	46
Atlantic	33,100,000	85,600,000	24
Indian	27,500,000	71,200,000	20
Southern	8,500,000	21,900,000	6
Arctic	6,100,000	15,700,000	4

10 LARGEST ISLANDS

	AREA			AREA	
	SQ MI	SQ KM		SQ MI	SQ KM
Greenland, North America	836,000	2,166,000	Sumatra, Asia	165,000	427,300
New Guinea, Asia & Oceania	306,000	792,500	Honshu, Asia	87,800	227,400
Borneo, Asia	280,100	725,500	Great Britain, Europe	84,200	218,100
Madagascar, Africa	226,600	587,000	Victoria, North America	83,900	217,300
Baffin, North America	196,000	507,500	Ellesmere, North America	75,800	196,200

10 LARGEST SEAS

	AREA		AVERAGE DEPTH	
	SQ MI	SQ KM	FEET	METERS
Coral Sea	1,615,500	4,184,000	8,107	2,471
South China Sea	1,388,400	3,596,000	3,871	1,180
Caribbean Sea	1,094,200	2,834,000	8,517	2,596
Bering Sea	973,000	2,520,000	6,010	1,832
Mediterranean Sea	953,300	2,469,000	5,157	1,572
Sea of Okhotsk	627,400	1,625,000	2,671	814
Gulf of Mexico	591,500	1,532,000	5,066	1,544
Norwegian Sea	550,200	1,425,000	5,801	1,768
Greenland Sea	447,100	1,158,000	4,734	1,443
Sea of Japan (East Sea)	389,200	1,008,000	5,404	1,647

Glossary

*Note: Terms defined within the main body of the atlas text generally are not listed below. Atlas page references are in bold (**125**).*

AFAR TRIANGLE hot, dry, low-lying area located in eastern Africa where the Great Rift Valley joins the southern end of the Red Sea (**100, 102**)

ANTARCTIC CONVERGENCE climate and marine boundary (roughly 55° S–60° S) where cold, slightly less saline Antarctic waters meet the southern extremes of the Atlantic, Pacific, and Indian Oceans; waters south of the Antarctic Convergence are sometimes referred to as the Southern Ocean (**125**)

ARID CLIMATE type of dry climate in which annual precipitation is often less than 10 inches (25 cm); experiences great daily variations in day-night temperatures (**20–21**)

ASYLUM place where a person can go to find safety; to offer asylum means to offer protection in a safe country to people who fear being persecuted or who have been persecuted in their own country (**34–35**)

BATHYMETRY measurement of depth at various places in the ocean or other body of water (**11**)

BIODIVERSITY biological diversity in an environment as indicated by numbers of different species of plants and animals (**118**)

BOREAL FOREST *see* Northern coniferous forest

BOUNDARY line established by people to separate one political or mapped area from another; physical features, such as mountains and rivers, or latitude and longitude lines sometimes act as boundaries (**10, 30**)

BREADBASKET geographic region that is a principal source of grain (**64**)

CANADIAN SHIELD region containing the oldest rock in North America; areas are exposed in much of eastern Canada and some bordering U.S. regions (**56, 62**)

CLIMATE CHANGE any significant change in the measures of climate, such as temperature, precipitation, or wind patterns, resulting from natural variability or human activity and lasting for an extended period of time (**29**)

COASTAL PLAIN any comparatively level land of low elevation that borders the ocean (**64**)

CONTINENTAL CLIMATE midlatitude climate zone occurring on large landmasses in the Northern Hemisphere and characterized by great variations of temperature, both seasonally and between day and night; continental cool summer climates are influenced by nearby colder subarctic climates; continental warm summer climates are influenced by nearby mild or dry climates (**20–21**)

COORDINATED UNIVERSAL TIME (UTC) basis for the current worldwide system of civil (versus military) time determined by highly precise atomic clocks; also known as Universal Time; formerly known as Greenwich Mean Time (**13**)

CULTURE HEARTH center from which major cultural traditions spread and are adopted by people in a wide geographic area (**90**)

CYBERCAFE café that has a collection of computers that customers can use to access the internet (**52**)

DEGRADED FOREST forested area severely damaged by overharvesting, repeated fires, overgrazing, poor management practices, or other abuse that delays or prevents forest regrowth (**28**)

DESERT AND DRY SHRUB vegetation region with either hot or cold temperatures that annually receives 10 inches (25 cm) or less of precipitation (**24–25**)

DIFFUSE BOUNDARY evolving boundary zone between two or more tectonic plates with edges that are not clearly defined (**17**)

ECOSYSTEM term for classifying Earth's natural communities according to how all things in an environment, such as a forest or a coral reef, interact with each other (**10, 15, 29, 68, 79, 118**)

FAULT break in Earth's crust along which movement up, down, or sideways occurs (**16–17**)

FLOODED GRASSLAND wetland dominated by grasses and covered by water (**24–25**)

FOSSIL FUEL fuel, such as coal, petroleum, and natural gas, derived from the remains of ancient plants and animals (**48**)

GEOTHERMAL ENERGY heat energy generated within Earth (**48**)

GLACIER large, slow-moving mass of ice that forms over time from snow (**26**)

GLOBALIZATION purposeful spread of activities, technology, goods, and values throughout the world through the expansion of global links, such as trade, media, and the internet (**50**)

GONDWANA name given to the southern part of the supercontinent Pangaea; made up of what we now call Africa, South America, Australia, Antarctica, and India (**16, 120**)

GREENWICH MEAN TIME *see* Coordinated Universal Time

GROSS DOMESTIC PRODUCT (GDP) gross national product, excluding the value of net income earned abroad (**10, 44**)

GROSS NATIONAL INCOME PER CAPITA a country's annual earned income divided by its population (**36–37**)

GROSS NATIONAL PRODUCT (GNP) total value of the goods and services produced by the residents of a country during a specified period, such as a year (**44**)

GROUNDWATER water, primarily from rain or melted snow, that collects beneath Earth's surface, in saturated soil or in underground reservoirs, or aquifers, and that supplies springs and wells (**27, 28**)

HEMISPHERE one-half of the globe; the Equator divides Earth into Northern and Southern Hemispheres; the prime meridian and the 180-degree meridian divide it into Eastern and Western Hemispheres (**5**)

HIGHLAND/UPLAND CLIMATE region associated with mountains or plateaus that varies depending on elevation, latitude, continental location, and exposure to sun and wind; in general, temperature decreases and precipitation increases with elevation (**20–21**)

HOST COUNTRY country where a refugee goes to find asylum (**34**)

HOT SPOT in geology, an extremely hot region beneath the lithosphere that stays relatively stationary while plates of Earth's outer crust move over it; environmentally, an ecological trouble spot (**28**)

HUMAN DEVELOPMENT INDEX (HDI) way of measuring development that combines both social and economic factors to rank the world's countries based on health, education, and income level (**36–37**)

HUMID SUBTROPICAL CLIMATE region characterized by hot summers, mild to cool winters, and year-round precipitation that is heaviest in summer; generally located on the southeastern margins of continents (**20–21**)

ICE CAP CLIMATE one of two kinds of polar climate; summer temperatures rarely rise above freezing and what little precipitation occurs is mostly in the form of snow (**20–21**)

INDIGENOUS native to or occurring naturally in a specific area or environment (**42, 116**)

INFILTRATION process that occurs in the water, or hydrologic, cycle when gravity causes surface water to seep down through the soil (**26**)

INTERNALLY DISPLACED PERSON (IDP) person who has fled his or her home to escape armed conflict, generalized violence, human rights abuses, or natural or human-made disasters; unlike a refugee, such a person has not crossed an international border but remains in his or her own country (**34**)

LANDFORM physical feature shaped by uplifting, weathering, or erosion; mountains, plateaus, hills, and plains are the four major types (**18, 22**)

LANGUAGE FAMILY group of languages that share a common ancestry (**40–41**)

LATIN AMERICA cultural region generally considered to include Mexico, Central America, South America, and the West Indies; Portuguese and Spanish are the principal languages (**33**)

LIFE EXPECTANCY average number of years a person can expect to live, based on current mortality rates and health conditions (**36**)

LLANOS extensive, mostly treeless grasslands in the Orinoco River basin of northern South America (**72**)

LOWLANDS fairly level land at a lower elevation than surrounding areas (**14**)

MANGROVE VEGETATION tropical trees and shrubs with dense root systems that grow in tidal mudflats and extend coastlines by trapping soil (**24-25**)

MARGINAL LAND land that has little value for growing crops or for commercial or residential development (**28**)

MARINE WEST COAST type of mild climate common on the west coasts of continents in midlatitude regions; characterized by small variations in annual temperature range and wet, foggy winters (**20-21**)

MEDIAN AGE midpoint of a population's age; half the population is older than this age and half is younger (**32**)

MEDITERRANEAN CLIMATE mild climate common on the west coasts of continents, named for the dominant climate along the Mediterranean coast; characterized by mild, rainy winters and hot, dry summers (**20-21**)

MEDITERRANEAN SHRUB low-growing, mostly small-leaf evergreen vegetation, such as chaparral, that thrives in Mediterranean climate regions (**24-25**)

MELANESIA one of three major island groups that make up Oceania; includes the Fiji Islands, New Guinea, Vanuatu, the Solomon Islands, and New Caledonia (**112-113**)

MELANESIAN indigenous to Melanesia (**116**)

MICROCLIMATE climate of a very limited area that varies from the overall climate of the surrounding region (**22**)

MICRONESIA one of three major island groups that make up Oceania; made up of some 2,000 mostly coral islands, including Guam, Kiribati, the Mariana Islands, Palau, and the Federated States of Micronesia (**112-113**)

MICRONESIAN indigenous to Micronesia (**116**)

MONSOON seasonal change in the direction of the prevailing winds that causes wet and dry seasons in some tropical areas (**94**)

MOUNTAIN GRASSLAND vegetation region characterized by clumps of long grass that grow beyond the limit of forests at high elevations (**24-25**)

NONRENEWABLE RESOURCES elements of the natural environment, such as metals, minerals, and fossil fuels, that form within Earth by geological processes over millions of years and thus cannot readily be replaced (**48-49**)

NORTHERN CONIFEROUS FOREST vegetation region composed primarily of cone-bearing, needle- or scale-leaf evergreen trees that grow in regions with long winters and moderate to high annual precipitation; also called boreal forest or taiga (**24-25**)

OCEANIA name for the widely scattered islands of Polynesia, Micronesia, and Melanesia; often includes Australia and New Zealand (**110-119**)

PAMPAS temperate grassland primarily in Argentina between the Andes and the Atlantic Ocean; one of the world's most productive agricultural regions (**70, 72**)

PATAGONIA cool, windy, arid plateau region primarily in southern Argentina between the Andes and the Atlantic Ocean (**72**)

PER CAPITA INCOME total national income divided by the number of people in the country (**36-37**)

PLAIN large area of relatively flat land; one of the four major kinds of landforms (**18**)

PLATE TECTONICS study of the interaction of slabs of Earth's crust as molten rock within Earth causes them to slowly move across the surface (**16-17**)

PLATEAU large, relatively flat area that rises above the surrounding landscape; one of the four major kinds of landforms (**18-19**)

POLAR CLIMATES climates that occur at very high latitudes; generally too cold to support tree growth; include tundra and ice cap (**20-21**)

POLYNESIA one of three major regions in Oceania made up mostly of volcanic and coral islands, including the Hawaiian Islands, Samoa, and French Polynesia (**112-113**)

POLYNESIAN indigenous to Polynesia (**116**)

PREDOMINANT ECONOMY main type of work that most people do to meet their wants and needs in a particular country (**44-45, 61, 77, 87, 97, 107, 117**)

PROVINCE land governed as a political or administrative unit of a country or empire; Canadian provinces, like U.S. states, have substantial powers of self-government (**63**)

RAINFOREST see Tropical moist broadleaf forest

RENEWABLE FRESHWATER water that is replenished naturally; the supply of freshwater can be endangered by overuse and pollution (**26**)

RIVER BASIN area drained by a single river and its tributaries (**72**)

RURAL pertaining to the countryside, where most of the economic activity centers on agriculture-related work (**38-39**)

SAHEL in Africa, the semiarid region of short, tropical grassland that lies between the dry Sahara and the humid savanna and that is prone to frequent droughts (**102, 104**)

SALINE/SALINITY measure of all salts contained in water; average ocean salinity is 35 parts per thousand (**125**)

SAMPAN flat-bottomed boat used in eastern Asia and usually propelled by two short oars (**98**)

SAVANNA tropical tall grassland with scattered trees (**24-25**)

SELVA Portuguese word referring to tropical rainforests, especially in the Amazon Basin (**78**)

SEMIARID dry climate region with great variation in day-night temperatures; has enough rainfall to support short grasslands (**20-21**)

SILT mineral particles that are larger than grains of clay but smaller than grains of sand (**78**)

STATELESS PEOPLE those who have no recognized country (**35**)

STEPPE Russian word for relatively flat, mostly treeless, temperate grasslands that stretch across much of central Europe and central Asia (**92**)

SUBARCTIC CLIMATE region characterized by short, cool, sometimes freezing summers and long, bitter-cold winters; most precipitation falls in summer (**20-21**)

SUBTROPICAL CLIMATE region between tropical and continental climates characterized by distinct seasons but with milder temperatures than continental climates (**20-21**)

SUBURB residential area on the outskirts of a town or city (**38**)

SUNBELT area of rapid population and economic growth south of the 37th parallel in the United States; its mild climate is attractive to retirees, and a general absence of labor unions has drawn manufacturing to the region (**60**)

TAIGA see Northern coniferous forest

TEMPERATE BROADLEAF FOREST vegetation region with distinct seasons and dependable rainfall; predominant species include oak, maple, and beech, all of which lose their leaves in the cold season (**24-25**)

TEMPERATE CONIFEROUS FOREST vegetation region that has mild winters with heavy precipitation; made up of mostly evergreen, needle-leaf trees that bear seeds in cones (**24-25**)

TEMPERATE GRASSLAND vegetation region where grasses are dominant and the climate is characterized by hot summers, cold winters, and moderate rainfall (**24-25**)

TERRITORY land under the jurisdiction of a country but that is not a state or a province (**57**)

TRANSIT CAMP place where refugees find temporary shelter before moving to a new location (**34**)

TROPICAL CONIFEROUS FOREST vegetation region that occurs in a cooler climate than tropical rainforests; has distinct wet and dry seasons; is made up of mostly evergreen trees with seed-bearing cones (**24–25**)

TROPICAL DRY CLIMATE region characterized by year-round high temperatures and wet and dry seasons (**20–21**)

TROPICAL DRY FOREST vegetation region that has distinct wet and dry seasons and a cooler climate than tropical moist broadleaf forests; has shorter trees than rainforests, and many shed their leaves in the dry season (**24–25**)

TROPICAL GRASSLAND AND SAVANNA vegetation region characterized by scattered individual trees; occurs in warm or hot climates with annual rainfall of 20 to 50 inches (50–130 cm) (**24–25**)

TROPICAL MOIST BROADLEAF FOREST vegetation region occurring mostly in a belt between the Tropic of Cancer and the Tropic of Capricorn in areas that have at least 80 inches (200 cm) of rain annually and an average annual temperature of 80°F (27°C) (**24–25, 78–79**)

TROPICAL WET CLIMATE region characterized by year-round warm temperatures and rainfall ranging from 20 to 24 inches (50–60 cm) annually (**20–21**)

TROPOSPHERE region of Earth's atmosphere closest to the surface; where weather occurs (**5**)

TUNDRA vegetation region at high latitudes and high elevations characterized by cold temperatures, low vegetation, and a short growing season (**24–25**)

TUNDRA CLIMATE region with one or more months of temperatures slightly above freezing when the ground is free of snow (**20–21**)

UNIVERSALIZING RELIGION a religion that attempts to appeal to all people rather than to just those in a particular region or place (**42**)

UPLAND CLIMATE see Highland/upland climate

URBAN pertaining to a town or city, where most of the economic activity is not based on agriculture (**38–39**)

URBAN AGGLOMERATION a group of several cities and/or towns and their suburbs (**38**)

Thematic Index

Place-Name Index

Map Data Sources

11 (Satellite Image Maps): NASA Earth Observatory. https://earthobservatory.nasa.gov

16–17 (Plate Tectonics): USGS Earthquake Hazards Program and USGS National Earthquake Information Center (NEIC). earthquake.usgs.gov; Smithsonian Institution, Global Volcanism Program. volcano.si.edu

26–27 (Water Stress): R.W. Hofste, S. Kuzma, S. Walker, E.H. Sutanudjaja, M.F.P. Bierkens, M.J.M. Kuijper, M.F. Sanchez, R. van Beek, Y. Wada, S.G. Rodríguez and P. Reig. August 2019. "Aqueduct 3.0: Updated Decision-Relevent Global Water Risk Indicators." Washington, DC: World Resources Institute (WRI). https://www.wri.org/publication/aqueduct-30

28 (Human Footprint): O. Venter, E.W. Sanderson, A. Magrach, J.R. Allan, J. Beher, K.R. Jones, H.P. Possingham, W.F. Laurance, P. Wood, B.M. Fekete, M.A. Levy, and J.E.M. Watson. August 2016. "Sixteen years of change in the global terrestrial human footprint and implications for biodiversity conservation." Nature Communications, doi:10.1038/ncomms12558; J.E.M. Watson, D.F. Shanahan, M. Di Marco, J. Allan, W.F. Laurance, E.W. Sanderson, B. Mackey, and O. Venter. November 2016. "Catastrophic Declines in Wilderness Areas Undermine Global Environment Targets." Current Biology, doi:10.1016/j.cub.2016.08.049, 26

28–29 (Fragile Forests): P. Potapov, A. Yaroshenko, S. Turubanova, M. Dubinin, L. Laestadius, C. Thies, D. Aksenov, A. Egorov, Y. Yesipova, I. Glushkov, M. Karpachevskiy, A. Kostikova, A. Manisha, E. Tsybikova, I. Zhuravleva. 2008. "Mapping the World's Intact Forest Landscapes by Remote Sensing." Ecology and Society, 13 (2). www.intactforests.org; Global Forest Watch. World Resources Institute (WRI)

29 (World Fisheries): V.W.Y. Lam, W.W.L. Cheung, G. Reygondeau, U. Rashid Sumaila. September 2016. "Projected Change in Global Fisheries Revenues Under Climate Change." Sci Rep 6, 32607. https://doi.org/10.1038/srep32607

29 (Climate Change): L. Hansen, A. Markham. World Wildlife Fund (WWF)

32–33, 60, 76, 86, 96, 106, 116 (Population Density): This product was made utilizing the LandScan 2018™ High Resolution Global Population Data Set copyrighted by UT-Battelle, LLC, operator of Oak Ridge National Laboratory under Contract No. DE-AC05-00OR22725 with the United States Department of Energy. The United States Government has certain rights in this Data Set. Neither UT-BATTELLE, LLC NOR THE UNITED STATES DEPARTMENT OF ENERGY, NOR ANY OF THEIR EMPLOYEES, MAKES ANY WARRANTY, EXPRESS OR IMPLIED, OR ASSUMES ANY LEGAL LIABILITY OR RESPONSIBILITY FOR THE ACCURACY, COMPLETENESS, OR USEFULNESS OF THE DATA SET.; (Urban Area Population) United Nations (UN), Department of Economic and Social Affairs, Population Division (DESA). 2018. "World Urbanization Prospects: The 2018 Revision, Online Edition." https://population.un.org/wup/Download

34–35 (Refugee Population): United Nations High Commissioner for Refugees (UNHCR), The UN Refugee Agency. https://www.unhcr.org/refugee-statistics/download/?url=E1ZxP4

36–37 (Life Expectancy at Birth, Human Development Index): United Nations Development Programme (UNDP). "Human Development Reports." http://hdr.undp.org/en/data#

38–39 (Urban and Rural Population): United Nations (UN), Department of Economic and Social Affairs, Population Division (DESA). 2018. "World Urbanization Prospects: The 2018 Revision, Online Edition." https://population.un.org/wup/Download

40–41 (Major Language Families) and 79 (Language Location and Endangerment Level): H. Hammarström, T. Castermans, R. Forkel, K. Verbeek, M.A. Westenberg, and B. Speckmann. September 2018. "Simultaneous Visualization of Language Endangerment and Language Description." Language Documentation & Conservation, 12, 359–392

42–43 (Dominant Religion) and 44–45, 61, 77, 87, 97, 107, 117 (Predominant Economies): Central Intelligence Agency (CIA). "The World Factbook." https://www.cia.gov/the-world-factbook

46–47 (Agricultural Land Use): Global Landscapes Initiative. Institute on the Environment. University of Minnesota. R.LeB. Hooke, and J.F. Martín-Duque. December 2012. "Land Transformation by Humans: A Review." GSA Today, Volume 22 (12): 4–10

47 (Low-Income Food-Deficit): Food and Agriculture Organization of the United Nations (FAO). http://www.fao.org/countryprofiles/lifdc/en

48–49 (Exports in Non-Fuel Mineral Resources): World Integrated Trade Solution (WITS). https://wits.worldbank.org/CountryProfile/en/Country/WLD/Year/2018/TradeFlow/Export/Partner/all/Product/25-26_Minerals

50–51 (Average Continental Globalization Index by Category, Overall Globalization Index): S. Gygli, F. Haelg, N. Potrafke and J.E. Sturm. January 2019. "The KOF Globalisation Index – Revisited." Review of International Organizations, 14(3), 543-574. https://doi.org/10.1007/s11558-019-09344-2; A. Dreher. September 2006. "Does Globalization Affect Growth? Evidence from a new Index of Globalization." Applied Economics 38, 10: 1091-1110

52–53 (International Tourism): The World Bank, World Development Indicators (WDI). https://data.worldbank.org/indicator/ST.INT.ARVL

59, 75, 85, 95, 105, 115 (Precipitation): National Oceanic and Atmospheric Administration (NOAA), National Environmental Satellite Data and Information Service (NESDIS), National Centers for Environmental Information (NCEI), Satellite Services Division (SSD). compiled by United Nations Environment Programme-Global Resource Information Database (UNEP-GRID)

69 (World Risk Index): B. Behlert, R. Diekjobst, C. Felgentreff, T. Manandhar, P. Mucke, L. Pries, K. Radtke, and D. Weller. eds. 2020. "WorldRiskReport 2020." Bündnis Entwicklung Hilft and Ruhr University Bochum–Institute for International Law of Peace and Armed Conflict (IFHV)

89 (Gray Wolf Range and Population): A.V. Stronen, B. Jędrzejewska, C. Pertoldi, D. Demontis, E. Randi, M. Niedzialkowska, M. Pilot, V.E. Sidorovich, I. Dykyy, J. Kusak, E. Tsingarska, I. Kojola, A.A. Karamanlidis, A. Ornicans, V.A. Lobkov, V. Dumenko, and S.D. Czarnomska. October, 2013. "North-South Differentiation and a Region of High Diversity in European Wolves (Canis Lupus)." PLoS ONE 8(10): e76454. https://doi.org/10.1371/journal.pone.0076454; Euronatur Foundation (EuroNatur), https://www.euronatur.org; Large Carnivore Initiative for Europe; The International Union for Conservation of Nature (IUCN) Red List of Threatened Species. https://www.iucnredlist.org

99 (Global Freedom): Freedom House. https://freedomhouse.org

109 (Tech Hubs): Briter Bridges. https://briterbridges.com; Afrilabs. https://www.afrilabs.com

119 (Forest Types): Australian Bureau of Agricultural and Resource Economics and Sciences (ABARES), National Forest Inventory (NFI). https://www.agriculture.gov.au/abares/forestsaustralia/forest-data-maps-and-tools/spatial-data/forest-cover

118 (Ice Sheet Thickness): Bedmap Project

119 (Antarctica Mass): NASA, Gravity Recovery and Climate Experiment (GRACE) satellites

Illustration Credits

FRONT AND BACK COVER
(Earth), adike/Shutterstock; (frog), Dirk Ercken/Shutterstock; (Golden Gate Bridge), JFL Photography/Adobe Stock; (trees), Chris Murer/Shutterstock; (fox), WildMedia/Adobe Stock; ("Christ the Redeemer"), Mark Schwettmann/Shutterstock; (butterfly), 135pixels/Shutterstock; (Neuschwanstein Castle), Alessandro Colle/Shutterstock; (seal), Richard Carey/Adobe Stock; (Cairo, Egypt), Prin/Adobe Stock; (Ha Long Bay, Vietnam), 12ee12/Adobe Stock; (lynx), Antonio Liebana/Getty Images

FRONT OF THE BOOK
2 (UP), k_tatsiana/Adobe Stock; 2 (CTR RT), R.M. Nunes/Adobe Stock; 2 (LO LE), Antonio Liebana/Getty Images; 3 (UP RT), Dean Turner/iStockphoto; 3 (CTR LE), 12ee12/Adobe Stock; 3 (CTR RT), JeremyRichards/Shutterstock; 3 (LO LE), Prin/Adobe Stock; 4 (LE), David Aguilar/NG; 4-5 (LO), NASA; 10, Belinda Pretorius/Shutterstock; 12 (LO LE), kai hecker/Shutterstock; 12 (LO RT), P.B. Houseknecht/Library of Congress/Corbis/VCG via Getty Images; 24 (1), Paul Nicklen/National Geographic Image Collection; 24 (2), Lane V. Erickson/Shutterstock; 24 (4), Raymond Gehman/Getty Images; 24 (5), John W Bova/Getty Images; 25 (6), Nic Watson/Shutterstock; 25 (10), EcoPrint/Shutterstock; 25 (13), FloridaStock/Shutterstock; 25 (14), EcoPrint/Shutterstock; 26 (LE), Jason Alden/Bloomberg via Getty Images; 26 (RT), Annie Griffiths Belt/National Geographic Image Collection; 27, COLLART Hervé/Sygma via Getty Images; 28 (LE), Steve McCurry/National Geographic Image Collection;28 (RT), Scientific Visualization Studio/Goddard Space Flight Center/NASA; 29 (LE), Ben Osborne/Getty Images; 29 (RT), MattGush/Getty Images; 32, Yann Layma/Getty Images; 34, Isaac Kasamani/AFP/Getty Images; 35, Mostofa Siraj Mohiuddin/iStock Editorial/Getty Images; 37, Sipa Asia/Shutterstock; 38, WH Chow/Shutterstock; 39 (LE), Simon Lowthian/Alamy Stock Photo; 39 (RT), Pius Utomi Ekpei/AFP via Getty Images; 40, Alex Segre/Alamy Stock Photo; 41 (LE), y&s creators/Alamy Stock Photo; 41 (RT), Silvia Kusidlo/picture-alliance/dpa/AP Images; 42 (LE), AP/REX/Shutterstock; 42 (RT), robertharding/Alamy Stock Photo; 43 (LE), Adrees Latif/Reuters; 43 (RT), Joseph Sohm/Visions of America/Getty Images; 44 (LE), Eitan Simanor/Alamy Stock Photo; 44 (RT), James L. Stanfield/National Geographic Image Collection; 45 (LE), Ariel Skelley/DigitalVision/Getty Images; 45 (RT), sofiko14/Adobe Stock; 46 (UP), Steve Raymer/National Geographic Image Collection; 46 (LO LE), stoonn/Shutterstock; 46 (LO RT), Merrill Dyck/Shutterstock; 48 (LE), Ayan82/Getty Images; 48 (CTR), Sarah Leen/National Geographic Image Collection; 48 (RT), Bob Krist/National Geographic Image Collection; 50, Joe Raedle/Getty Images; 51, RUNSTUDIO/Getty Images; 52, Rich LaSalle/Getty Images; 53 (LE), Jodi Cobb/National Geographic Image Collection; 53 (RT), Sergio Pitamitz/Alamy Stock Photo

NORTH AMERICA
54-55, k_tatsiana/Adobe Stock; 68 (UP), R.M. Nunes/Adobe Stock; 68 (LO), Courtesy the International Institute for Sustainable Development

SOUTH AMERICA
70-71, R.M. Nunes/Adobe Stock; 78 (UP), Michaela/Adobe Stock; 78 (CTR RT), Norberto Duarte/AFP via Getty Images; 78 (LO LE), Eduardo Blanco/Alamy Stock Photo

EUROPE
80-81, anko_ter/Adobe Stock; 88 (UP LE), fegari/Adobe Stock; 88 (CTR RT), Nadtochiy/Adobe Stock; 88 (CTR LE), Nadtochiy/Adobe Stock; 88 (LO RT), Antonio Liebana/Getty Images

ASIA
90-91, 12ee12/Adobe Stock; 98 (UP), Isaac Lawrence/AFP via Getty Images; 98 (LO), Ahn Young-joon/AP/Shutterstock

AFRICA
100-101, Prin/Adobe Stock; 108 (UP), i_am_zews/Shutterstock; 108 (LO LE), Khaled Desouki/AFP via Getty Images; 108 (LO RT), ogbechie triumph/Shutterstock

AUSTRALIA & OCEANIA
110-111, AtomicZen/Getty Images; 118 (UP), Dean Turner/iStockphoto; 118 (CTR LE), Jean-Paul Ferrero/AUSCAPE/Alamy Stock Photo; 118 (LO RT), redleg/Adobe Stock

ANTARCTICA
120-121, Andy Mann/National Geographic Image Collection; 125 (UP RT), JeremyRichards/Shutterstock; 125 (CTR LE), Jean-Paul Ferrero/AUSCAPE/Alamy Stock Photo; 125 (LO), Sergey/Adobe Stock

Published by National Geographic Partners, LLC.

First edition copyright © 2001 National Geographic Society
Updated © 2005, 2009, 2014 National Geographic Society
Updated © 2019, 2022 National Geographic Partners, LLC

Since 1888, the National Geographic Society has funded more than 14,000 research, conservation, education, and storytelling projects around the world. National Geographic Partners distributes a portion of the funds it receives from your purchase to National Geographic Society to support programs including the conservation of animals and their habitats. To learn more, visit natgeo.com/info.

For more information, visit nationalgeographic.com, call 1-877-873-6846, or write to the following address:

National Geographic Partners, LLC
1145 17th Street NW
Washington, DC 20036-4688 U.S.A.

For librarians and teachers:
nationalgeographic.com/books/librarians-and-educators

More for kids from National Geographic: natgeokids.com

National Geographic Kids magazine inspires children to explore their world with fun yet educational articles on animals, science, nature, and more. Using fresh storytelling and amazing photography, *Nat Geo Kids* shows kids ages 6 to 14 the fascinating truth about the world—and why they should care. **natgeo.com/subscribe**

For rights or permissions inquiries, please contact National Geographic Books Subsidiary Rights: bookrights@natgeo.com

Designed by Kathryn Robbins

Hardcover ISBN: 978-1-4263-7244-5
Trade paperback ISBN: 978-1-4263-7343-5
Reinforced library binding ISBN: 978-1-4263-7245-2

Acknowledgments
The publisher would like to thank everyone who worked to make this book come together: Chris Bickel, writer and geography educator; Grace Hill, project editor; Angela Modany, editor; Hilary Andrews, associate photo editor; Mike McNey, map production; Maureen J. Flynn, map edit; Anne LeongSon and Gus Tello, associate designers; and Alix Inchausti, production editor.

Printed in Hong Kong
22/PPHK/1